THE DIRECTORS LAB

THE DIRECTORS LAB

TECHNIQUES, METHODS, AND CONVERSATIONS ABOUT ALL THINGS THEATRE

EDITED BY EVAN TSITSIAS

PLAYWRIGHTS CANADA PRESS
TORONTO

First edition: December 2019. Second printing: February 2022.
Printed and bound in Canada by Imprimerie Gauvin, Gatineau

Playwrights Canada Press
202-269 Richmond Street West, Toronto, ON M5V 1X1
416.703.0013 :: info@playwrightscanada.com :: www.playwrightscanada.com

Jacket design by Leah Renihan
Author photo by John Gundy

LIBRARY AND ARCHIVES CANADA CATALOGUING IN PUBLICATION
Title: The directors lab : Techniques, methods, and conversations about all things theatre / edited by Evan Tsitsias.
Names: Tsitsias, Evan, editor.
Description: First edition.
Identifiers: Canadiana (print) 20190190035 | Canadiana (ebook) 20190190922 | ISBN 9780369100511 (softcover) | ISBN 9780369100528 (PDF) | ISBN 9780369100535 (EPUB) | ISBN 9780369100542 (Kindle)
Subjects: LCSH: Theater—Production and direction—Handbooks, manuals, etc.
Classification: LCC PN2053 .D57 2019 | DDC 792.02/33—dc23

Playwrights Canada Press operates on land which is the ancestral home of the Anishinaabe Nations (Ojibwe / Chippewa, Odawa, Potawatomi, Algonquin, Saulteaux, Nipissing, and Mississauga), the Wendat, and the members of the Haudenosaunee Confederacy (Mohawk, Oneida, Onondaga, Cayuga, Seneca, and Tuscarora), as well as Metis and Inuit peoples. It always was and always will be Indigenous land.

We acknowledge the financial support of the Canada Council for the Arts, the Ontario Arts Council (OAC), Ontario Creates, and the Government of Canada for our publishing activities.

Canada Council for the Arts | Conseil des arts du Canada

ONTARIO ARTS COUNCIL
CONSEIL DES ARTS DE L'ONTARIO
an Ontario government agency
un organisme du gouvernement de l'Ontario

Canada

ONTARIO CREATES | ONTARIO CRÉATIF

This book is dedicated to all the theatre dreamers and creators out there, who toil and twist and sacrifice in pursuit of their art. Who stand together against, and for, ideas. Who bravely fight to create, to be heard, and to voice their opinions in this ever-challenging world in which we survive. To those who bring questions, new thoughts and perspective, beauty, and illumination to everyone. Who allow themselves to be vulnerable. A radical act. Who let us peek into their soul. This is for you. Continue to puncture, provoke, lure, enlighten, and inspire. And, of course, continue to fight for it all.

CONTENTS

FOREWORD

BY ANNE CATTANEO

The idea of a directors' lab began as a search for a new way for a theatre of a certain size to open its doors to a sizable group of emerging artists. The theatre in question, of course, was Lincoln Center Theater in New York, and the birth of the Directors Lab took place at a special moment in time.

In the 1970s many theatres in the US were part of a burgeoning new play movement. Ford Foundation money had jump-started the creation of regional theatres in the late 1960s and not-for-profit theatre took hold across the country. And soon alternative theatres too were founded in many cities. For these new institutions, their repertory was an open question. But by coincidence, or luck, as these theatres were slowly staffed and repertory decisions made, a groundswell of playwriting emerged from the likes of Sam Shepard, David Mamet, Irene Fornés, Tina Howe, Steve Tesich, Beth Henley, David Rabe, Wallace Shawn, Charles Fuller, Ntozake Shange, Lanford Wilson, Michael Christofer, Corinne Jacker, David Henry Hwang, Michael Weller, Spalding Gray, and countless others that came to dominate the theatres' repertory. In New York, this was reflected in the flourishing of the Off-Off Broadway movement with its countless theatres devoted to new plays, all working cheaply under the Equity New York Showcase Code.

Many current theatre administrators—artistic directors, dramaturges, and literary managers—began their careers in this freewheeling atmosphere, where space was cheap, shows could be put up for very little money, and a thousand flowers bloomed.

New play agents were few, and most theatres read literally hundreds of scripts sent in over the transom each year. Important new play development centres such as the Eugene O'Neill Theater Center under George White and Lloyd Richards, and the Northwest Playwriting Lab at the Empty Space in Seattle, focused their efforts on discovering and supporting new writers. The idea that the newly created regional theatres would, based on a European model, be homes to the classics, evaporated in the rush of new play submissions from across the country.

By 1980, this groundswell had turned into a fully-fledged, mature movement—plays were transferring from showcase theatres to Broadway. Financial success was eating away at many of the previous share-and-share-alike assumptions of collaborating with modest resources. At this moment in time, Lincoln Center Theater (LCT), built with Ford money in the late 60s to assume the role of an American national theatre went dark. Considered a failure, the theatres were shuttered for six years and there was discussion of turning the building into a parking lot or a skating rink. But thanks to a newly revived board created by former mayor John Lindsay, Lincoln Center Theater reopened in 1985. Led by Gregory Mosher and Bernard Gersten, it became a miraculous success almost immediately with both new and classical play programming. The artistic philosophy was to give free rein to a small number of master artists—from David Mamet (*Speed the Plow*), Wole Soyinka (*Death and the King's Horseman*), Julie Taymor (*The Transposed Heads*), John Guare (*House of Blue Leaves* and *Six Degrees of Separation*), and Mbongeni Ngema (*Sarafina!*) among others. These were seasoned artists and their successes assured the stability and popularity of the revived LCT from 1985 to 1990.

When Andre Bishop came aboard as artistic director in 1991, he arrived from Playwrights Horizons, one of the premier new play theatres of New York City. He and I had known each other as literary managers during the late 1970s when I was at the

Phoenix Theater producing new work. Bernard Gersten continued at LCT as Executive Director and, as co-founder of the Public Theater, he too had a storied history with emerging artists. So very soon the discussion turned to doing what we knew how to do best: working with emerging writers as we had with our many friends at Circle Repertory, the Negro Ensemble Company, the American Place Theater, the Wooster Group, INTAR, La Mama, and countless other theatres. But as we set out to do this, we discovered that in the intervening decade everything had changed.

Summer play development retreats had multiplied. New play agents were everywhere and very few scripts came in over the transom. Almost every play we read had already had a reading in a theatre, though very few had had productions. Authors were wary of comments (rightly so) from establishment theatre administrators. The evident and discernable artistic characteristics of each theatre were now blurred. It used to be easy to tell a Circle Rep play from a Public Theater play, and there was a distinct regional character evident in the work of many writers—a Chicago school in David Mamet, Sam Shepard's western writing at the Magic in San Francisco, Beth Henley's southern sensibility, etc. Now everyone was reading the same plays and many playwrights' resumés overlapped in ways we hadn't seen before.

Andre and I found ourselves mostly dealing with agents, and with scripts that had had a lot of contact with other theatres without yet finding a home. We also had many new limitations. One of our two theatres was way too big for premiering new work, with its 1,100 seats and relentless pressure from close to a hundred opening night press reviews. Even a very good new play had trouble withstanding the pressures of opening in such an arena. And LCT's powerful membership plan, pioneered to throw out the old subscription model, had generated a base of forty thousand members, and seats in the three hundred–seat

Mitzi Newhouse Theater were hard to find. Our minimum runs came close to sixteen weeks, which gave us the option of producing only three plays and musicals each year in the space. (Since that time, we have inaugurated a new space, LCT3, with one hundred seats, devoted to young writers, but this took decades to realize.) So where would the emerging writers work? By the mid 1990s, we declared ourselves defeated on this front. We were producing the new work of Jon Robin Baitz, Mustapha Matura, Michael John LaChiusa, and Spalding Gray, but we had then run out of room.

And of this dilemma the Directors Lab was born. It came from a desire to open our doors to many artists, to artists we didn't yet know, with the idea of welcoming them as equals and putting some of the resources of a large theatre at their disposal. "What if we think about doing something with directors?" said we. And in what we now know to be "the Lab way," we inaugurated a series of meetings with everyone we could think of who had experience and understood the changing challenges of making new work in the '90s. Over a year we gathered actors, many directors of course, designers, playwrights, and other theatre makers—ranging from JoAnne Akalaitis, Garland Wright, Laurie Anderson, Lois Smith, Novella Nelson, Chris Durang, Michael John LaChiusa, Mark Lamos, John Conklin, Dan Sullivan, Marsha Norman, Steve Carter, to Graciela Daniele—in a series of discussions about what a theatre like LCT could do in a new way to bring young artists into the tent.

Beginning there, and with our first Lab in 1995 ("ARE there even a hundred young directors in the US?" asked Andre Bishop as we set out!) we worked by trial and error to experiment and reinforce our successes as the years, and the Labs, passed.

Most of what characterizes the Lab, like all good theatre experiences, originated from the work itself, and the Lab over the first years was our crucible. I drew conclusions from watching what seemed to work best and what the directors responded to. As I say in my opening speech to the Lab each year, the Lab is like a small ship set sail by a large hand, but once afloat it goes where its crew takes it.

The importance of the Lab's size became immediately apparent, as did the artistic diversity of the group. We discovered immediately that what had characterized our own early time in the theatre, the cross-fertilization that came from personal friendships between people working in totally different kinds of venues, was rich and unpredictable and powerful. The Lab's activities were at first generated by me and by the contacts I had through LCT to artists and work I felt would interest each group. A large theatre has many such connections. But this became a big responsibility and one that was too centred on me, and I discovered a way to focus each Lab and to ask the applicants what they knew, who they knew, and what and who they would LIKE to know pertaining to each year's focus. Then with Lincoln Center's resources, together with the directors' connections, I could often get to these people. And I was, and remain, ever surprised by the generosity and willingness of master artists to participate and bring what they know into the Lab. I've been surprised from the very beginning how eagerly the directors have embraced one another. Directing is usually the loneliest job in the room.

My task—to create an intense Lab, devoted to artistry and ideas, where each director could be as active as possible and would have the opportunity to contribute—is not an easy challenge to meet when seventy-plus directors are in residence. Through this challenge I learned that the Lab was most appreciated by directors who were already underway, who were making an active life in the theatre (not thinking of doing so, or still in school), and wanted a place to reflect and experiment and refresh. It did not work so well for directors who had been in the profession for several decades with diminishing successes who sought a reboot. It did not work at all for directors with no experience—only dreams. These applicants now get a gentle letter of thanks from us for their application and an invitation to reapply a few years down the road. In a world that tilts in the opposite direction, I came to underline the non-competitive nature of the Lab. No one is singled out, no one's career is advanced—only each director's artistry is expanded.

Word of the Lab, which LCT has never advertised and which has always been free of charge, spread quickly and applications were soon arriving from across the US and then from around the world. In 2014, thirty-four countries were represented and for some time we have been working with a number of arts agencies, foundations, and embassies to make it possible for directors from abroad to attend. My focus has remained on diversity of work—small ensembles, Broadway, opera, regional representation, classical theatre, experimental theatre, theatre in theme parks, churches, and—my latest favorite—directors who are starting theatres in places that have not had a theatre before. That's a challenge!

Of course, the most wonderful surprises are what happens in the Lab and who meets whom and who ends up working together. This is something I have no part in, and it always surprises me. Our Los Angeles lab was our first offshoot because a community of theatre artists was so sorely needed in a city where theatre was considered a second-tier art. Several directors from our early years founded the Lab there. And I'm grateful that the Directors Lab West soon found a home at the Pasadena Playhouse, where it has thrived for twenty years, in its own form: like ours in some ways, but also responsive to the scene there. The Directors Lab North began as an idea when three very talented directors from Toronto met for the *very first time* in the basement of Lincoln Center, and ever since it has been successful by staying close to the working theatres of Canada, and the directors who administer it—including generous site host Richard Rose at the Tarragon Theatre—have kept it close to the evolving professional theatre scene. It is that continuing change and enrichment with current trends that has kept it lively and relevant. Its nature is quintessentially Canadian. But its core principles of artistic diversity and sharing, and its focus on artistry carry the DNA of the original Lab. We have a Lab in Chicago, and a newly created Mediterranean Lab, which began in Beirut in 2019 and will move to Barcelona in 2020, and Cyprus in 2021. Many Lab members have created associations and produce work together in different forms of collaboration—often across the globe in different countries.

There are a few important conclusions I have drawn over the years as I've watched the boats sailing away. I have come to understand from watching the directors that, as we know from the history of our profession, all important theatres have been created by artists who are peers and friends, who see the world in the same way, who usually dislike the theatre that exists and seek to change it, and who have taste and talent and can attract good collaborators. From the Lord Chamberlain's Men to the Moscow Art Theatre to the Group Theatre to Steppenwolf in our time, no one in a generation above chose these artists. They made their own path. I never forget that the Moscow Art Theatre was founded in an all-night session in a bar. So, in essence, what the Lab has inadvertently provided is a "scene," a social gathering place where like-minded individuals can get to know one another. Exactly this existed for so many of us in the 1970s new play scene. Now in a world of unlimited contact via social media, somehow it still works only when the bodies are in the room. And some directors can thrive and enlarge and refine a vision, and others will not—just as in life. Part of the challenge of directing programs is how to discern who is a good director: unlike actors who audition, or playwrights who submit a script, the director's portfolio is useless unless the work can be actually seen, and often in early career stages that work is limited and compromised by financial and other restrictions. In the Lab there is no need to assess this—the application provides proof of artistic "reach"—and the personal side, the ability of a director to marshal resources and inspire others, is left to each director. Some can follow this through and some cannot. Some will direct, others will produce, and still others will move into other aspects of theatre.

And, of course, to return to the beginning, the Directors Lab has by now been involved with literally hundreds of plays by emerging writers, as well as the contributions of an equal number of emerging designers, who are paid to come into the Lab and think with the directors, to spend time in the room, and not to shop or build *after* all the decisions have been made. Each year an acting company of about two dozen joins the Lab—so in a way, we "went around" as the Boyg says in *Peer Gynt*—and returned to face the initial challenge that began our journey so many years ago.

As we look to the future, I think one of the unexpected successes of all the Labs is their total flexibility to be able to radically refocus each year on issues of collaboration, on new ways of making theatre and artistry from the past that are suddenly being rediscovered. Our world is changing so rapidly, and one of the questions I have is whether what I consider the age-old model of making theatre—a true and open and free collaboration in the rehearsal room between artists of skill and imagination—will be viable in the future. Will there be things we can't say in those rehearsal rooms and on our stages? Who will determine who is in the room? How will artists speak to one another, first of all in the content of the new plays being written and then in the process that brings them to life? To me, the idealism of the working environment of the Lab, its inspiration from great models of the past—we *are* an apprentice tradition after all—and a joyous sense of community will be the key factors in the continued success of all the Labs. And that success will result in audiences—new and old—completing the circle.

THE LAB

OPENING REMARKS

BY EVAN TSITSIAS

Every summer, for over twenty years, deep in the trenches of Lincoln Center Theater, through the maze of hallways that lead to the rehearsal studios, lies a secret. A secret society of directors—strangers—brought together as the year's "chosen ones." They convene in this theatrical crucible to spend three weeks filled with conversation, dialogue, discourse, workshops, master classes, exchanges, technique sharing, frustration, agitation, and passion. They nurture, support, incite, inspire, recalibrate, and renegotiate all they think they know about their art and craft, all with one common goal: to explore the art of directing. This is the Directors Lab.

I was fortunate to participate for two consecutive summers in this exhilarating and all-consuming program at Lincoln Center and one year in the Chicago Directors Lab before co-founding the Directors Lab North in Toronto, Canada, in 2011 with my colleagues Esther Jun and Elif Işıközlü. I had no idea what was in store for me that first year. Not a clue that it would drastically alter the trajectory of my career and artistic life. That the people and ideas I encountered there would radically alter the landscape of my theatrical terrain, adding extensively not only to my directing toolkit, but providing me with an opportunity to widen my theatrical lens beyond recognition, exposing me to a broad spectrum of techniques and methodologies that would normally take a lifetime of international travel to experience.

After years of amassing an epic pile of notes, memories, and experiences through these labs, I was left with a tremendous amount of knowledge . . . and computer files. I felt the need to share this incredibly rich experience with those directors who might not have the means or time to travel and experience it themselves. And so the idea of this book was born.

Directing is a lonely, insular profession. The director's process is even more elusive. Some directors are intensely methodical while others have a completely instinctual and organic way of entering the work. Whatever the approach, each director has their own unique process, utilizing various techniques to achieve their goals. One thing they all share is thorough preparation in order to leave all that at home and focus on the moment in rehearsals. This book examines and dissects their techniques and processes, allowing both emerging and established directors to be inspired by other directors' techniques or reminded of their own or perhaps, even, create a new hybrid. It is an artistic and logistic exploration into the mechanics of theatre creation through the lens of a director.

I don't want this book to be a "how-to" manual. I want it to serve as inspiration, to ignite a creative spark and add to the communal theatrical flame that we as theatre artists perpetually attempt to keep lit. It's a call to action, a decree of passion, of connections both personal and artistic. It's an encapsulation of what theatre is, in this space and time. And yes, fine, perhaps even a manual. Allow it to create connections within your own work and remind you of your own methodologies while inspiring new ones. This is the only way in which theatre can and will survive.

Throughout the last decade of these Labs, I've been privy to the musings and ideas of hundreds of directors from dozens of countries and continents who openly share their passions, methodologies, and practices with one another. It's been fascinating yet overwhelming to realize how many variations and techniques are out there. How do you decide on your own? How do you trust that your method is the right one? What I've learned after my many years of the Labs is that there is no one magic "how to direct" manual. Each director's method is as singular as their fingerprints. But what I've also discovered is that most methods are variations of the others. You borrow here, you steal there, you combine or massage or manipulate one exercise into the next until you can't remember where you first heard of it or if you even came up with it on your own in the first place. But this is what is so incredible about exchanging ideas with other directors. Each idea influences the next until it becomes part of our own directing DNA.

Having multiple directors in a room together is daunting. But it's also utter magic. The collective respect and yearning to learn from others is palpable each year. The biggest surprise has been the discovery that directors truly want to share their techniques with other directors. The atmosphere is one of complete camaraderie, touched not by competition but instead, a willingness to engage with one another. I've been making my own connections through these artistic collisions of techniques, pedagogy, and methodologies over the years. It's been thrilling to also watch all these other directors share their own discoveries with other directors.

For me, spending this many years at the Labs allows the privilege and luxury of retrospection and the exploring of connections. I've noticed similar questions emerge and reoccur year after year, along with new ones that correlate with the social-political climate of each successive year. Questions like: How can theatre evolve with the times? Does theatre have to evolve with the times? Is it our job as theatre creators and artists to maintain theatrical traditions or create theatre for the Netflix generation? As theatre seems to live in a state of constant peril from becoming irrelevant in this technologically obsessed world, how do we keep its resonance and relevance in the modern age?

How can we as theatre artists, respond to the world we live in at that particular time to use theatre as a vehicle for change?

I've also noticed through these connections how narrow our idea of what "theatre" is and how heavily we rely on these crutches, as audiences, that play on our expectations. Can we call it simply "expression"? How can we widen the lens? We've trained audiences in Western theatre to rely so heavily on linear narrative, and we expect them to "understand" every moment and constantly negotiate and make connections. How can we release those expectations and just experience the moment like we experience music or visual art? Is this possible?

What has also struck me throughout the process of listening to artists talk about their work after seeing their pieces is how, often times, it's much more interesting and thrilling to listen to them discuss their ideas of inception and rehearsal of the piece than it is to watch the piece itself. It leads to a very pertinent question: If the intention does not match the execution, have we "succeeded"? What constitutes a "successful" production? Should the words "success" or "failure" even be part of the theatrical equation? How do we quantify art and the process of creation?

Another series of questions I noticed over the past ten years has gained tremendous traction and relevance to the art of theatre is "Whose story can we tell?" Appropriation has become a very hot topic since I started these Labs as we continue to reflect on what stories we've been telling and the lens through which it's told. This has been a heated topic of debate within the lab and among the participants (Labbies) over the years. Do we have the right to tell stories of cultures outside our own? Why do we choose to tell these stories? Specifically in Canada, do we as Canadians, understand that we are telling a "Canadian" story on Indigenous land? Do we acknowledge this? How do we acknowledge this? How does that history affect and reflect the stories we are telling? I'm sweating even typing this. These are huge but important questions with no definitive answers. But they're definitely worth the asking.

It also dawned on me while watching the Labbies over time, what a massive juxtaposition lives between the highly intellectual, academic, and cerebral talk and the ridiculous child's play in many theatrical exercises. We discuss psychological intentions while at the same time executing guttural animal sounds as we flop all over one another as lions. So where does theatre practice live inside that vast spectrum? How do we find that balance?

These are some of the questions that are explored and covered in different forms through the various chapters and the transcribed interviews in this book. I urge you to ask yourself the same questions as you read through this, and I hope you come up with some answers.

A word that seems to re-emerge and repeat every year is "rigour"—the rigour it takes to create and persevere through creation and, also, career. This book has taken a rigour of my own. It's been a labour of love, just like the Lab itself. The endless hours of transcribing interviews we've conducted has gifted me with a truly intimate experience of words and reading. What a gift it has been to revisit the last decade of all these phenomenal ideas and conversations.

This book is assembled from Lab experiences I've amassed around the globe. Although it's divided into stand-alone sections, I've done my best to curate and structure a cohesive reading experience that covers all the relevant questions, ideas, and concerns that percolate each year during the Lab. The chapters are divided into the various components that are incorporated into the annual Lab—from our invited guest artists, workshops, master classes, and panel discussion to chats between Labbies addressing questions they want answered. All of the contributors in this book have been involved in the Lab in some capacity. I've chosen some of our most successful sessions and asked those guest artists who led them to write their own sections of the book. From heightened language to new play development to the art of collaboration, I wanted to stay as true to the nature of the Labs as possible, doing my best to recreate the experience as precisely as I could. If this book captures even an ounce of the magic and alchemy that occurs in these Labs, these years of work will be worth it. This is a compilation of ten years of research, conversation, and exchange. It's a book I myself would have killed for when I started directing. I also think it's a great tool for actors, playwrights, designers, and dramaturges. The more we know, the better the creation.

Theatre is my religion and I wanted to create my own Theatre Bible. I'm hoping this book will have many disciples.

HISTORY OF DIRECTORS LAB NORTH

Directors Lab North is an annual event held in Toronto at which invited directors gather from around the globe for workshops, master classes, dialogue and discourse, technique sharing, and networking. It is inspired by the Lincoln Center Directors Lab in New York City, where the three founding members, Evan Tsitsias, Esther Jun, and Elif Işıközlü met in 2010. The Lab exposes its participants to a network of colleagues that they would not have had the opportunity to connect with otherwise. We began the Lab in Toronto on a whim and a prayer. The inaugural event was three days in the Tarragon Theatre studios (generously donated by Richard Rose since 2011) and, almost a decade later, has expanded to eight days and a fruitful partnership with the supportive and generous Luminato Festival. We've hosted over two hundred international directors through the program and continue to build our network and Lab family.

Each year at the Lab, we begin the week by reading a speech that Anne Cattaneo wrote for us to read to the Labbies. I want to begin the journey of this book with that speech.

ANNE'S OPENING SPEECH

Hail, Directors,

I was so happy to be able to come to Toronto years ago to inaugurate the Directors Lab North, and I am with you in spirit this year. In fact, you don't need me at all. That—in a nutshell—is what I said when I traveled to Toronto to meet the first Directors Lab North, and it's what I say each year at greater length in my orientation speech here in New York.

You are here because you need one *another*—and you want to be with one another. And what you have to share with one another will keep you intrigued, fascinated, and irritated and will change your artistic life forever.

Your hardworking steering committee has been mainly devoted to the task of finding ways to weave a variety of plays, techniques, shared sessions, and guest speakers together—and now what you do with it all is totally up to you.

I always feel it's important to say that all the Labs are the opposite of showcases—showing off what you know. Instead they are about sharing what you know and doing what you don't know, what you haven't had a chance to do or explore. And being open to things you thought you weren't interested in. And meeting new people. I believe Evan told me that one of the reasons the Directors Lab North began was that three directors from Toronto met for the very first time in the basement of Lincoln Center Theater. Thank goodness that is not the case any longer.

So the Lab has a social function and it has an artistic function—not a career function. Each of you will make your way through the Lab differently, finding some things revelatory, some people fascinating, some techniques boring, and some speakers sparking new ideas and insights you can use in your work. Take all of this as grist for your mill and you will be astonished at how all of it—good and bad—will affect your work in the coming year. Be open to everything. I don't know how many times I've heard directors say, "I thought I was one kind of director and so I could skip over this other session. And then it was the afternoon I thought I would find irrelevant that changed the course of what I do. And I didn't realize it until the following December."

Be open to it all. Keep notes of your thoughts. Remind yourself to look into things you don't know that are mentioned or referred to. All these things will enrich your future work. Share your reactions honestly and openly and in a kindly fashion. Find new partnerships. Together you will have a wonderful time.

Anne

BREAKOUT SESSION

Three Vital Questions for a Director

WHAT DOES A DIRECTOR DO?

- Directing lives on the spectrum of allowing and guiding people to grow and then letting them go—much like being a parent.

- A director creates the world of the play for the entire team and allows them a safe place to play and explore on this playground created for them.

- Ultimately, being a director is empowering people to be their best.

- It's managing relationships.

- It's a process of fixing problems.

- You are the captain of the ship. You have to lead a group of people towards their final destination.

- You must be a facilitator. In a sense you are the least important person in the room. The playwright and actors are the ones that live on. You are the negotiator.

- A director tells the story as clearly as possible.
- A director nurtures, supports, and encourages the team so they can open up.
- You're an investigator, an architect, a mechanic.
- Your job is to inspire, clarify, guide, and lead.
- You are the host of the party.
- You are a conduit, sculptor, orchestrator, conductor, and filter.
- You are the filter into which all the ingredients are poured, allowing the cleanest and purest story to emerge.
- A director ignites the spiritual fire and inspires others to keep the fire burning.
- Directing is an editing process.
- A director manages panic attacks.
- You stimulate, then you watch.
- Your job is to clarify.
- You merge all the elements.
- Being a director is partly being a psychologist.
- A director creates action in time and space by putting characters in conflict with one another.

- Leadership is 100% willingness to communicate 100% of the time.
- You empower everyone so they feel safe to take risks.
- A director's job is to keep an eye on the journey of the play while negotiating the lights, sound, costumes, and all other elements.
- Directing is interpreting. The creative impulse already existed.
- You are there to support the actors' discoveries, not give them the answers.
- Your job is to mask your anxiety.
- You have to be a good collaborator, especially with very disparate groups of people. But you must be the boss, the person who adjudicates the ideas. You need a certain amount of diplomacy and a significant ability to articulate.
- You have to know what the motor of each specific project is. Each play and musical has an engine driving it that is very different from another.
- A director liberates the actor completely in the work and allows the actor's nature to guide rehearsals.
- You have to have deep ambitions—interested in being great with no ego. Be at the service of your work with strong ambition.
- Your job is to work with all the best ideas available, and shape them into a production.

- A director always makes the room feel like it's moving forward.
- You are the writer of the "production."
- It's about recognizing a good thing in others and molding it into something. It's managing the chaos factor or anarchy factor.

WHAT IS THE ROLE OF THE THEATRE AND THE THEATRE ARTIST?

- To bring people together in outrage. It's one thing to be a loud radical voice, but you have to connect with your truth. Then you can bring people into the truth of your radicalism.
- As theatre artist, to speak truth and not be afraid to speak the truth and provide opportunity for other artists to speak their truth.
- To bring your peer group into the theatre—and young people!
- To be in constant search for the truth, no matter how muddy it is.
- To always be curious and to investigate that curiosity through a well-researched, educated, and objective lens.
- To contribute to the vitality of the world.
- To ask questions about what it means to be a human being.
- To be closer to a poem than a novel, and provoke unanswered questions.

- To be about transcendence, unlocking something inside us.

WHAT IS THE ROLE OF THE AUDIENCE AND HOW DO YOU INCLUDE THEM IN THE WORK?

- I am always thinking of the audience. I want to elicit certain reactions.
- I always seek to entertain, interrupt, disrupt, and educate.
- You cannot compete with TV or film. An audience is hungry for theatricality, so give it to them.
- They come to see themselves represented.
- They want a conversation and to feel part of the experience.
- The audience needs it to be an event.
- I am always trying to put the audience in the position of the character.
- I try to chisel away at the audience's defences.
- I want the audience to see people in complex ways. There's truth in that, to start off normal and then change from that. In the same gesture there is both evil and good. I want to allow people's view of reality to become more complex.
- I want to give the audience maximum opportunity to make their own experience. People want a journey.

- The more specific it is, the more people think it's their story.

- Remember that audiences are not bad people. They're a benevolent witness. They want to have a nice time. They want us to do well. So if we can have that sense of a witness that is kind, then we can start being activated that way.

MASTER CLASS

Heightened Language and the Art of Listening: Director as Guide

BY JEANNETTE LAMBERMONT-MOREY

It's a rehearsal. About ten actors make up the "crowd" listening to a long speech delivered by the main character. They know their job is to give the speaker something to work for and against. They are doing their level best to make the scene come alive. "Do I understand you to mean . . . " is heard, quietly, over and over from the crowd. The speaker steps up his game, connects with them on a new level, with all the powers of the language at his command, and suddenly something massive shifts in the room. He makes a point, and they listen. They receive it and question it. They shout for more. They shout for corrections, in real time, without stopping the flow of the main monologue. The scene bursts into life. A face in the crowd, Sarah, suddenly breaks the fourth wall and turns to me with a look of shocked delight. She makes a gesture of explosion coming from the top of her head, "Boom!" she says, and her voice rises above the rest in excitement, "Oh my god! I get it! I get it! I get it!"

What she got was the concept of truly, *truly* listening.

* * *

When casting a heightened text play, I expect the actors to have a basic understanding of how poetic structure works and to be confident in technical aspects such as the metric line, scansion, punctuation, and so on. They need to arrive in the rehearsal room with a solid basis in technique, which allows an uninhibited freedom to explore. As we rehearse the play, we work together to make the heightened text become active and alive.

First of all, I should clarify what I mean when I say "heightened text." I am generally talking about language that has a more formalized structure, often verse, and employs an advanced vocabulary. It frequently uses figures of speech for rhetorical or persuasive effect (e.g., metaphor, alliteration, etc.). Obviously Shakespeare's classical writing in iambic pentameter is a good example, but heightened text can actually take any number of forms. There are plenty of modern writers who employ some version of what we might call heightened text. Maybe it's just easier to say it is writing that relies on poetic expression rather than common vernacular.

As a director, I have a very particular and detailed relationship with the text I am about to put into rehearsal. My prep process literally takes months. I begin by reading and re-reading the play multiple times. Then I type the whole piece into a word document to tackle any cutting or editing that needs to be done. As I type out the words, they become more tangible to me. After editing, I print out a copy of the text to begin creating my image script. (I have occasionally created the image script before editing, but only if I have plenty of time, because I will end up doing work on text that later gets cut.) This is the most time-consuming part of my journey because I go through the text line by line, word by word, and examine any images that come to mind. They can be literal images, as prescribed by the playwright, or the result of word-associative riffs. Then I find pictures that best express what I am "seeing" (sourced from Google images, art books, magazines, etc.). I cut them out and paste them into a thick collage on the facing page. Occasionally I draw a squiggle or two myself. Sometimes I also add snippets of poetry, or word definitions, or other textual associations and stick them in the collage too. I go through the entire script this way, and usually end up with a wonderfully fat and crunchy 3-D script, thick with collages on every page. You can see why the process takes so long—but it is an undertaking I absolutely adore. I often find myself pulled into strange and wild tangents I never would have found had I only paid attention to the face value of the text.

Looking at the end product, it is impossible not to see themes emerging, leaping to life through all these images. I remember some years ago, for example, when I finished my image script for *The Tempest*, I was struck by the overwhelming preponderance of drowning imagery. I did not expect to find that. Of course I was aware the play opens with a storm, a tempest (the event for which the play is named), in which a ship is wrecked at sea and sailors drown, but I was unprepared for the sheer volume of powerful underwater images that followed. I had no idea how insistent this theme actually was. It was embedded in the entire script. Before you laugh and tell me I had merely missed the obvious, think about how easy it is to get distracted by plot points, blindly taking the themes for granted. Sometimes we have to dig for the thing that is right in front of our face.

After the image work is complete, I break the script down into blocks (which I name) and action beats, identifying the climax of every scene and its relationship with the climax of the whole play. And finally, I work through the script one last time with coloured highlighters, identifying key words and critical passages that I want to convey to the actors.

My director's script ends up looking a bit like a creative art project! I guess this makes sense since poetry is art, after all.

Of course, my image work is most useful in feeding my overall concept, and it helps me identify the atmosphere I am trying to create for the show. Conversations with the design team are enriched by my ability to articulate these feelings. This ability to put my thoughts into words also becomes a great benefit in the rehearsal room. The image work gives me a rich vocabulary with which to address the actors. (It is perhaps ironic that my prep practice starts with words, passes through a visual exploration, and is then turned back into words—only now they are my words, coming from deep within my own process.) I make my director's script available to my acting company if they are curious, but I do not insist. This work is really my own private research and, as such, is not designed as a demonstration tool. I would be happy if it simply served as inspiration for each artist in the room to create their own personal script-expression.

So, finally, here we are, gathered in the rehearsal hall to bring these magnificent words to life, each actor passionate and invested, homework done, ready to act.

There are so many factors that go into directing or staging a play with heightened text. I am not going to attempt to plunge into that entire process right now (I could likely fill a whole book with my thoughts on that), but rather, I am going to focus on one particular aspect of what is needed to bring this kind of material to life: listening.

It seems some actors are skilled at activating the text assigned to them but have trouble truly hearing the information that they are supposed to be receiving. I am very sensitive to the subtlety of this. I recognize when a scene lacks the organic give-and-take of real conversation. The links in the chain of communication are almost tangible, and if one of the links is missing, well, then the communication is not real. Gears move in our brains when we process thoughts. Those gears are what an audience is watching, or experiencing (although they don't realize it). Acting is the practice of attempting to replicate the human operation of communication, which is, believe it or not, wildly interesting for an audience to see, because it makes the character seem real, dealing with an immediate situation . . . in the very moment that is now.

I also refer to this as the need for an actor to land their intentions. What a character says must touch down in the scene, tangibly engaging with the other characters (in as far as thoughts and words carry physical energy—and they do!) in a way that feels organic and true.

If the actions aren't landing, we need to back up a few steps to find out why. Chances are that it is because the actors are having trouble receiving the data they need to act on. Metaphorically speaking, you need to *catch* the ball before you can *throw* it again. If I detect a problem like this in rehearsal, I take a moment to try to help the actor learn to listen better.

I have developed some exercises that go hand-in-hand with rehearsal and might serve to illuminate the process of listening just a bit. Of course, exercises are not an end in themselves—I am not telling the actors how to act—nor can I make them listen, but I can help them to explore what to listen for.

I am sure you agree that when we communicate we, of course, listen to many things, not just to words. We listen to body language, energy, tone, intensity, and even the rhythms of our own heartbeat. However, when it comes to heightened text, it is an inescapable fact that the language itself, the words, are the lead vehicle. Listening enables comprehension and opens the door to discovering how ideas are carried very consciously by the very words themselves (choice, arrangement, weaponization). The language one chooses is born from the data received. Step one: before an actor can even think of responding, they must truly understand what is being said to them.

So, as with any text in a scene, poetic language needs to spring from context. What a character chooses to say comes directly out of what has happened before they speak and, since with heightened text the action is very often conveyed through words, particular attention needs to be paid to any words directed at them. In simple terms, what is being said to a given character is arguably even more important than what they say back—or, at the very least, equally important.

Since, in the case of heightened text, the language itself is challenging, the tendency is for actors to focus on the text they have to speak—to analyze it expertly and completely—and to forget that they need to know why they are speaking in the first place. What are they reacting to? Are they receiving data that will affect what they have to say? How can they hear what is being said to them as if they have never heard it before, and, as if the very core of their argument depends on it?

I humbly invite you to step inside the shoes of an actor for a moment: Imagine I am lucky enough to be working with you and that you are interested in learning more about the process of listening. I think the best way to understand the full value of these ideas is to try to experience them yourself.

I invite you to test out some of my exercises.

DO I UNDERSTAND YOU TO MEAN . . . ?

One way to experience listening is to find a way to make the communication exchange feel personal and intimate. Somehow it needs to get deep inside you. It is not enough to have the words bounce off your ears. When we speak to one another in life, it can be argued that we are trying to reach inside each other to affect change, to make a difference, to be *felt*. So, as actors, we must find a way to replicate that exchange: for one speaker to *cut into* the other with their intentions, and for the listener to feel the words on the *inside*.

I have discovered that it is possible to approximate that sensation by speaking the received words aloud. You will be amazed how deeply this affects you.

For example:

Your scene partner says: I love you.

And you reply: Do I understand you to mean that you are telling me that you love me?

You will find that making those words your own instantly personalizes them. Notice how "I," "me," and "you" play in this. The concept of someone loving you becomes real because it is now inside you through your own voicing of the concept of "me."

The construct of this experience is important. It needs to be phrased from your own point of view: "Do I understand you to mean . . . ?" Because you cannot read the other person's mind, or know exactly what the other means, you must ask from within the context of your own understanding. It must be phrased as a question in order to lead to the need for an answer.

Imagine, in all the following examples, that your reverse paraphrase of understanding is *improvised*, on your feet, as a result of information you have just received. This is about listening, not pre-planning. And it must be spoken *out loud*.

And if the exercise has connected, you will find a very natural and easy segue into your next scripted lines.

EXAMPLE ONE

Here is an example from the opening scene of Shakespeare's *King Lear*, where Lear is dividing his kingdom among his three daughters in exchange for their public expressions of devotion. The youngest daughter, Cordelia, has just listened to the professions of love given by her two older sisters.

LEAR: . . . Now, our joy,
Although our last, not least; to whose young love
The vines of France and milk of Burgundy
Strive to be interess'd; what can you say to draw
A third more opulent than your sisters? Speak.

CORDELIA: *Do I understand you to mean that you are turning to me now, and that my existence gives you joy, and that you are addressing me last because I am the youngest, and not because I am less than my sisters; and that my youth and capacity for love has attracted the best of France (known for great wine) and Burgundy (where there are good pastures for milk cattle) who are competing to be connected to us through me; and that you want to know what I can say that will inspire you to give me a larger and more luxurious third of the kingdom than my sisters? And you want to know what I will say now to obtain that?*

Nothing, my lord.

From this example you can see how much information goes *into* Cordelia before her short three-word answer. It sheds light on why she replies to her father the way she does. It is important for the actor playing Cordelia to paraphrase her understanding on her feet, in the moment. This is not an exercise that should be done intellectually, in writing, or as homework. However, it is important to remember that, since we are working with heightened text, the actor may encounter words they don't understand or syntax they find confusing. Clearly their script prep needs to include everything that is spoken in the scene, not just their own lines, so they can truly understand what is being said to them. I would recommend reinforcing that with your company.

As a director, you have maybe experimented with paraphrasing in rehearsal—it is a great tool for testing whether or not your cast understands a piece of heightened text—but in all likelihood you have asked your cast to paraphrase only the words assigned to them, not those of their scene partner. The difference is that, in addition to clarifying what the words mean, this exercise also *reverses the intention* so that they experience the incoming data personally (as it is felt by "me"). Take a look at how "you" and "me" play off each other.

Let's pursue the scene a bit further.

CORDELIA: Nothing, my lord.

LEAR: *Do I understand you to mean that you have nothing to say to me?*

Nothing?

CORDELIA: *Do I understand you to mean that you can't believe I have nothing to say to you, and need me to confirm it?*

Nothing.

LEAR: *Do I understand you to mean that you are again insisting that you have nothing to say to me?*

Nothing will come of nothing: speak again.

CORDELIA: *Do I understand you to mean that my insistence on having nothing to say will result in my getting nothing from you; and that you want me to say something that pleases you in order to get my reward?*

Unhappy that I am, I cannot heave
My heart into my mouth: I love your Majesty
According to my bond; no more nor less.

LEAR: *Do I understand you to mean that although you feel bad about it, you cannot manage to find words of love; and that you only love me as much as ordinary child/parent duty requires?*

How, how, Cordelia! Mend your speech a little,
Lest you may mar your fortunes.

So we experience, through the text, the *action* from Lear that elicits Cordelia's *response*, which is in itself also an *action* in need of a *response*: a continuous chain.

This segment may seem a bit laboured and perhaps a tad obvious, but think about it: What goes into this chain of "nothings"? In handing back and forth between them the simple idea of having *nothing to say*, the incredible stakes are revealed. The exchange must be loaded with meaning for father and daughter. Both are measured and sure of what they say, and as a result the action of the play is catapulted into being. This exercise shows you how much you can hear in one simple word and how personal it can feel.

EXAMPLE TWO

Okay, let's dig a little deeper and look at how the choice and arrangement of words can become weapons. This time we look at Shakespeare's *Hamlet*—in the scene where, after recklessly reacting to evidence of Claudius's guilt, Hamlet is called in for a dressing down by his mother.

QUEEN: Hamlet, thou hast thy father much offended.

HAMLET: Mother, you have my father much offended.

QUEEN: Come, come, you answer with an idle tongue.

HAMLET: Go, go, you question with a wicked tongue.

These two sets of paired lines are completely balanced in every way, including the metric length (the first pair having an extra foot in each). Word by word, Hamlet transforms his mother's simple sentence into a weapon, which he could only do if he has truly heard her, specifically and clearly. He makes no mistakes.

Hamlet/**Mother,** thou/**you** hast/**have** thy/**my** father/**father** much/**much** offended/**offended.**

Come/**Go,** come/**go** , you/**you** answer/**question** with/**with** an/**a** idle/**wicked** tongue/**tongue.**

In the second pair of lines, Hamlet takes pains to match her words, particularly the action words (verbs), with their *opposites* in order to challenge and provoke. Literally, this weapon is only available to Hamlet because he has listened so intently that he can use her *exact* wording against her. This is the launch pad for a sequence that becomes increasingly more aggressive as the scene progresses.

Combining this discovery with the personalization of the "do I understand you to mean" exercise enriches the exchange even more:

HAMLET: Now, mother, what's the matter?

QUEEN: *Do I understand you to mean that you want to know why I called for you and want to know what is bothering me.*

Hamlet, thou hast thy father much offended.

HAMLET: *Do I understand you to mean that you are referring to my uncle Claudius as my "father" and that I have upset him?*

Mother, you have my father much offended.

QUEEN: *Do I understand you to mean that you are childishly quibbling on my use of the word "father" in order to distract from the issue at hand?*

Come, come, you answer with an idle tongue.

HAMLET: *Do I understand you to mean that you think that my concerns about who can be called my "father" are frivolous?*

Go, go, you question with a wicked tongue.

QUEEN: *Do I understand you to mean that you are accusing me of some sort of evil intent?*

Why, how now, Hamlet?

HAMLET: *Do I understand you to mean that you are surprised by my accusation of wickedness, and want to know what I am talking about?*

What's the matter now?

QUEEN: *Do I understand you to mean that you are questioning the subject of our conversation and that you don't respect my authority?*

Have you forgot me?

HAMLET: *Do I understand you to mean that you think I am being disrespectful and have forgotten who you are?*

No, by the rood, not so.
You are the Queen, your husband's brother's wife,
And, would it were not so, you are my mother.

QUEEN: *Do I understand you to mean that you swear by the holy cross that you know exactly who I am. That I am the Queen who married my husband's brother, and that you wish I wasn't your mother?*

Nay, then I'll set those to you that can speak.

HAMLET: *Do I understand you to mean that you don't think I am listening to you properly and you are going to go get someone who will get through to me in a way that will make me listen?*

Come, come, and sit you down, you shall not budge.
You go not till I set you up a glass
Where you may see the inmost part of you.

QUEEN: *Do I understand you to mean that you are forcing me to sit down until you make me face some flaw within me?*

What wilt thou do? Thou wilt not murder me?
Help, ho!

Imagine forming these paraphrased responses in the heat of the moment, off the top of your head, as a result of what you hear. You will find that in order to paraphrase your understanding in detail, you will truly have to listen closely. You can't fake it, because you have to say it out loud to your scene partner who can confirm or deny if you have understood clearly!

The stakes of the scene jump when a third person is introduced—Polonius hiding behind a tapestry—but the exercise continues:

POLONIUS: *[behind the arras] Do I understand you to mean that Hamlet is threatening you with physical violence?*

What ho! Help!

HAMLET: *Do I understand you to mean that you—probably Claudius—are hiding behind the arras, calling for help because I am threatening my mother?*

How now? A rat! Dead for a ducat, dead.

[Thrusts his rapier through the arras.]

POLONIUS: *Do I understand you to mean that you think I am a scoundrel for hiding here and you bet that I will soon be a dead scoundrel and so you have deliberately stabbed me?*

[behind] O, I am slain.

QUEEN: *Do I understand you to mean that without thinking you have stabbed Polonius?*

O me, what hast thou done?

HAMLET: *Do I understand you to mean that you want to know what I have just done?*

Nay, I know not.
Is it the King?

[Lifts up the arras and discovers Polonius, dead.]

QUEEN: *Do I understand you to mean that you thought it was Claudius?*

O what a rash and bloody deed is this!

HAMLET: *Do I understand you to mean that my action was reckless and murderous?*

A bloody deed. Almost as bad, good mother,
As kill a king and marry with his brother.

QUEEN: *Do I understand you to mean that stabbing Polonius was indeed vicious and barbarous, but not as bad as murdering a king and marrying his brother?*

As kill a king?

Hamlet and Gertrude can feel how they battle directly with words that affect each other's choices. Hamlet needs to truly understand what Gertrude means by "a rash and bloody deed." It needs to hit home in a personal way, which will affect how he repeats, "A bloody deed." They have been driven to the very core of the issue, and the next thing out of Hamlet's mouth is, "Almost as bad, good mother, as kill a king and marry with his brother." This is the first time Hamlet actually says this out loud to someone else. It is a turning point in the play. And it will be understood as such if they really hear each other.

This exercise is intended to help an actor understand what they are listening for. It is not something that plays in real time, of course, because during performance there is no time for paraphrasing. Most of the understanding would be taking place simultaneously while your partner is speaking. In quick action such as this, the concepts strike you instantly; there isn't a pause. But for the purposes of the exercise, it is important to give yourself time to address the full spectrum. Trust the thoroughness of the exercise, because you will often find surprises that might slip by at playing speed if you haven't opened your receptors.

The following example from Shakespeare's *Richard III* shows even more clearly how the language you choose is born from the data you have received. This is listening at its most scientific. Elizabeth in particular uses Richard's own words against him, at lightning speed. You will see how the returned paraphrasing leads directly to the wording of each reply. Notice how different it feels when you say it out loud.

EXAMPLE THREE

After clearing all obstacles to the throne and now wearing the crown, King Richard wants a private word with his sister-in-law, Elizabeth, widow of his deceased brother King Edward IV.

KING RICHARD III: Stay, madam; I must speak a word with you.

QUEEN ELIZABETH: *Do I understand you to mean that you want me to wait because you have something to say to me?*

I have no more sons of the royal blood
For thee to slaughter: for my daughters, Richard,
They shall be praying nuns, not weeping queens;
And therefore level not to hit their lives.

KING RICHARD III: *Do I understand you to mean that I have killed all of your sons but you will make sure your daughters will be nuns rather than miserable, victim queens; and that you are warning me not to target them in my plans.*

You have a daughter call'd Elizabeth,
Virtuous and fair, royal and gracious.

QUEEN ELIZABETH: *Do I understand you to mean that you are identifying my daughter Elizabeth and that you are describing her as good and beautiful, and a noble princess?*

And must she die for this? O, let her live,
And I'll corrupt her manners, stain her beauty;
Slander myself as false to Edward's bed;
Throw over her the veil of infamy:
So she may live unscarr'd of bleeding slaughter,
I will confess she was not Edward's daughter.

KING RICHARD III: *Do I understand you to mean that you are begging me not to kill your daughter? And that in order to save her you are willing to spoil her character, make her ugly, falsely assert that she is illegitimate; and that, to keep her alive, you would destroy her reputation by dishonestly claiming you cheated on your husband and gave birth to a bastard?*

Wrong not her birth, she is of royal blood.

QUEEN ELIZABETH: *Do I understand you to mean that you don't want me to tell lies about her birth, because she is a royal princess?*

To save her life, I'll say she is not so.

KING RICHARD III: *Do I understand you to mean that you think you can save her life by denying her birth?*

Her life is safest only in her birth.

QUEEN ELIZABETH: *Do I understand you to mean that you are saying only by the fact of her being born royal is she safe?*

And only in that safety died her brothers.

KING RICHARD III: *Do I understand you to mean that her brothers were born royal but they were not safe, they died?*

Lo, at their births good stars were opposite.

QUEEN ELIZABETH: *Do I understand you to mean their births were cursed by bad omens?*

No, to their lives bad friends were contrary.

KING RICHARD III: *Do I understand you to mean that they had enemies in life?*

All unavoided is the doom of destiny.

QUEEN ELIZABETH: *Do I understand you to mean that no one can escape their destiny?*

True, when avoided grace makes destiny:
My babes were destined to a fairer death,
If grace had bless'd thee with a fairer life.

KING RICHARD III: *Do I understand you to mean you are accusing me of having deliberately tampered with fate by avoiding my responsibility as a noble person? And that if I had lived my life better, your sons would have been destined for better deaths?*

You speak as if that I had slain my cousins.

QUEEN ELIZABETH: *Do I understand you to mean that you can't believe I would imply that you could be capable of killing your own cousins?*

Cousins, indeed; and by their uncle cozen'd
Of comfort, kingdom, kindred, freedom, life. . . .

The key concepts swirl and twist through the spine of the scene: sons/daughters, die/live, virtue/infamy, birth/life/birth/death, fate/omens/doom/destiny. They are more than key words; they are weapons thrown, caught, transformed, and returned. Richard holds on tight to the idea of family—calling Elizabeth's sons his cousins. This is clearly strategic, and Elizabeth pounces on it; yes, they are his cousins (kin) and he, their uncle, deceived them (cleverly using a homonym to ramp things up a notch—cousins/cousin/uncle/cozen'd).

Okay, now you have had a chance to see how this exercise can open up the listening receptors of your actors. You may have already realized that there is an equally exciting extra bonus outcome that comes hand-in-hand with this work: clarity!

How we shape what we say affects how it is understood, of course. **Do I Understand You to Mean** is a *two-way* exercise. Actors quickly become aware of the need to deliver their lines with the utmost care and intelligibility if there is going to be any hope of being understood. They have immediate feedback on their success through whether or not their scene partner is able to paraphrase back. The relationship between them becomes teamwork of the highest order. The connection becomes tangible and urgent and very much alive in the moment. You might just see theatrical sparks fly.

All right, you have now tasted what it might be like for your actors to receive their partner's intentions in a way that counts (*Are* you *doing this to* me*?*). So, now what? How does this affect their subsequent response? We have seen how clear comprehension leads smoothly into the wording of the reply, but how can that reply further deepen the actors' intentions? How can we explore what fuels the return fire?

Now you have your cast listening, but the exchange is still not flowing with as much organic life as you would like. It might be necessary to address the reverse angle, so to speak— what do they want to hear back?

A note: the following exercise, **I Want You To Say,** should be enacted *separately* from Do I Understand You To Mean. It isn't possible to attempt both at the same time as it would take you too far away from the core text being examined and would be confusing.

I WANT YOU TO SAY . . .

When we speak, we all wish, however unconsciously, for the ideal response. Agreed? That wish absolutely informs how we construct what we say. Actors need to experience that same act of construction, even though the playwright has crafted the thoughts for them. How is that possible? In this exercise we take that notion to the extreme, allowing the actor time to *insist*, to *fantasize*, to shape the response they want by *force of will.*

Once again, I invite you to step into the shoes of an actor . . .

ACTOR A: I love you.

> *(Actor A, through the sheer force of willpower, imagines the response they want. The more detailed the better. Really look at your scene partner's face, imagine the lips moving. Truly, but silently, insist on the exact wording you want. Perhaps, something like: "Oh my dearest darling, I love you too!" When you have it clearly in focus, invite your scene partner to speak by saying "speak.")*

ACTOR B: You disgust me.

Okay, whoops, that wasn't the response you wanted. The clearer you are about what you want to hear, the more powerful the moment will be when you receive the answer. Remember, your fantasy of what you want the other person to say is private. Do not speak it aloud, but rather keep it inside you as a silent wish.

Here is an example of a scene from Shakespeare's *As You Like It* in which the actors have many choices and the "want" of the scene may not always be immediately obvious. I can imagine that the actors involved might wish to try different options . . .

EXAMPLE ONE

In this scene, Rosalind and Orlando encounter each other for the first time in the Forest of Arden. She is in disguise as a boy and he has been hanging love poems dedicated to her on all the trees.

ROSALIND: Do you hear, forester?

I Want You To Say: Yes, I can hear you. I am listening.

ORLANDO: Very well: what would you?

I Want You To Say: Sorry for disturbing you, but I have an important message for you.

ROSALIND: I pray you, what is't o'clock?

I Want You To Say: Time to get to know you better.

ORLANDO: You should ask me what time o' day: there's no clock in the forest.

I Want You To Say: How clever and wise you are. You are smarter than me, I will leave you alone.

ROSALIND: Then there is no true lover in the forest; else sighing every minute and groaning every hour would detect the lazy foot of Time as well as a clock.

I Want You To Say: How clever and wise you are. You recognize that I am in love. You are smarter than me and I could listen to you all day.

ORLANDO: And why not the swift foot of Time? had not that been as proper?

I Want You To Say: Ah, you got me. I don't have a snappy comeback for that.

ROSALIND: By no means, sir: Time travels in divers paces with divers persons. I'll tell you who Time ambles withal, who Time trots withal, who Time gallops withal and who he stands still withal.

I Want You To Say: You absolutely fascinate me. You are incredibly smart and intriguing.

ORLANDO: I prithee, who doth he trot withal?

I Want You To Say: Darn, I was bluffing. I don't know.

ROSALIND: Marry, he trots hard with a young maid between the contract of her marriage and the day it is solemnized: if the interim be but a se'nnight, Time's pace is so hard that it seems the length of seven year.

I Want You To Say: What a brilliant example. You know a lot about the impatience of young maids.

Of course, this example only explores one set of possible wishes, but the point is to entertain options that can open the scene up. This is particularly important when you don't know yet where the scene might be headed. What does Orlando want to hear back when he asks, "Very well: what would you?" Good question. Is it possible for him to be completely neutral, in limbo, truly waiting for Rosalind to explain what she wants? Or, is it more interesting for him to have a point-of-view right from the beginning? Of course it is, because this gives Rosalind something to work against, which is always more active. Really, Orlando has two obvious choices: either he wants this person to explain why they are calling out to him or he doesn't (perhaps he just wants to be left alone). Is he curious at all? If so, what is the nature of his curiosity? If he is hoping, as in the above example, for an important message, he will be disappointed when the boy only asks him what time it is. Rosalind, on the other hand, apparently gets her initial wish because Orlando's reply is very close to what she hoped for . . . and this encourages her to go further, leading to the sparring one-upmanship that follows. They eventually become quite evenly matched and even occasionally wish for almost exactly the same thing, which could support the idea of a balanced pairing between them later in the play.

In contrast, let's look at a scene where there is a sense of dread about what might be revealed—where what I *don't* want you to say may be as strong an impulse as what I *do* want you to say. The two may go hand-in-hand.

EXAMPLE TWO

In this scene, taken from *The Trojan Women* by Euripides (adapted by Ellen McLaughlin), Talthybius, a Greek herald, is bringing a chilling message to the captive Trojan women. Queen Hecuba and her daughter-in-law, Andromache, protect young prince Astyanax, the last surviving Trojan male.

TALTHYBIUS: Do not hate me.

I Want You To Say: You appear to be kind. We do not hate you. You are only a man, a soldier. You are forgiven in advance. Speak.

HECUBA: You are only a Greek. Give me more reason.

I Want You To Say: I am not like the others. I am a kind and compassionate Greek and will not harm you. I am unique. Speak.

TALTHYBIUS: I speak for others. They send me here to do this thing, I can't say . . .

I Want You To Say: You are forgiven because you are only a soldier following someone else's orders. You are not responsible. We forgive you in advance. Speak.

ANDROMACHE: What could you possibly do to us that is worse than what has already been done? Kill us? We would sleep in surrender of our misery. Rape us? We are already tagged for parcel to our different rapes. There is nothing we have left to fear.

I Want You To Say: You are right. When you put it that way, I see I have nothing more to say. You are strong and fearless and my mission here is useless. Speak.

TALTHYBIUS: I have come for the child.

I Want You To Say: Oh that's not a problem. Take him. Speak.

HECUBA: Which child?

I Do Not Want You To Say: Astayanax. Speak.

TALTHYBIUS: Dead Hector's child.

I Want You To Say: Of course. This is not your fault. We do not blame you. Speak.

ANDROMACHE: Must he go to another master than the one I serve?

I Want You To Say: No, he will go with you to live with Achilles's son. Speak.

TALTHYBIUS: There is no way to say this—the council decreed . . .

I Want You To Say: Oh! Of course, the council decreed that he must be killed. No problem, we respect the council and accept their decree. Speak.

ANDROMACHE: What? Must he be left behind in the ruined city, all alone?

I Want You To Say: The council would never be that cruel. He will not be left alone. Speak.

TALTHYBIUS: Worse, terrible. I can't say it.

I Want You To Say: Don't worry. You do not have to say it. We will spare you. We understand what you mean. You mean that he must be killed and we accept that fate. Speak.

ANDROMACHE: What did the council decree?

I Do Not Want You to Say: That he must die! Do not say it! Speak.

TALTHYBIUS: That he must die.

I Want You To Say: Yes. That is just. Speak.

HECUBA: How?

I Want You To Say: As an old man in his bed some day. Speak.

TALTHYBIUS: He must be hurled from the battlements of Troy. The top of the city walls.

I Want You To Say: That is fair. We accept. Speak.

Again, I reiterate that each actor keeps their fantasy-hopes to themselves. They do not speak them aloud. It is a *private* wish. Only they understand if they get their wish or not. Knowing what they want will colour how they hear the reply, and this brings complexity and detail to the scene.

In rehearsal, you want to pay close attention to whether or not an actor seems to *care* about what effect their words have on other characters and the action of the scene. You may feel that it is difficult for them to find the shape of the scene, the beats, and the climax. You might be yearning for higher stakes and a clearer build of tension in the scene. If you are worried that the thread of the scene keeps snapping, if you sense an actor *disconnecting* after they finish speaking, it is a good idea to remind them of the need to hope for a perfect response. When I have experimented with this exercise, allowing a shorthand to be established in the room, I find I can simply call out, as the actors are working, *"I want you to say . . . "* and the reminder is alive. You might wish to wait and address the problem in notes after rehearsal, but I, personally, like to inject it into the room in the heat of the necessary moment.

COMMUNICATION AS SCIENCE

I hope that through these exercises, you can start to illustrate for your actors how communication is actually a science: the meticulous, exacting art of finding the perfect mechanism for conveying an idea. Science before emotion.

Clean, clear listening skills are the basis for this science. But listening is a two-way street. When we speak, we want others to listen, and so it becomes equally important for the speaker to be clear and precise. Heightened language can deliver ideas with mathematical precision.

By its very definition, poetry is capable of reaching inside us and grabbing hold of deep emotions. Sometimes it is difficult to control the emotional rush that these powerful words and images unleash. In fact, it can feel extremely satisfying to connect to such raw emotion—for many actors, heightened text gives them access to emotions they don't experience in other work and they fall victim to a seductive pull to give in to those emotions.

Our objective when speaking is to persuade and teach and change the person we are speaking to. We are arguing, sometimes passionately and fiercely, to be understood. It is important to remember that emotion is a by-product, and not (usually) the aim.

For this reason, encourage your actors to think about what they say in scientific terms, to be clinical and exacting in how they express themselves. To make themselves understood by precision. If there is emotion, let it fall to the sidelines. It can be there, but it is not the point.

In the words of one young actor I had the pleasure of working with on Goethe's *Faust*:

> . . . I remember feeling deeply overwhelmed at the prospect of the role and the process. I was twenty and was not familiar with this material whatsoever. I felt like every second word on the page was a word I had never heard before. I worked very hard to prepare the text and began to feel this enormous emotional connection to the material. In our first rehearsal Jeannette and I were working through the massive opening monologue. She let me do one pass and then she gave me a very gentle but incredible note. She told me, when approaching sections that were particularly emotional, not to try to muscle the emotion, but instead to think of the text as facts. It made complete sense to my whole body and unlocked a profound understanding of the material in a way I didn't think was possible. She was very quickly able to get me to stop working so hard and to find the moments from an authentic and truthful place.
>
> I really think it was a moment where I felt what it was to be an actor. It remains one of the most cherished artistic moments of my life.
>
> —Alessandro Costantini

The following brief passage from Faust's opening monologue illustrates the point. He is describing, in elaborate detail, a profoundly emotional and sensual experience that hits him as he reads a passage from a book of magic. He is not merely experiencing it physically, but he is attempting to describe the experience as accurately as he possibly can. As a drug-like sensation courses through his body he notices something happening to him. It swamps his senses, and he can literally feel it travel through his veins and nerves. He describes it as an injection of youth tonic.

FAUST: Ha! as I look, what sudden ecstasy
Floods all my senses, how I feel it flowing
Through every vein, through every nerve in me,
Life's sacred joy and youth's renewal glowing!
Did not some god write these mysterious
Signs, by whose might my soul is filled
With peace again, my poor heart healed,
And by whose secret impetus
The powers of Nature all about me are revealed?
Am I a god? Light fills my mind:
In these pure lines and forms appear
All Nature's workings, to my inner sense made clear.

He tries to analyze the source (some god?) and through scientific deduction he arrives at the conclusion that he himself has god-like powers of understanding now.

The facts of the speech are:

1. At the same time as my eyes read the words on the page of this book, I feel a corresponding physical sensation, which is extremely pleasing.

2. The physical sensation is speeding through my physical body, specifically travelling through my blood-veins and nerve endings.

3. I believe this warm sensation means I am becoming young again.

4. I think this is coming to me via the actions of a supreme being who has the power to cleanse my essential soul of past troubles and give me back a long-lost sense of serenity, which, in turn, by some magic, has opened my understanding of all the laws of nature.

5. I think this must mean that I am now a god too.

6. I am suddenly filled with intellectual clarity and can easily understand the signs and symbols on this page.

Following this path of logic helps the actor avoid the pitfall of "getting velcroed to the ceiling" (my phrase) in a generalized emotional state. I see it often when actors give in to that sensation of awe and excitement that has no foothold, nothing to keep it grounded: breathing gets shallow, the face gets red, veins bulge in the neck and temples, and the voice goes up and up in pitch. Ultimately it is very disconcerting for an actor to find himself up there, hanging in the air, with no idea how to get down to finish the scene.

Tracing the *facts* keeps the thoughts grounded.

* * *

The world of the play is determined by the language used to construct it. The play will not *live* if that language isn't handled in a completely truthful way. It must be delivered as part of an organic exchange that makes sense. Something coming in and something going out: listening and responding.

In preparing to direct a heightened-text play, I pay close attention to the themes, mood, and message of the story revealed by the *poetic language* in which it has been created. As part of my script prep I identify how that story might be delivered by the characters in the play. Through rehearsal I try to guide my acting company to a place where the *language world* empowers them.

I offer these exercises as an illustration of how actors can listen to heightened text.

In taking their scene partner's challenging language deep inside, an actor has a better chance of truly hearing it. Personalizing the experience brings them to a clearer sense of urgency and clarity about what they might want in return. In order to get what they want—to make a difference, to affect change—they must demand with scientific precision. Ultimately those electrical impulses of communication work together to create the extraordinary *moment that is now*.

And this gives me the fabric I need to start creating the production that I yearn for.

BREAKOUT SESSION

To Table Work or Not to Table Work

Every year we conduct the same session with each new group of Labbies. We call it "To Table Work or Not to Table Work." We spend time discussing the pros and cons of the practice. There are so many opinions and theories behind its effectiveness, but the overarching answer to this conundrum always seems to be "it depends." It always depends on the piece, since table work means different things for different people. It also varies if the piece is devised, a classic, a new play, a movement piece, or something in between. The consensus over the years has also been that a blend of table work and up-on-your-feet play yields the best results. Here are some of the highlights over the years of opinions, practices, and theories. I hope some resonate with you and you can implement them into your future work.

- Table work tells you where the actors are at with the piece. I need to see if we're all on same page. A scene is hard to block when we don't know what is going on. The scene will block itself if you've done the work ahead of time.

- It gives some structure and boundaries. All actors are different in what they like and some need this.

- We empower our actors by being intellectual and analytical. It can be as liberating as being physical. Being physical is vulnerable.

- Table work allows you to address all the questions before the scary proposition of moving bodies in a space.

- It allows us the time to create a living encyclopedia of questions, going through with cast and designers to gradually answer all the questions.

- It's a jumping off point. Yes, it is decision. It's a launching pad, but we're not auctioning the entire text ahead of time.

- The goal is to make sure we are in the same world. References in the play need common understanding. I do steer away from making decisions at the table as things will change in the space itself.

- I don't like term "table work." It's all rehearsal; a welcoming process to the world so we can play in it.

- It allows for fact finding.

- Scene-read, then up . . . then read . . . then up.

- I keep a table close by so any time we may have a stumbling block we can all sit around the table and dig into the questions.

- I like to fuel the actors with some table work. Otherwise I feel like they are floundering in chaos.

- It's a great way to make sure you are all collectively grasping the playwright's vision and digging into what they are saying.

- We read through together once, then read a scene, talk about it, and loosely block it.

- It's about identifying intention, making a decision.

- Time around the table is necessary to an agreement about who these characters are, what they are looking for, what they want. This must be agreed upon.

- It depends on what the project is, but text lives in our bodies. I expect them to come with the text memorized to blocking rehearsal in the second week. It's active analysis, exploring themes of the show. We create scenes around this, connected to play.

- I like devising on our feet. Energy can get low at the table. It can get boring and become repetitive. Instead, I read while moving in space, being active, and having energy.

- If it's a social, intellectual piece, table work asks why the piece is relevant now. I bring in articles and talk about the big idea, reigniting the fire of the piece for myself and for the cast.

- I do a mix of the two. We move through the space knowing intention without words; then the words just come.

- For me it's a combination—table read in morning: what are the facts, make a huge list, character to character. Then the afternoon I guide through huge improvisation, emotional work, walking improv for an hour and half, which drops them in emotionally and creates a huge jumping off point: how are you connected, what is your feeling towards one another?

- The first couple of days we set the tone for the culture of the room.

- I found that breaking the script down into beats, and titling and "verbing" everything—all the things I was taught in school—didn't work for me. I found it rigid. I found that the overarching ideas were more important to me, and that's what I implemented into my table work.

- I use table work to make sure we all understand where we are—time, place, and so on—and have the opportunity to uncover and ask questions about what's going on in this moment or in that one. Here's the secret that's revealed, and here is the lie. I try not to set up any structure but more to have an opportunity for actors to feel like they're not performing yet or worry about being on their feet or what their bodies are doing. We pull apart the script and talk about themes, not to over intellectualize but to have a familiarity with the text and what is underlying the text before going into specifics.

- It's an opportunity to answer questions and think about our characters and our relationships.

- I used to work as an actor and I need to work in stages. If I'm thrown onto my feet on the first day with no discussion and no searching of the text, it's difficult for me to intellectualize while I'm trying to physicalize, and to conceptualize while trying to intellectualize. So I find it a great benefit to talk about the play, make some preliminary investigations and then start to build a physical structure for it. Then we can discover where we might have gone wrong. Keep it flexible at every stage. But I crave any kind of framework.

- It's a way to make sure that everyone is in the same play. To bring all the questions and collaborate at the table with the performers gives them an opportunity to invest and feel part of the process so when we're on our feet, there is a base.

- You're also using table work to figure out who is in the room with you. You need to suit the play to the people who are working on it, to ask what is this work that only the bodies in this room can make, that another group wouldn't.

- I find table work exhausting. I experiment with loose blocking and talking, which I find more effective. I like to try things rather than talk in circles.

- Text lives in our bodies. So we need to know what we're talking about.

- It helps to set the context. It's about meeting the people and their minds. But I do try to keep it limited. It has to serve everyone in the room, but it doesn't have to be at an actual table!

- For me the rehearsals start when we're on our feet. The rest is just dialogue.

- So many juicy stories come out of that table work. Sometimes people's sharing of their own experiences from reading this work is the most fruitful part. And it does create a bond with the ensemble.

- Table work mixed with games works best for me. So it's a balance of playing and intellectualizing.

- I often work with dense scripts and heightened poetic language, so I tend to do longer table work intentionally. We often do a couple of weeks, if time permits, where the entire team is there, talking about it and interrogating the script. Simultaneously, we do physical work, but it's not with the text or the script in your hand. It's more experimenting with organic moments, where we explore the sounds we talked about that relate to the script or images we've discussed.

- It's not about "verbing" individual moments pedantically, but about distilling down a script to essential story points. There's confusion when there's not a conversation about how to chart a story simply. It's about giving a subjective framework in which to play. I also spend a lot of time listening to each individual actor's vocabulary, and I note a lot of it because I know that, in the process, I can reflect some of that back. Half of my job is about finding common vocabulary.

- I used to do table work because that's the system I'd been taught. I was trained in a literary process. I found I would do all that work myself at home for weeks on end, then repeat it again with actors, knowing already what I wanted, so it felt false. I also think that some actors are not comfortable doing that work. I think they spend a lot of time trying to get good at it. What actors are good at is getting up and doing stuff on their feet. I like to work with actors who think on their feet. I found that what I was doing around the table was blocking that process. I now start on day one up and in the space.

- When you sit down and figure it all out "intellectually," then you've stomped on it. The surprises are not there. The things you discover as you play don't come to you because you've already decided what it is in advance through logic. But if there are questions that need to be answered, I'm not opposed to table work. For me, you establish trust by playing. I'm not so interested in the real life stories of my actors. That's not where the trust comes from for me.

- I usually go into the room and see who my tribe is and cater to that specific group. I'm a big fan of throwing everything out the window and jumping up on our feet, but there are actors who don't respond well to that, so you need to communicate things to the actors you have in the room and respond to their needs.

- We need to think about table work as part of a dramaturgical element in the process as opposed to its own separate thing.

- I think we can all agree that dogma is poison. Any book or theory or learned process is a tool. You have to be flexible because each actor is unique, and you have to work with each of them.

- The more you discover at the table, the more it's going to help the production.

- Sometimes late table work is helpful. We can't figure it all out on the first days of rehearsals.

- Table work is an opportunity to notice layers and make connections, explore what's beyond the surface.

- Table work establishes commonality and makes connections between you and the characters.

- It allows you to also see the personalities of the people you are working with.

- It's about *posing* questions, not answering them. What are you curious about at this point? What's there for the director to answer?

IN CONVERSATION

with Directors

THE ART OF ADAPTATION: PETER HINTON INTERVIEWED BY ELIF IŞIKÖZLÜ

This interview took place in 2016. Peter had just adapted and directed Alice in Wonderland *at the Shaw Festival, and the Labbies had gone to see it as a group. Much of this interview is based on his adaptation of this particular piece.*

ELIF: I wanted to delve right into this question of adaptation. I know that you directed the show but you also adapted it. I'm wondering if there's a particular meaning that adaptation has for you that's different than perhaps writing a piece that's original?

PETER: That's an interesting question because my instinct to write and my instinct to direct come from the same place. Because I feel that directing is working with a different language of storytelling—with actors, with design, with elements in time. And my directing is really centred on the premise of the play and its ideas, its words, and so where the writing starts and the directing takes over is always a very fine line for me. I've been very fortunate in my time in the theatre of directing, in equal measure, new original work and classical plays. Adaptation could be a whole discussion within itself, because how something works in one form and how it works in another is a dramaturgy of constant trial and error and experimentation. And one in which you're trying to bring elements of a theatrical dynamic to a literary form. You're emphasizing the literary nature of the theatre versus where you're changing it, so it's such a huge question for me. I've done a lot of adaptations and I'm interested in what it asks of the *auteur* aspect of directing. What I don't prescribe to is the idea that the director is an interpreter alone—an invisible, neutral voice. I feel that's a kind of false thing. I think that how we interpret and how we see something is always a question of adaptation. I don't believe there is a neutral way, or an invisible way. I don't believe that "good" directing is if you "don't" see it. I think that's stage management. What I'm interested in doing is opening up for an audience a way of seeing something. And directing is a writer's form: you're always writing. You're just writing with different things.

ELIF: There's a field that's gaining steam called adaptation studies. They're actually looking at adaptation quite critically, because it's starting to happen so often now on Broadway and television and film. And one of the tenets of the field is exactly what you said . . . that it's not a neutral act. In fact, to adapt something is to engage critically with it, and in some ways to interpret it in the moment of adaptation or to comment on the work critically. I'm wondering if a critical commentary or a critical engagement with *Alice* was part of your approach?

PETER: With *Alice* it's interesting because *Alice* is such an iconic piece that is perhaps more well-known through how others have interpreted it than the actual book itself. And I was very interested in the relationship of Charles Lutwidge to Alice, and the idea of intimacy, and looking at the way a child might see a very complex idea. The thing that moves me about *Alice in Wonderland* is the premise that you're not the same. You can never go back to who you were yesterday because you were a different person then.

I think that's a very complicated idea. Virginia Woolf wrote novels on that subject. I think that's what Lewis Carroll explores in that story, and I wanted to investigate it in the theatre. I think that's a very serious and mortal idea. And I love that it's done through a language of fantasy and illusion and nonsense. So it was very compelling to me. Most people know this piece through a very sanitized vision of it or a very suspicious take. Lewis Carroll was unique in terms of creating the first work of literature for children that had no reliable moral compass. It was the first book for children where there was no adult character sanctifying the child's experience with a moral judgment. The pre-eminent children's author before Lewis Carroll was a chap called Isaac Watts, and there's some of his influence in *Alice*. No one today would recognize it as Watts's, but his contributions are very familiar. Children's TYA is full of these tropes still today. If you ask someone working on a TYA show what it's about, it usually has a moral lesson attached to it. It's about the dangers of bullying or accepting all sides. It has a moral agenda. They make them about morals I share and agree with, but it's very rare to do a TYA show without a moral purpose. We somehow distrust children to be on their own and to make up their own minds about things. We feel we must teach them something. This is very scary. You get a bunch of kids together and if we don't tell them something cogent, then anarchy will break out. And Lewis Caroll was against it. He was an ordained minister and he was faculty at Christ Church Oxford where at the time everyone had to be ordained to teach there. And he was a professor of mathematics and logic. And I think it's very interesting that for a book from his theological background that God is never mentioned in *Alice in Wonderland*. Ever. Satan is, but God is not. And he was quite challenged about that in his own time. To which he said, "God is everywhere in *Alice in Wonderland*." There's a whole series of biblical allegory and allusions. Falling down the rabbit hole is like the fall from the Garden of Eden. In the original story Alice's neck grows like a serpent and invades a pigeon's nest. The great flood of tears is like the deluge with Noah. It runs throughout the book. He created this story for a real little girl, Alice Little, who was the daughter of Henry Little who was the dean at Oxford. And the book is full of riddles and allegories that operate on a large mythic level. It's a way of comprehending European literature and classical mythology on a local level. Every scene in *Alice* has a correlation to a location at Oxford. One of my favourites is the hall that she lands in where she tries the key is the replication of the Radcliffe Camera where the students arriving to Oxford are matriculated. So when you arrive at Oxford your welcoming ritual is in the Radcliffe Camera. So when Alice arrives in Wonderland her welcoming ritual is to get through doors there. He's created this incredible puzzle to live with that attempts to arm a girl with her own resources to take on an adult life that is approaching. I thought that was a natural and wonderful resource for adaptation and theatrical thinking.

ELIF: I wanted to pick up on something you mentioned about morality. Does morality have a place in the theatre today?

PETER: Yes. The theatre is a very moral form. But there's a difference between the inherent morality of a play and characters telling you what to think of it. Plays that have messages, plays that have advertisements in them, I think are insulting to the audience. We say in theatre that you have to create an experience that you can comprehend in one viewing and that's antithetical to what I try to do, because I think great plays require multiple viewings to comprehend them.

ELIF: So why is that idea pervasive?

PETER: I think it comes out of a very capitalist system that says that you have to write about what you know. Give people a product. We have to recognize something. Our whole language of creating theatre in the twentieth century was taken over after the war largely by acting teachers who created a theory about it and theatre was being written for theory, and it's all about set up, pay off—it's a theatre of wanting. You run into anybody and they go, "what do I want?" in this scene and I oppose all of that. I think that is a very cynical way of approaching life and the depiction of humanity. Like, what do you want right now? Wanting supposes that I'm trying to get something from you and I either get it or I don't. It's a very capitalist exchange. And there's something different and more in a play. It's about not understanding. I believe you should write about what you *don't* know. Characters do not explore what they want. I think they explore what they *need*, which is very different. Curiously, the original meaning of the word "want" was to "lack." So when an actor says to me, "Well, what do I want?" in a scene, I ask, "Well, what do you need, actually?" If I *want* you to understand me, I could *not* want you to understand me. It's just a choice, who cares, but if I *need* you to understand me, then it commits me to you in a very different way.

ELIF: "Want" is also very binary.

PETER: It is. But I think that's just very capitalist language we've developed, and it's largely through American culture.

ELIF: Have you ever had to direct a work that you felt was moralizing?

PETER: All the time. And so you have to try to counter it. You have to find the ambiguity in something. Great theatre moments are never one thing; they're always two things. I spent eight hours today talking about why King Lear divides his kingdom into three. I'm coaching someone who's playing him. And if we were to follow this logic, that there is only one answer to that and it's good or bad, then the play is ruined. The play keeps posing that question all the time. And to me that is a great theatrical problem. Everybody wants life to be familiar. I do. I want life to reassure me that I know things, that I have a compass or a bearing for something, yet that is an impossibility. That's the great delight in Lewis Caroll. He understood the nonsense of it.

ELIF: Is ambiguity then an artistic choice?

PETER: I think it's a theatrical condition. It doesn't mean characters don't make choices. You have to do one thing. That's the brutal thing of life. You have to make a commitment. I'm going to sleep with her, or I'm not. I'm going to invest in this, or I'm not. I'm going to kill this person, or I'm not. You have to do one thing—but how it plays out and what it means, a conscious person wrestles with the ambiguity of it. Lewis Caroll does that. For a lot of reasons we are very nervous of doing this with children. Our age looks at the Victorian age with such suspicion. We hate the Victorians. And this is a very twentieth century idea. My belief is that we don't like to associate with the Victorians because we like to believe that we've progressed, that we're beyond them. We don't want to identify with them. There's a lot of scary stuff to identify with. It's dangerous because we like to say, "We're not like that." We use the term Victorian synonymously with anything being uptight, sexually repressed, colonial, and cruel. Yet there are many incredible qualities of the Victorians that I think we still share and can learn from enormously. It's dangerous to say we're not like them. People say the silliest things to me. Like when I direct Shakespeare, they say, " I really love the Elizabethan temperament. I would have loved to have been Elizabethan." I'm like, "Nonsense." You would have hated to be Elizabethan. That life was much more brutal. The Victorian age was a much more interesting time. I acknowledge that there were horrors of the Victorian age—slavery horrors. But that's not to say we can't identify with them. I think it's imperative. It's an important age to look at and reconsider. The twentieth century invented adolescence. The Victorians didn't have this sense and so a girl of thirteen was a woman. And we don't know what to do. We're terrified. Capitalism and the industrial revolution failed the economy and the families so deeply we had to prolong [adolesence]. So we invented things like high school, a teenager, invented these enormous things to put off child-bearing as long as possible and created this huge gulf called adolescence. So I'm inviting you to understand from a different habit of mind. I was trying to capture how a child hears things. I was trying to use impressionism as a theatrical mode in contrast to fantasy and whimsy in the story and the idea of realism, which is a really important ideology to nineteenth century drama. There is definitely a method to my madness. That's just part of how I think of creating something. History is a really interesting thing to contend with in our own time. I think this notion of our suspicion and hatred of Victorians—I think we're very pompous about the Victorians. That's what I don't like. We allow ourselves to feel quite smug about our sense of progress. I don't think we're that far from it. And I certainly think there are many aspects of our culture today that are far more conservative than they were in the 1860s. And I'm interested in those things.

ELIF: Is that aspect that you wanted to push more in the piece, or was the amount that was there quite deliberate? Because it was like you say, subtle. Or was it just the right amount? Or is there another version or adaptation of *Alice* lurking somewhere?

PETER: No. I was trying very much to play within the codes of its time. That's what I meant by the impressionism. To me it's a play about a girl who gets in a boat and steps out of it a young woman. It's a play about the death of childhood. And that's inevitable. It must happen to all of us.

ELIF: This idea of mortality, I'm hearing that again. And it's interesting because the word "adaptation" or "to adapt" in biology is something we must do to survive as a species. So I'm wondering if, in a way, the adaptation of the Alice story—does it need to continue to adapt in order to survive in our contemporary culture? Is that part of the reason it's important to revisit it or re-adapt it?

PETER: I don't think it's important to re-adapt it. I think it exists. Most people's experience with *Alice* is not through reading it. This is my new thing. I've stopped teaching acting. When a theatre school speaks to me, I say I will come to teach reading. That's what I teach. I teach reading. I'm a reading teacher. And that's true of my directing master classes too—they're about reading, how you read something, because that's what I think we don't know how to do. People don't have the discipline of reading. They think reading should be shoved in between other things. That it should be easy. That a book or a play does all the work and entertains you. It's a very entitled, selfish way of approaching a work. I think reading a play should be like reading a piece of music. Words require playing. It's a very active engagement. Last year I did an informal survey among my students to ask them what they read, when they read, if they had a reading habit and where they read, and how much time they devoted to it daily. I can tell you that most people told me they read in transit between one place or another, or in bed. This is as sensible to me as saying "I want to be at my height of physical fitness and I do my workouts on the bus and my bed. Most people don't dedicate time to read. Those are skills that are really needed by actors and directors. So in my adaptation of *Alice* is a reading that I think is true to it. I'm being criticized because I didn't interpret it. Because I didn't say this means this or that Alice was abused. In other works I've directed I've been more demonstrative, but I didn't want to do that with this.

ELIF: Your adaptation is in a way a dialogue?

PETER: I think so. I can argue very much why things are there. And what people see and what people don't. It doesn't mean it's successful or that it's perfect. I learned that on this. My directing is very popular when I'm more demonstrative to my public and very flattering to my public. As Oscar Wilde said, "The theatre does not reflect life, it reflects the spectator." My plays that are very popular tend to do that more. This one is more asking the audience to come to *it*. Which is interesting because it's a very showy piece with an enormous design. I nearly died when we were teching it. But it does demand the audience come to it. We used to live in an age where you had an artist's depiction. You go on a trip to Rome and you'd have an artist's depiction of the Colosseum. Then, innovation-wise, you'd be able to take your own photograph of the Colosseum. Now you take a picture of you at the Colosseum. We are the centre of our narrative. And *Alice* is not about that. It's not about trying to put you in it. It's asking you to come to her. It's asking you to go outside of yourself, so it's difficult.

ELIF: There are two threads here. One is what you mentioned about teaching reading and, in a way, espousing a more contemplative approach to art, which is something we've distanced ourselves from for a long time. I feel we're coming back to contemplation or giving contemplation weight in our society. And that's what you're asking the audience to do, to engage in a contemplative mode with the piece, not meaning to sit back, but to let the work be received.

PETER: I think reading is very active.

ELIF: Right. But it requires a kind of stillness, a mental stillness. Or a state of mind in the spectator that you're hoping for?

PETER: I think it's more a skill necessary to create something. Reading is a lost art form that we need to be rigorous about as practitioners. I can't do anything about the audience. But as a creator of theatre—and you know, I've got ten years left to do it, so I want to really be rigorous about it.

ELIF: Is this a new thread directing-wise? Or is it production specific?

PETER: I just discovered it because I realized I'm not teaching acting or directing; I'm teaching reading.

ELIF: But when you direct—this question of ambiguity, that's something you're going to actively engage in?

PETER: I always do. It's always part of my working practice. I make rules in my rehearsals about what language I like to use. And the others are free to reject it when they leave the room. They can go to the bar and say I'm full of whatever, but they don't. The actors are very stimulated by it. And this want/need thing—they love it. At first they're like, "What do you mean? I've trained in my wants." And then I say just replace it with needs. The thing about "I want and need" that I find interesting is "I want, I want, I want" makes it all about need. Need means I have to look at you. If I need something from you, I can't just *need* need. I want to be loved is all about need. I need to be loved, well, from where? All of a sudden I have to actually look at you. It takes the artist outside of themself. Most directors or actors or writers believe that creative stimulus comes from inside you, which I don't believe is true. Creative stimulus comes from outside of you. And as soon as you accept that then creation becomes much freer. If you get up there and think, "Oh, I have something brilliant to say," you're going to get tongue-tied really fast. But if you want to have a conversation with someone and actually disagree with somebody or change their mind about something or let them know that you think something, as soon as it's outside of you, then you have something to say. But if I get all fixated on myself, then I get very boring.

ELIF: It becomes the idea of self-expression.

PETER: Yes. That's very detrimental to the theatre. I think of it like dating. Like, a really bad date is the guy who says, "Well, in 1985 I did this, this, and this," while a great date is the guy who says, "Tell me all about you." Because he's interested in *you*. Not the person who talks only about himself. So a play's like that.

ELIF: So Peter, why only ten years?

PETER: Because I'm fifty-four. I believe directing has a shelf life. That's my bias. I don't want to be a director when I'm seventy. Theatre is a young person's game and I'm in my last ten years. I've got ten years of vigour, then it's kind of like a legacy, laurel, sitting-on-my-work type thing. There needs to be space for young people. I really think that. And there are plenty of universities I can go to to do my thing, share what I know. That's why I'm very committed to mentoring—committed to passing on what I know to another generation and having my ass kicked by young people. It's very important to me. But I don't like this generation of sixty-year-old directors running everything. People running theatres for twenty-five years, that's crazy. So I really have ten years where I can be vital. And I want to be vital. I don't want to just rehash. I want to be meaningful.

ELIF: Do you think there's going to be a work that's going to define who you are as a director? Is that something that you aspire to, or do you just want to continue working?

PETER: I just want to continue working. I know there are plays I want to do. I do want to direct Shakespeare again. And I would like to do a Greek tragedy. And I have to do a Restoration. So I have my little list. But you know, time is ticking.

ELIF: Why is theatre a young person's game?

PETER: Because it's alive. And it requires a lot of physical and mental energy. And it needs young people. We are not doing terribly well at opening our theatres to young directors. Stratford is probably the most exemplary. There are young people. I want all generations speaking to the art form. And every now and then have the old master whip it out. I think theatre needs more young people in the big institutions, on the big stage, with all the resources. It needs the perspective of the millennials. Because that teaches me a lot. How are you going to be good unless you get the shot? I grew up in a time where I got shots. All the time. And I'm not trying to say the '80s were the heyday, but they were better than now. And not because I was more talented, but I had more opportunities. I went into a theatre and said I want to direct and I was pointed to a pile of scripts. It wasn't hard because I was white, and male, I was in Toronto, and I was ambitious. It's not true of my female counterparts, and it's not true of my brothers and sisters of colour. They're not around anymore. There were no opportunities. Things are different now. We have a higher consciousness about that now, and yet still no opportunities. We need to make room. The problem with our theatres is that they're being run by people who have nowhere to go. So they hold on and they make the dialogue about quality. It's not about that. I'd be foolish to say

I get my opportunities because of my talent. It suggests that others don't because of their talent or lack of it.

ELIF: Are there other skills you think are lacking or need guidance from you, or a gap that needs to be filled in relation to directing?

PETER: Problem solving. Reading, problem solving, and maybe something to do with delegation. Reading is enormous and covers many things for me. Many young directors get very obsessed with the interpretation right away without having full access to the skills of accumulating the information to interpret. I was working with a director today who was very excited with the idea that the coxcomb in *King Lear* would be a bowler hat, in reference to Beckett. It was all very interesting, I suppose, but I thought about what a coxcomb is—and one of the things about a bowler hat—yes, it's true that clowns wear them and Beckett has them, but to me they're kind of cruel. I also have images of Sally Bowles and *Clockwork Orange*. What I understand a coxcomb to be is one thing. It's a signature of a fool. It says you're an idiot. You should look foolish wearing it. You're the clown. It doesn't mean you have to do a court jester from a cartoon book, but the director has to find something that functions in a way it's intended in a script. And this director felt I was infringing upon his aesthetic. And I said, "I'm not infringing I'm trying to say it's a singular meaning in the text, so no matter how you translate that, it's a singularity of shame." Especially when there is a crown and fool's cap. It's a very particular thing. I don't know what the equivalent is, but one should feel like a ridiculous person wearing it. That's why the fool gets away with such wisdom, because he looks like an idiot saying it. That's an example of how interpretation and innovation and actually gleaning concrete information comes from reading. And by reading I don't just mean ABC. I mean how to *read* something. How to read the room. How to read your crossed arms, or your great shoes. How to read all the clues that are full of paradox and contradiction. That's what I think we do as directors.

ELIF: Our primary function?

PETER: Yes. I get the privilege of watching a lot of young directors go into a room, and what I see—I've sat down and had an amazing coffee with this person prior to this and they have these incredible ideas—and then they go into the room and they're completely boring. They become a cardboard cutout, because they're so terrified of being approved or judged or liked or interesting. I'm no different when I'm directing a play as I am right now. I hope. So it's how do you stay yourself? You were right, there is an element to reading— Someone once told me a very beautiful thing a long time ago, to imagine in your head the picture of a director, and what is that picture you see? A lot of people see a guy—maybe not, maybe that's not true anymore—and they're pointing and their mouth is open. And what is the picture of you directing? Is it you? And how is that person receiving, listening, watching? That's largely what reading is. How do you be in a room? I took on this incredible experiment this year that's really tiring, which is to direct without my book. What it means is I prepare in a way so I really know what I'm going to be working on that day, so when I come in I never have my script. It means I can see what you're doing. It's very risky to direct a scene with your head in a book. You can get very attached to what is happening on the page. My biggest problem as a director is that I fall in love with actors' problems. I especially love heterosexual male actors who are emotionally tortured. A straight guy who cries? I'm done for. A dramaturge I worked with said it's because I don't have to fuck them. And it's true, because there's no sexual dynamic. The problem is I can fall in love with that problem, but it doesn't mean they've overcome that problem. Or that they're any good. I can love someone struggling with something. I admire an actor's struggle so hugely. But I do need someone to say, "Yeah, they have that struggle, but they're losing on it. It's not helping the play. So you have to have a degree of "seeing" that's objective, that acknowledges it's a really legitimate struggle you're having, but the play demands this. The play demands that person overcome that particular struggle I might be in love with. So this business of directing from "seeing" required an incredible amount of discipline. And it means that I'm only assessing what works by what I'm seeing in front of me, not what I'm imaging or hoping or what I'm told it is, but what I'm "seeing." It's really hard. And you have to go back to the script to go, "There's a great scene going on here but, oh, that's not written." You have to balance the homework part with the actuality part.

ELIF: I almost feel like you're describing a state of mind when you enter the room.

PETER: I try to respond to what's actually happening in the room. Not what I want to happen in the room, or what I hope is happening in the room, or what I fear is happening. A lot of directors are terrified of a boring rehearsal. It drives me nuts. As an artistic director I got to see this a lot when I'd visit the rehearsals. A scene would go terribly bad and the director would go, "Good. Good. It's all good." And I would think, "Why did you just say that? It wasn't good. It sucked. It was horrible." And the actors think, "Oh God, he thought that was good?" The actors know. It's so liberating if you get the tone right, if you're present and with them, if you are a problem solver and have an idea of what we're going to do. If you say to your actor, "Wow, we're not going to do it that way," they think, "Thank God, he knows!" *Now* what are you going to do? That's your job. You're job isn't to know the right way, you're job is to have another solution, to try. You go, "Well, I said we'd get to the Falls by two o'clock. We're still not there, but I think we should unpack this inflatable raft I have" or whatever your analogy is. But that's about a real presence of mind. You're actually seeing what's going on. Some directors do this sort of Socratic method of questioning. "How was that for you?" That's making the actor do all the work. Happens a lot. If you're an actor you know that one. You've been there. We have to come to the table with more than that. I need to be responsive by really seeing what's happening in the room. That goes hand in hand with a very comprehensive reading. A lot of the time I'm saying, "There's this signpost, this signpost, this signpost"—that's the reading. Then you have to be present to see how the actor is managing those signposts.

ELIF: Thank you, Peter. Let's open this up to questions.

LABBIE: How do you feel about assistant directing? What their job is and what that entails and how that contributes to the process of younger directors?

PETER: I work a lot with assistants. It depends on the person, but I try to give the assistant a meaningful function or a role in the room. I'm not big on the observer position, because I would find that painful. So I give them a role and that will immediately unload a lot of work that I don't need to do anymore. I used to be a very controlling director. I'd have to do all the research, and I would have to decorate the room. I don't do that anymore. I think it's important to endow that AD with a relationship to the room, make sure they're actively engaged in it. There has to be a constant checking in. There needs to be dialogue and discussion. With my assistants I try to talk a lot during the day. Every day at some point. It's not easy to do.

I once was assigned an assistant and it was a play with all two-hander scenes, and it was tough because there was this feeling of privacy that I needed.

LABBIE: I'm curious to hear about the process of the evolution of your vision as a director—adjustments you have to make as it progresses in relation to problems or challenges you find along the way, in terms of production and design and so on, and how you reconcile your original vision to accommodate changes as you go along.

PETER: I don't have that issue because I don't have an original vision. I have a compromised vision. There are definitive things about it, but my vision is constantly in flux. So what's on stage is what was intended. It goes back to directing the play you are directing and not the play you wish you were directing. It is the expression of what I had envisioned.

LABBIE: I'm curious when you use the word "devised," how collaborative is that, with a new piece and how it's different when you're using an existing piece that's not your own? What does the word "devised" imply for you?

PETER: It depends a lot on the piece and the circumstance, how long we have, the caliber and quality of the collaborators, did I pick them—all of that stuff. With *Alice* there was a lot of collaboration. There was a lot of improvisation with the company. But it's a very guided collaboration. That's what I think the role of the director is. When is it great when the director doesn't know, and when is it not good? No company wants to feel like they're on a bus driving to the Rocky Mountains and no one's at the wheel. It's scary. That's not collaboration. So how do you guide? I returned to acting last year and I learned a lot. I learned that when the director asks me what I thought, I was thinking, "Does he really want to know or does he just want me to say I love it?" I thought, "Why doesn't he just ask me if I love it?" That would be useful. "Do you like what you're doing right now? Does it give you pleasure?" (As the actor) "Yes. I do. And this costume makes me feel sexy." "Okay. But is it right? Is it what the play needs?" That is part of the language of devising.

ELIF: Is it important to not be precious about things or moments when you're directing?

PETER: Definitely. But it's also important to fight for what *must* be there. It's hard for a director to know what is vision and what is stubbornness.

ELIF: How much failure do you think we're allowed, and how much failure do you think we tolerate with ourselves?

PETER: You just have to keep standing and working. I really don't know what failure is. I know what I assess in my work, what I think is successful or not. What worked or didn't. But if I believe that critical response is success or failure, I'd be insane. I want to be respected. I allow that some of you can see my work and not like it. So I don't prescribe to an idea of failure or success. I don't like awards. I don't believe in those things. I'm suspicious of them. There's an argument that it's about celebration—celebrating our community—and I agree with that. I don't know what the solution is to that.

LABBIE: You talked about impressionism as a theatrical mode. I'd love to hear more on that.

PETER: It's about using an aesthetic of beauty to convey realism. So on one level—I can talk about it really technically—it's to take something that traditionally would have enormous detail and reduce it to its essential dimension. It has to do with what I think is the major, most important, ideological shift that took place during the Victorian period—the abandonment of idealism for realism. Most people think realism is a response against artifice, which I think is untrue. I think realism is a response to idealism. That when we did away with idealism we were left with reality. And reality is impossible to bear. That's what *Alice* is about. So impressionism to me is how to create the impression of the experience and not its reality. That might be an unsatisfying answer to your question, but that is the answer I can provide. It's a lot.

ELIF: Peter, you've given us so much to think about. We really appreciate you sharing your thoughts. Thank you so much.

YVETTE NOLAN INTERVIEWED BY NANCY MCALEAR

This interview took place in June 2017. Yvette's dance-opera, Bearing, *which she created with Michael Greyeyes, had just premiered at Luminato in Toronto, and much of the conversation stems from that performace.*

NANCY: I'm wondering what led you into the arts?

YVETTE: Much to the disappointment of my parents—we actually moved around a lot when I was a child because my father had to take different jobs. When we moved to the city in Winnipeg when I was six years old, my parents gave me all the things they'd ever wanted—as an Indigenous woman from a residential school and an Irish immigrant from the working class—I got ballet lessons, theatre school, books, piano lessons, and that was a mistake on their part because I thought I was going to be an artist. They wanted all that stuff to make me a well-rounded person, not to be an actor. Then I went to university to get a real useful degree in English and French, and while I was there I got sucked into the Black Hole, which was the name of the theatre at the University of Manitoba. And by the time I graduated, I was already working. I wrote my first play, which was in a fringe festival, and I couldn't find anyone to direct it, so I directed it myself.

NANCY: How much acting did you do?

YVETTE: I wanted to be an actor, but I wasn't very good. And there are no parts for women. There are parts for women of a certain age, then there's nothing, then there are parts again. And I didn't have the patience to wait in between. And because I look like this, right? I wouldn't get cast as "Native"—as we would call them in those days—because I read white. So I'd go out for a "half-breed" role and they'd say, "You don't look like an Indian," and I'd say, "This is what a 'half-breed' looks like," but that wasn't acceptable.

NANCY: We've talked to many director/playwrights this week who have very fierce ownership over directing that first production. Is that something that's very important to you?

YVETTE: No. I never wanted to. I wanted someone else to, because I believe in the multiplicity of vision.

NANCY: But do you want to be in the room for that first production?

YVETTE: Yes, I do. I love to be in the room.

NANCY: I'm interested in the process of creating *Bearing*. Can you speak to everyone here about residential schools, because it is very close to you?

YVETTE: I'm the daughter of a woman who went to residential school and an Irish immigrant. My mother was taken from her reserve in Quebec when she was seven years old. My father was her math teacher in residential school. He came from Ireland and couldn't get a job as a draftsman, but he could get a job as a math teacher at the residential school. When she graduated the nuns gave her away. I am a product of the residential school system, literally and figuratively. The residential school system existed for about 120 years of what we are celebrating in Canada as our 150th anniversary, which means that our country is built on the idea of taking Indigenous people and assimilating them, destroying—the idea was to kill the Indian and the child—that's the idea of the residential school. That was articulated. We weren't allowed to speak our languages. We weren't allowed to practice our traditions, our culture. Kids went away and sometimes they didn't go home. They didn't get to go home for summer. Some never saw their families again. And when some made their way back to their families, so much was gone, including their language. You were punished for speaking anything but English. My mother was a polyglot. Her first language was Algonquin, Anishinàbemiwin. Her second language was French, and her third language was English. When my mother died ten years ago she was a master at English but had mostly lost her Anishinàbemiwin tongue. The last residential school closed in this country in 1996. At that time I was thirty-five years old. I'm the first one in my family not to go to residential school, but it doesn't mean it didn't affect me. When my mother died she was estranged from both my brothers, who are both younger than I am. She never saw her grandchildren, my brother's kids. That brother and I are working that stuff out. And he asks me questions all the time. My brother at fifty-two years old is starting to track backwards to find out what his history is. That's what the legacy of the residential school system is. We've all lost in some way or another and are finding our way back. Because if you're on this territory and you don't know what went on before, then you're also lost.

NANCY: *Bearing* was a three- to four-year process from fruition to production. I'm curious how you went from taking that idea and manifesting it to such a massive production.

YVETTE: Because I'm the child of a residential school survivor, I have that history and there's no way to not bring that into the room with me, but it's never been so foregrounded in the work. Music was the entry point for us. Then we began to generate the dance. I threw some text at it at some point, but then I didn't think there was any room for text, because the music is saying this and the movement is saying that, and what we ended up with in text was what you saw on the floor, the scripture, which plays a big part in our colonization.

NANCY: Knowing that as part of the Luminato Festival you'd be playing to a mostly Caucasian audience, did that influence the direction of the piece creatively in any way?

YVETTE: You do think as a director who your audience might be. We have an advantage of being a multicultural company already, so we always have those eyes in the room with us. We were aware of that. And often, because I'm a dramaturge as well, I also put that into the air in the room. And with the dancers I'd say, "Okay, we're doing this, so what's happening in this moment for you? The way this is going to be received is like this." So we can tweak it that way. So we knew it was going to be a really mainstream audience. But we don't do cultural informancy much. I'm done with that. I'm pretty impatient and I want everyone to move along with us now. I'm not interested in having a discussion from point A anymore; I want to start at F or G or H, because 120 years is a lot of time. Let's move on. I don't want to do race relations 101 anymore. I don't want to teach you what the four directions are, what those things mean. Educate yourself. There's lots there. I'm willing to do some stuff like lexicons and talkbacks.

NANCY: The other thing I'm curious about. How do you negotiate the co-creation/co-directing relationship in the room?

YVETTE: It's pretty fluid. That's indicative of the way we work. We're always checking with one another.

NANCY: Are you finding that the responses from the audience are useful and helpful in the evolution of the piece?

YVETTE: Audience response is always the final part of the equation. But first production is always just part of the development.

NANCY: So I have a quote from you: "I found that the way to strengthen the connection to my roots and to my culture was through work. Through education, through my elders, and my teachers." And from Michael Greyeyes: " It's not sufficient that Indigenous voices are present in creation. It matters actually much more that Indigenous voices have their hands on the levers of control. That we have a means to change the story. To tell the story in a way that is authentic to us."

I'm curious—Are the stories more important than who's telling them?

YVETTE: I feel like more makes more. There's room for so many. Part of the challenge is the "one and only-est" of everything. Like one Tomson Highway, so we don't need another Native playwright for twenty years, even though there's twenty playwrights coming up behind Tomson, or under or beside him. And if you track that artistic genealogy, you get one all the time and you miss all the others. Which is what the challenge has been in the work. If there were twenty productions and ten of them were directed by Indigenous directors or the creative team was primarily Indigenous and five of them were white folks and five of them multicultural, then we'd be having a real discussion. But all we get is one. And still the five white folks. And that's where things get out of balance. If there was enough, if more makes more and there's room for everybody, then we can have discussions in the art. But we end up with just one thing representing all of us. And we're not monolithic. Indigenous people aren't monoliths. So one experience can't be representative of us all. Which is why we need more opportunities to tell our stories, because if you look at the mainstream, the "white" stream, everyone is telling stories of everybody's experiences and we should have the same opportunity as well and then we would be able to have the discussion in the art.

NANCY: I'd like to open it up to questions from the Labbies.

LABBIE: This is something I grapple with in my work: when I'm creating art that centres on the experience of a culture that's not the mainstream, but then trying to balance and making the work understood or palatable to a larger outside group. Do you struggle with that? And how do you ignore it or address it or work with it?

YVETTE: I used to work harder to make it more accessible to the mainstream and then the mainstream seemed resistant so I gave up on that and I said, "I'm just gonna do the work. You're welcome to come along on this journey with us."

LABBIE: What is one thing that I can do in terms of decolonizing a rehearsal space?

YVETTE: She says quoting a dead white guy—Jonathan Swift—who said the vision is the art of seeing the invisible. And I think that is the primary thing as far as decolonization, is being in a room and seeing who's not there and then behaving as if they were. If you can bring those who aren't there into the room, then you have a witness. You have a way of being both there and with those who can't be there. That seems too simple.

[Laughter from Labbies.]

LABBIE One tool.

YVETTE: One tool? One tool! Educate yourself. There's ton of great reading now. Once you've got it in you, you've got it in you.

AKRAM KHAN INTERVIEWED BY ELIF IŞIKÖZLÜ

This interview took place in June 2017, the day following Until the Lions, *an award-winning piece Akram choreographed and directed, was performed as part of the Luminato festival in Toronto.*

ELIF: I think what struck me yesterday [after watching Akram's performance in *Until the Lions*] was thinking about what it's been like for you to do four of those shows in succession. What kind of mindset or physical state do you need to be in to keep that going for four consecutive shows as a performer but also as a creator?

AKRAM: I would say I'm in survival mode. I'm forty-two so in dancing terms that's like 110. I have to prepare pretty heavily physically and it gets harder and harder, so next year is the premiere of my last solo. Then I'll retire after that. It's quite strenuous. Emotionally, stamina-wise, it's fine. I go more into my theatre experience and let go of the body, since my body can't always do what I want to do. And since I'm the choreographer/director I get to change stuff to accommodate my body, especially the stuff that I can't do anymore. I have to negotiate with my body throughout the four shows, and I negotiate more and more.

ELIF: So it sounds like the body is moving one way, yet the mental endurance seems like it's going the other way. Would you have been able to endure this kind of performance twenty years ago, mentally?

AKRAM: No. I relied on my physicality, so there's an ego that goes along with that because I was pretty strong. So everything to me was external. There's a space between the body and the physical space within the room that I was interested in. Now I'm interested in the space within the body. Those are very different spaces that you focus on. And as I got older I started to focus more internally. I started to work a lot with Simon McBurney. He studied with Lecoq and we spoke a lot about the internal space, which is limitless. And that's where all the emotion and intention of each action lives. That's what I became more interested in as I got older. Twenty years ago I would not have even been interested in this.

ELIF: This sounds like execution mode. What does it mean to execute from a different place technically?

AKRAM: I feel it's more in your body. And also, you can't win, so you just fuck it. I remember I did a duet with a flamenco dancer, and I discovered I was not alone in the experience; before the show there was a ritual and I realized he was doing the same ritual, so we talked about it. And the ritual was, for an hour before the show we were trying to find wonderful excuses for the presenter to cancel the show. This became an everyday activity. Every performance we were doing this, and around the seventeenth show we discovered we were doing the same thing. And that was because as we get older our mind is in fear mode. And it's in fear mode because it's on two timelines. One is in the past, of the injuries that we've had, and one is in the future, of things that can go wrong. But the funny thing is that, once we got on stage, everything disappeared because we were in another time zone, which was the present. And it's the "fuck it" present where you say, whatever happens happens, you're just gonna go for it. So all that fear just disappeared and you just go with the present. That kind of thing can happen, for example, when I ruptured my Achilles tendon, which was in 2012 just before the Olympic ceremonies, so it would not have occurred to me before. So when you go into the present you become more the performer, whereas before I was a performer but also a witness, because I was also on stage being a director. I was observing the other performers and I was judging them. I was thinking, "Oh, that could be different." I was analyzing them. Which means I was not in the body, which is a very, very different shift. A huge shift.

ELIF: So, when you're in the present what are you relying on to make sure that you execute or deliver?

AKRAM: There is a faith and a trust that my training is properly done. I hate the gym; it's so monotonous. It's not creative or artistic, but I got into doing a lot of preparation to prevent injury, so I carry that with me. But I also do an hour and a half of physical preparation, physical meditation, before I get on stage. There was once when I overslept—because I usually take a nap a few hours before the show—but I overslept and it was half an hour before the show, so I cancelled it because I was terrified. Now I make sure I have five alarms. But that's what I rely on—an hour and a half of getting slowly into it physically.

ELIF: You touch on two things we discuss a lot in theatre, and one of them is relying on your technique and your training so it's there and you don't question it. The other thing is preparation. Often something we talk about at the Lab is this idea of preparing. Do you engage in any kind of warm-up with your cast—your actors or dancers—or do you think that's theirs to follow through on?

AKRAM: I push for the group to prepare together. So the musicians prepare separately, the dancers prepare individually, then they come together. That's a culture I adopted from Peter Brook when I was a kid. There were thirty, forty actors and we would do an intense preparation. One example that inspired me as a child was, when I first came to Peter Brook I was very excited, of course, because it was Peter Brook. I thought, "Okay, we're gonna get to the script" and the script was just lying there, and we got into the space and he said, "Okay, I would like you all to go home now." I was quite shocked. Then he said, "But from the moment you leave the door, you're going to go in slow motion, and when I say slow motion, I mean like this—

[Akram demonstrates extreme slow motion.]

Until you arrive back at rehearsal the next day." Of course I was thirteen, and I wasn't going to do that. I didn't do it at all. I just left the theatre and went on with my day. I was thinking, "What's going on? I thought we were gonna do scripts." And the next day we came in, and I could feel the energy of all the people that had done the exercise had changed. They were in the same zone, one of exhaustion, and one of immense respect for time. And that was his point. That was his first exercise, before we even started rehearsal. He wanted us all to be in the same zone. I think what he was trying to achieve was that he wanted all the actors to experience a sense of a lengthening of time, because that's what *The Mahabharata* is. It's not a clock time. Clock time is Westernized. It's horizontal, it's Christianized, it's man-made, it's industrialized, and it's money time. And then there's the vertical time, which is a spiral time, and that is life-and-death time. It's ritualistic time, it's sacred time, it's seasonal time, it's feminine time, and it's Eastern time. So he wanted us to shift from horizontal time to vertical time. That really had an impact on me and how we prepare before a show. But saying that, I'm still always stuck in my room like a boxer, but I insist that they'll be together.

[Huge laughter from Labbies.]

ELIF: To do what? To just be together?

AKRAM: To do whatever they need to do as a group. They will hold hands. They will sing. They will also do movement while they're singing, so we try to connect the human body, not just through movement, but also as a musical instrument. Each artist will lead it, but I'm stuck in my room. Then I come out and I hug everyone before we go on stage. It's a bit like a boxer: they don't want to see any of it, they zone in, then they just go out into the ring. I've always been a lone wolf. I'm my own teacher. There is the classical world, like classical ballet you learn from a teacher. There is one teacher and many students. In classical Indian dance you train yourself. As an example, when I came back from the Peter Brook *Mahabharata* after touring for two years, I was in chaos because I couldn't adapt to normal life. It was a gypsy life. There was no homework; it was all about theatre. And I was a kid and I was absorbing all that, so when I came back to London, suddenly I have to do exams. I have to follow a timetable, and it was very tough for me. So I used to leave home in my uniform, then I would go around the back and climb over the fence to my parents' garage. I would wait for ten hours, then climb back over the fence, and go back home as if I'd gone to school. So I became very, very good at telling stories, a master of lying, telling stories from that period. I did it for a year. My mother found a letter. She was sick that day—and I usually claimed all the letters from school, there was a whole plan—and she said, "Oh, there's a parents' evening." So she went, and my mother said to the teacher, "I'd love to hear about my son." And the teacher said, "Oh, what's your son's name?" and my mother said, "Akram," and the teacher said, "Oh, I'd like to hear about your son too." And that was the end of my hiding. My mother said, "Where were you?" And I said I'd been in the garage all day. She asked me what I'd been doing and I told her I was training. I was training ten hours a day. I only did it for one year, I've never trained like that again. I took my father's VHS player, and I collected VHS copies of all the people I admired, mostly classical artists. And I learned to memorize the show, their behaviour, so I mimicked them. I could do their entire show.

ELIF: Can I ask which artists?

AKRAM: Michael Jackson, Beckett talking in an interview, Bruce Lee. Classical dancers, their concerts, and how they behaved. I became obsessed with wanting to be like them. And my mother forgave me because she thought, it takes some kind of will to want to train in technique, to just keep doing something over and over again. So I became obsessed with repetition.

ELIF: We saw that last night. But there's also something else you're touching on here, which is how many hours you spent observing. Also, doing. Watching others, absorbing that in. Seeing what you can learn from them. Sometimes I wonder—I don't know if it's the world we live in, or our time—but it seems that with your touring, and later in that garage, you're carving out this time that you can be in to enter an artistic space. How do we do that now? How do we find time to carve that out? It seems to me you had these formative years where you could throw your energy into being in that space, and we can see the accumulation of that in your work. A lot of us struggle with, how do we carve out that time?

AKRAM: It's a difficult question. If you ask a choreographer friend of mine, he doesn't get much funding. So him carving out time is very different for me carving out time. My producer and I have decided that reflection time is expensive and playtime is expensive, but if you invest in that, the result will be that it will have depth. Whether successful or not publicly it doesn't matter, as long as we feel it has depth. To have that depth we invest a lot in everything that leads up to the beginning of creation, which means going into a studio. So if I work backwards, we will have three months before the premiere either with the set or without the set—most often with the set. A year before that we will be collecting poetry, imagery, from all the lead collaborators and the dancers. And in that year we also have a thing called "playing with the absurd." So we would have two weeks, where we bring everything in: costumes, props, everything regarding that subject, because sometimes it's random. Wherever you are, if you like something you bring it in. Then we have a month off, another two weeks and then a month off, and another two weeks. So we design it very carefully. The touring fits around everything. The new creation strategy is very important. And then a year before that, the collaborators and I are meeting regularly and I'm collecting the collaborators and the dancers. So it's a three-year process. And it comes down to money because bodies cost money. With dancers you can't just go into a room. You need a studio space, and that costs money. We're heavily subsidized. We talk to co-producers, so when they invest, they're investing in the whole production, which means they're investing in the whole creation . . . the playtime.

ELIF: What I'm hearing you saying is that you are in a place where you can demand that as part of your artistic integrity.

AKRAM: Yes, we can, but it's also a choice. I have friends who are very big in the theatre and dance world who are happy to just make the work in four weeks. But I'm very slow, or that's my excuse to demand more time. We need to dive deep into it and that takes time. Because we have to shed our normal life, our everyday life, and in order to do that, it takes time. And that takes money.

ELIF: Speaking as an artist here to directors in the room, who perhaps can't filter the outer world as we might like, what do we do in that space between being outside the studio—I like to think about entering the studio as entering a threshold—what needs to happen between here and entering the studio?

AKRAM: Well, I learn a lot from theatre directors. The theatre directors I know prepare a whole load before they get to the studio, and that I have a lot of respect for, and I realize that I have to adapt to them as well. I have to do my own work. Because I'm the kind of person, or personality, that acts like I know where I want to go, and I convince the dancers and all my collaborators that I'm completely in control, but I have no idea.

[Huge laughter.]

And I make them also believe that I've done a lot of homework. But it's a little bit in my nature to be that kind of a risk taker. And it's very risky. I got good at letting them think I know where I'm going, that I know where the narrative is. And I just pray and trust that the narrative will emerge. And it usually tends to emerge two weeks before the premiere.

ELIF: So what are you doing until then?

[Huge laughter.]

AKRAM: I'm teasing the narrative out. I'm teasing scenes out, or things that I like. Every director, when you're into a project, you're consumed by that subject. So when you look outside you see the subject. It's the same thing in the studio. When I see someone doing something that narratively connects with me, I create a scene. It's a bit like storyboarding. We give names. I leave the beginning of the scene open, and the end of the scene open. Because I may want to put it in a different order. So when it comes to the last two weeks, we just throw around everything. And we say, let's do this and this and this and then we do a first run, and we say that didn't work. I look at it in terms of energy and intention. And my dramaturge comes from theatre. I owe her a lot, Ruth Little. She's responsible for some of the great writers of today. I can communicate very confidently after the work is done, but during it I don't have words. I can physicalize what I want, but I can't express in words. She can express it in words. She's been with me since 2008.

ELIF: So again, before you enter the room there's already been so much shared language between you. You're not starting from zero.

AKRAM: Yes. The only thing that used to be consistent is that I come with no preparation, which drives Ruth mad. Because she's come in having done a lot of her own work. She comes with a lot of preparation, but I tell her not to tell me, we'll discuss it later. I don't know if it's an actor's thing or dancer's thing, or a Kathak thing. Kathak is an old Indian dance form. One of the greatest aspects of it is to improvise, which is to create a narrative at that moment.

> *[Akram demonstrates this to the group, creating a mathematical musical equation.]*

So while I was on stage I thought I'd like to create something because, you see, in Kathak I love the sense that you are creating a narrative, and that also came from Peter Brook. Because we used to do workshops in which we would improvise, create a narrative, so it's devised in many ways. And I thought, well, in Indian music there is a huge mathematical calculation going on, so between each syllable I'll put seven spaces, and once I finish the cycle of seven, I will take one count out. Then I would take another count, so the syllables start to accelerate because you're making the gap shorter. So I thought, well, this is laborious. And I thought, can I put a groove to it? So the pattern is—we rehearsed it while we're on stage—

[He demonstrates to the group.]

—so it's mathematical calculations, it makes no sense to me. It has no narrative.

Patterns became a huge part of my narrative. A lot of choreographers think in patterns. And then I discovered, at a very late stage, Stravinsky and I studied him and realize that he wants to evoke emotion through patterns, and I found a similar process. So I wanted to tell stories to patterns, and Ruth really connected with that.

ELIF: I love this because it comes back to things that I rely on, which is technique, timing, pattern, and training, and if we just go through that without explanation, we still find something to connect with without actually knowing the exact dialogue. I find that it's interesting that you didn't start with emotional place. You didn't say, "I want to translate this dialogue and the pattern or rhythm." You entered it mathematically with technique, through timing and training, and you found a way to connect to emotional narrative. That's a process that you definitely find more in choreographers and dancers than with directors in the theatre. So this comes back to a thing that we talked about before, which is directors and choreographers, and is that a continuum? Is it two different things—what's happening that's similar and what's quite different between them?

AKRAM: I think it depends on which cultural perspective you're looking at it from. If you look at it from the Western perspective, then the critics say everything. You have a theatre critic for theatre, dance critic for dance, and a music critic for music. In India everything is one—musician, the storyteller, and the movement. So we don't see actors as actors—a choreographer is a director, a director is a choreographer—but from the Western perspective, director is a director, choreographer is a choreographer, and there's a hierarchy that plays into it as well. Whereas from an Indian cultural perspective, it's not. A director is a choreographer. To me, Simon McBurney is a choreographer. He understands rhythm. He choreographs his shows; he's not just directing. So it just depends on how you are looking at it, really. Yes, primarily director's main source is text, and primarily choreographer's main source is movement, so perhaps that's where the separation is. For *zero degrees*, for example, the choreographer asked me to tell a story the first day of rehearsals that I had never spoken about. So I told him about a journey, that was true, of me travelling from Bangladesh to India and seeing a dead body, and nobody reacted to it. Everything was normal. I had my passport and I thought I was powerful because I was British—the arrogance of me—because I had a red passport and all the Bangladeshis had a green passport and, of course, the guards thought, "We can make money out of this." So I told him the story on camera and he said, "Well, it's not my story. How do I now make it my story?" So he came up with this ingenious idea. Why don't we relearn your talk from the camera, word by word, rhythm by rhythm, gesture by gesture.

[He demonstrates.]

For each phrase it took us a week. It was horrible because I move my hands a lot, so I started to hate myself because it was so idiosyncratic, so codified in my own way, and it happened subconsciously with each phrase.

[He demonstrates for us again the rehearsal technique.]

We treated it like a score, and suddenly it was the first time in theatre you saw two people do the text simultaneously and move simultaneously and I think that's where our career shifted, because suddenly the theatre world was coming to see dance. There was music and it was the first time we thought, "Well, this isn't just dance or music or text." We found a way that was culturally interesting. The writer kept on asking me, "Why did you tell this story." He said it was a confession. He said, "You feel guilty because you didn't do anything about seeing a dead body on the train," and I think he was right. It's funny because I think with actors, sometimes they're incredible and sometimes they drive me crazy because it's just a process of thinking. I understand there's two ways of approaching it. There is a physical theatre director—I won't mention his name—but he said, "I need to know. I need my actors or dancers to know what the fuck they're doing—what the intention is; what the history is; the psychology of the parents and grandparents; what school the character went to—before I even get them to move." There's this whole philosophizing, conceptualizing, psychology process that happens. Then there's a visual artist who said, "Akram, just fuck it, just do, instinctive, just go for it and then discover the character." One isn't better than the other. They're very different processes. Dancers generally tend to jump in. They're not afraid to discover something and look stupid. Especially contemporary dancers. It's not like ballet dancers or Kathak dancers who have more fear of looking like a fool.

They have such a sense of perfection.

ELIF: Well, you're measuring yourself up to a technique and a tradition.

AKRAM: Yes, the perfect technique, where in contemporary dance it's looking for the imperfections. It's looking for the flaws. And that's where I was very fortunate to come across contemporary dance, because I was running away from my community. They wanted me to be a mathematician. My mother became a literature expert, which is where I got all my narratives from Greek mythology, Hindu mythology, all the myths. When I was born they said, this boy is gonna be a mathematical genius, so I was burdened with the responsibility of being a math student, so by default I became fascinated by patterns. My parents didn't know what to do with me, and I thought I've got to get out of London. And what was beautiful about the contemporary dance course was about looking for the imperfections, the flaws, what makes us human. Whereas everything else I'd been training for until that point as a dancer was trying to be godly. But what was interesting many years later is that technique is crucial. When I see great masters perform, you can't describe that they're doing a particular classical form. Because they're going beyond that form. The reason they can command it, or twist it and test it and break it is because they know that form.

ELIF: They're transcending the form. Their technique is allowing them to transcend that form.

AKRAM: And they cannot transcend it unless they know that technique.

ELIF: This is my next question about contemporary dance and contemporary dancers. There is a trend sometimes where contemporary has been confused with sloppy.

AKRAM: I have huge respect for classical because I was trained as a classical Indian dancer. Perhaps there are rumours where classical artists feel that contemporary dancers really wanted to be classical artists but they were not good enough. So they ended up doing contemporary dancing. There was this hierarchy. Contemporary dancers, you think, well, they're just rebels.

ELIF: Well, historically they were.

AKRAM: There is that huge tension between classical and contemporary, but then there's Martha Graham's technique, lots of contemporary dancer techniques, but, of course, it's not as rigorous. But we're not searching for the same thing. For me, personally, I had the rigour that let me train ten hours a day. Because what classical gets you is the sense of rigorous training, and that is about fine-tuning the body, and making it like a weapon, like a warrior.

ELIF: I want to ask you what you're looking for when you're casting your dancers, because of this commitment to rigour and training.

AKRAM: They have to be technically strong. Full stop. It's a three-stage process. First, I have to know they are a technically strong dancer, unless there's someone incredibly interesting with no formal training, someone that is so gifted they have their own technique. Then the second stage is where I enter, and usually I make them stand and not move and see if they're telling me something. That's really hard for a dancer because all their lives they're trained to move. So to me, it's "Are they carrying something in that moment that is being physicalized even by standing?" Sometimes they're speaking volumes, so you can feel it. It means nothing to me if they don't have an emotion. So when I'm looking at a dancer's body, I'm trying to see if I can feel something from them. In Indian dance it's all about storytelling. It's a place of worship, so you're dancing for the gods. So from the moment I enter the space, the first thing I was taught as a child, the first thing is, I touch the floor in respect and immediately the space becomes holy. Sacred. It's a place where we're all going to come in to which we have to commit ourselves and give ourselves fully. The second I leave, I touch the floor and say thank you and go. In contemporary dance that doesn't happen. It's a scientific laboratory. I'm interested in both, but one doesn't exist without the other. I'm interested in scientific movement, but in the end I'm not trying to show scientific movement to the audience. I want to tell them a story. The third stage in the process of audition is: I have a camera so I give them a very strict task. I say, "I'm turning the camera on," but I only pretend to turn the camera on, and I say, "I'm going to film this. I would like you to improvise around that task." Probably in small groups. And then I'll say to my rehearsal director, of course so they can see me, "I'm gonna go get some coffee," and I don't come back for a few hours. It depends on the level of dancers because the more experienced they are, the more they have to express. So I wait and I look through the window. And I see if they're all just standing and tired and don't know what to do anymore. And then I walk back in and turn the camera on and say, "Let's improvise." Because up to that point they're getting rid of everything that they're good at. Sometimes they're showing me everything, all their tricks, but never committing to the task, so they're bending the task to suit their gifts. And I wait till they run out of ideas and then the improvisation continues. And then we begin. Sorry, there is another part of the process, the fourth part. I invite them to be with me for a few weeks of playtime, so I'm still not committed to them, but I pay them for six weeks. Because I need to know if they have mutual respect, respect for other performers, because it just takes one unhappy performer to fuck up an entire tour or company. Just one. I have to protect the group and have to feel there is compassion and a sense of empathy for one another. I also don't follow the classical rule. There are principles like in the ballet. So when I made *Giselle*, the ballet, I made my rules very clear when I signed the contract. It was unheard of. The first thing I said is "First of all, everyone's a principal here and everybody's a corps de ballet and everybody's a Giselle." So, of course, there was a huge outcry, but they kept it internal. You could feel the tension and you could feel the liberation from the corps de ballet who had always just been the corps de ballet who are there for scenery. They were really there to decorate the stars. And suddenly you felt liberation but you also felt fear from the principals. My second rule was that everyone had to be there all the time. Even if you're not working with me directly you have to embody the process. If I'm saying something to you, it matters to you as well. Even if you're Giselle, it matters to you as well, because you are part of this journey.

ELIF: It's a very contemporary ideal, this idea of equality.

AKRAM: I think it's never been quite done like that in the ballet. Until last year, and now they're writing about it, because I think the ballet needs to change from within. Dancers are generally self-sacrificing. They will break their bones for the work. I want my participants to bleed for me, for the work. I don't mean physically, I mean everything is for the work. I think the same with Simon McBurney, when we're in the studio. He's still like a child. Some of the great people are. He acts all-knowing and super eloquent but in the studio, if you ever saw him there with his object, his set, he's constantly running around like a child. All his boundaries melt away. I'm interested in bringing the actor back to the child's body, where we were full of "anything is possible." That's why I do the play of the absurd. We go through a process where we shed being Akram Khan, or whoever, or being a principal dancer and just play.

ELIF: What are some internal principles that we can enter the work with that have nothing to do with the external situations? So in the absence of our ability to exact change in the external world, what can we commit to internally that you think might be useful to enter the work?

AKRAM: That's a hard question. Everyone should have a bible, their own internal narrative. It can't be the same for everyone. One of the things would be rigour. It changes with each process. Rigour stays the most consistent. It's harder for me now to be more internal because I'm an artist that's involved in politics, because I'm dealing with the big guns, co-producers. I'm fighting myself all the time, thinking, "Do I make a particular kind of work that that co-producer would like, that I can get money from?" Which I never had an issue with before. But as you get more established, then there's the audience expectation and the critics' expectation. And I know some artists are like, "Fuck it. I do what I do. I don't make it for them." But I *do* make it for them. I do make it for people, and I care what people feel. Otherwise I can just do it in my living room. I want people to be moved. I want to provoke them or make them think or take them away from their normal lives just for a moment to that space. That's something that I take with me in every process—to find a human story I can connect with and the audience can connect with. But it gets harder and harder, because there's a lot of external powerful voices involved more and more, so I'm having to negotiate with the Akram Khan the choreographer or the Akram Khan that is curious as a child and is instinctual, so that negotiation is very fascinating. And I keep a very few people close to me who say it as it is. One of them is my wife, who is the unofficial dramaturge of my work, and the other is Ruth Little, who is the official dramaturge of my work. They're the voices in my head, like a coach to a boxer. I also find, more and more, bringing in children to see my rehearsals helpful.

Because they are so honest, so primal and you can see when they know it's fake. They know truth very quickly. So I always build in a moment where I will bring children into the process.

LABBIE: I was fascinated by what you said about classical versus contemporary because there are classical actors that say, "Don't worry the text will do it all," which always scares me. Are there similarities between the emotions that are brought to the creation of the piece and the emotions that happen on stage? And do they go too far or not far enough?

AKRAM: It's a good question. A lot of my thinking was formed by what I learned from Peter Brook. I was only thirteen. One of the things he said was that text has to shed itself. We had a lot of text in that piece, so what we did is that we slowly shed the text bit by bit every day until we were left with a skeleton of the text. Perhaps it was because he believed—it's quite philosophical—that the space between the text is where the story is told. The text is the skeleton to arrive at the journey. So what you're going to feel each time you take the journey is going to be different and you need to allow that to happen. The power of dance is that it has the possibility of being ambiguous. Yes, it can be literal but text is loaded. Words are loaded. So Peter was more interested in how to physicalize the text then how to say it.

LABBIE: Do you feel the emotion every time you're on stage?

AKRAM: No, I feel different things. I just allow it now. When I was younger I'd be frustrated that I wasn't feeling it every night and then a great classical master in her seventies said to me, "You're going on stage full. Your cup is full. How are you going to be a vehicle if you don't empty it first? Go empty. The text is there. And it will come. Just go with it." And so sometimes I'm in love with the other character or sometimes it's extremely violent. It depends on how I feel. And we adapt. Sometimes she's extremely violent, so the intention is that we know where we need to be at the end to commit to the narrative to move forward, but in between, how that plays out, it's the same movements but it's done differently. Emotionally different.

ELIF: Unfortunately, that's all the time we have. Thank you so much for your time and sharing your art with us.

MASTER CLASS

Dramaturgy and New Play Development

BY ANDREA ROMALDI

For fifteen years, I worked in new play development. Ten of those years were spent as Literary Manager at Toronto's Tarragon Theatre—a leader in the development of new Canadian plays—where I practised dramaturgy every day. This is a luxury in my field and it served me well, exposing me to a variety of dramaturgical visions, processes, and practices. This chapter draws primarily from my experience as a working dramaturg. In sharing my insights, I hope others can make use of them to support the creation of their own unique theatre.

This chapter is also informed by my contributions as a panellist to the Directors Lab North and questions asked by its participants. As such, it speaks to the relationship between playwright, dramaturge, and director, and it is intended to offer guidance to directors engaged in new play development and/or the premiere of a new play.

WHAT IS DRAMATURGY?

Dramaturges are frequently asked, "What is dramaturgy?" and I would be remiss not to attempt an answer. However, just as each director, playwright, actor, and designer would define their role and practice differently, so would each dramaturge.

In reading my response below I encourage you to add to it whatever you already know of dramaturgy. In my theatre community, I have sometimes observed a tendency to parse definitions, conventions, approaches, theories, and styles, and split along certain aesthetic lines. My approach has always been more of an additive one: I try to layer whatever new theory, thought, or tool I encounter into my practice in the hope of making it richer, deeper, and more versatile in its application.

I work in new play dramaturgy, which is distinct from production dramaturgy. My understanding and experience of the latter is relatively limited. Production dramaturges tend to work on plays that have been produced previously, often, but not always, historical plays, or plays set in a time or place less than familiar to those working on it. They frequently engage in historical research and bring relevant materials into the design and rehearsal process to support the creative team and cast in their interpretation and performance of the play. When a classical text needs to be edited for a specific production, a production dramaturge will often work with the director to reshape the play in support of the directorial vision.

In new play dramaturgy, a dramaturge's role is to help a playwright or group of theatre creators identify and address the gaps between what they want their play to communicate to an audience and what the play actually communicates. When a person (or group of people) creates new work, they experience two major hurdles. The first is that they possess a glut of information. They know much more than any reader or audience member about their play, its world, its characters, and its artistic aims. A dramaturge helps to ensure that such relevant information—basic facts of the play's world—reaches the audience instead of remaining only in the creators' minds. A dramaturge might ask: What is happening? Why? How do I know that? What do I need to know about this world and these characters in order to follow the story, in order to emotionally invest in the play? The second problem play creators face is a lack of information. Like most of us, they are frequently unaware of their own subconscious drives in creating art. In following the emotional life of the play, a dramaturge can often point to clues in the text that hint at a playwright's deeper obsession, the moral or metaphysical question lying unacknowledged in the heart of the writing. In pursuing both lines of questioning, a dramaturge can help a playwright realize their vision of their play.

WHAT MAKES A PLAY?

In selecting a play to develop, I look for two primary qualities in a play or creation proposal. They are remarkably simple, but difficult to find. The first is an understanding of theatre as a medium, and the second is the presence of a unique voice or perspective on the part of the playwright or theatre creators.

Theatre is a dramatic medium and a live art form, which means it has a very specific relationship to time and physical space. It is not uncommon to read texts offered up as plays that are not theatrical. When reading a play, I consider the following questions as to its theatricality:

- Is the play written to be a live art form, experienced in a particular space over a particular span of time?

- Does the play acknowledge the scale of theatre, or is it written in the equivalent of filmic "close-ups"?

- Does the text conjure a visual world, or is it sparely written to convey primarily character intention, as in film?

- Is the text written dramatically, or does it sit in description or contemplation as prose and poetry are apt to do? Does it embrace plot and conflict, character development and arc, and transformation—of its characters and world—over time?

- Is dramatic action the primary means of generating the play's theme or meaning?

The more plays you read and see, the more immediately clear it will become to you whether or not a text is theatrical.

One important consideration, especially given the rising prevalence of alternative performance conventions in theatre, is the fact that theatre is a durational art form. That means a viewer should have to experience the play over time and that each moment of the play—regardless of how it is conceived and staged, and regardless of whether each audience member views the same content in the same order—must be integral to the artistic experience. If you can imagine leaving and returning during the performance without anything substantial changing in the interim, I would submit that the text is not essentially dramatic.

On a basic level, what I look for in a play or theatrical creation is a series of dramatic events, each of which creates a transformation, however small, in the world of the play. This chain of events and transformations (event → transformation → event → transformation) should achieve two things. The first is to draw a reader or viewer more and more deeply into the world of the play, increasing intellectual and emotional investment over time. The second is to allow the reader or viewer to begin to construct a precise and play-specific meaning to the progression of events; this meaning should be *felt* as much as or more than it is intellectually understood. A great way to test whether a play is working dramatically is to ask yourself, at any given point in the play, if you can identify and remember the series of events and transformations that immediately preceded it. In dramatically written plays, regardless of whether they are linear or non-linear, conventional or unconventional, this should be relatively easy to do because the events and transformations should accrue in impact and meaning such that one could not occur without all the others leading up to it. If you are still in doubt as to a text's theatrical potential, ask yourself if you could more easily imagine it in another medium: prose, poetry, performance art, essay, television, or cinema. If your answer is "yes," then you are likely not reading a theatrical text.

In addition to a play's theatricality, I am most compelled by the playwright or theatre creators' unique exploration of the human condition. By "human condition" I mean those experiences and struggles that form the core of our shared humanity. They point to something deeper and more inescapable than individual, social, and political categories—something that is capable of generating profound meaning in our lives. This, for me, is the central purpose of any art, including theatre. I want to be surprised—by new thoughts, new feelings, and new arguments, or old ideas in new contexts and new interpretations. If a play offers up a simplistic and immediately recognizable world view that is a severe limitation for me. Likewise, if a play offers up an uncomplicated view of a political or ideological dilemma, and allies with a single character or perspective throughout, that is also a severe limitation for me.

I search for plays that engage with moral questions, human questions, and, yes, universal questions. Each of us wants to be seen, loved, valued; each of us wants to belong, somehow. However imperfectly the concept of universality might have been (and still be) understood or applied, it remains a very powerful aspirational concept for me. Art must be created with an underlying compassion for the human beings represented in it and viewing it. If it is dark and despairing (and frequently the most compelling plays are), it must be in search of a significant truth and offer some glimmer of redemption for humanity.

NEW PLAY DRAMATURGY—PRINCIPLES AND GUIDELINES

Because I am writing for directors, my goal in this chapter is not to offer a comprehensive methodology on text analysis and new play dramaturgy. Rather, it is to provide some basic techniques and questions for reading and developing new plays collaboratively, with playwright, director, dramaturge (or director/dramaturge) and, when possible, designers and actors.

While every play follows a different development path, there are certain essential steps that effective dramaturges—and other collaborators implicated in play development—can take to support a positive and productive experience. They help to ensure that collaborators communicate clearly and consciously in service of the same set of artistic objectives and with self-awareness and respect for one another's work.

Here are my suggestions for how one should approach dramaturgy and new play development.

Formulate a vocabulary around text analysis, dramatic action, genre, and style with your collaborators. Communicate clearly what your terms mean to your collaborators and then invite them to share their own. There are an overwhelming number of theatrical and literary terms, and many artists use identical terms to mean different things. Each artist speaks their own theatrical language, and it is crucial that a group of collaborators develop a shared language of terms with agreed-upon meanings. These terms are the tools of play development: they allow collaborators to point to specific parts of the text to determine how it functions and how it could function differently. If you are still relatively new to text analysis, dramaturgy, and new play development, I would suggest that you turn to *Backwards and Forwards* by David Ball and *Story: Substance, Structure, Style and the Principles of Screenwriting* by Robert McKee for basic plot structure and vocabulary. (Of course, there are many, many other options that you might prefer.) Both books are extremely useful, and even as you embrace alternative methodologies throughout your career, you will regularly return to the first principles laid out in these books.

Identify your own obsessions. Any artist's work involves self-examination. Know your own obsessions, not just external to yourself (social, political), but internal. What are your emotional obsessions? What are the most painful moments in your life? What is the issue or struggle you see everywhere over and over again? That you are compelled to explore endlessly? That you avoid exploring at all costs? If you were a writer, I would tell you to begin writing based on your answers. If you were a dramaturge or a director supporting new play development, I would tell you to become acutely aware of when you see these obsessions in other people's work and ask yourself: are they really there, or is it just you?

Identify your own theatrical preferences. Do you enjoy musicals? Do you revile one-person shows? Each of us has preferences about theatre and how it is made. Do not confuse what you like with what is well done. You might not enjoy a theatrical form or device, but it might yet be useful to a playwright structuring a play, and that playwright will almost certainly make choices based on preferences different from your own. Although there will always be arguments for and against a choice, ensure that they are substantive—based on the specific needs of the play—and not simply reflections of differences in taste.

Listen clearly to the play, with awareness of your own biases and prejudices. This follows closely from my last two points. I cannot count the number of times someone has described a play to me, and their description bears little resemblance to what was written: they simply inserted their own obsessions into the work. Are plays open to interpretation? Yes. Can a play be interpreted to mean anything? No. As a dramaturge or a director supporting new play development, part of your work is to discover what the play is communicating. You will never be objective—that is impossible—but you can become increasingly aware of your own subjectivity and better able to identify what a play is exploring and support that exploration. Remember too that there will be room in the process to share your own subjective experiences; they in part fuel your creativity and so are essential to any productive creative collaboration. The key is to be aware of when, how, and why you are communicating them.

Feel deeply. One major misconception about dramaturgy is that it is an intellectual exercise. Text analysis is an essential component of dramaturgy, and it is largely an intellectual endeavour, but what drives text analysis? Why ask a question about a piece of text? Because you feel something powerful, or you feel something surprising, or you want to feel something but cannot. Text analysis is a tool, but our emotional journey is the bar by which we measure a play's effectiveness. Track how you feel throughout a play, especially those places where you feel deeply connected to it, feel indifferent to it, and feel frustrated by it. Then, using your own personal insights and agreed-upon vocabulary, attempt to articulate what incited those feelings to your collaborators.

Remain mindful. A good dramaturge sits in the tension between feeling emotionally connected to a play and maintaining professional distance. During play development, do your best to regard your emotions as another source of information rather than allowing yourself a full audience experience of the play each time you read it or see it. If you find yourself responding strongly (laughing, crying) steadily throughout the process, you are probably not paying close enough attention to what the play is doing and how it is working. Are you moved because a passage is superbly written, or are you responding to sentimental treatment of subject matter? Take a step back, become mindful of your feelings, and use them to drive your analysis.

Identify boredom. When you read or listen to the play, when do you stop paying attention? What parts of the play do you *dread*? Do not disparage yourself for feeling this way: your experience as an "audience member" is valid and will frequently provide insight into how a future public will respond to the play. Moreover, boredom is a strong indicator of a lack of dramatic action. The dialogue might be lively, the images might be beautiful, the characters might be seductive, but are the play and its characters pursuing something, or are the scenes merely repeating action? If you remove the parts that induce boredom, what would you have to insert for the play to make sense? Often, your answer will be nothing, or only a small part of what you removed, or an entirely different scene covering entirely different terrain.

Identify familiar content. Is there an argument you recognize, that you can speak almost along with the character? From where do you recognize it? The answer is frequently the news, an ongoing public debate, or another piece of art. If this is the case, chances are the play is treading familiar ground. Forget about whether you agree with the argument or not. Ask the playwright: how can you complicate it? How can you humanize it? How can it be rendered surprising? How can it upset our notions of right and wrong, sympathetic and unsympathetic? If something is familiar to you, chances are it is well-trodden ground for your audience too. The play must rise to the challenge of offering the unexpected and/or the unwelcome.

Track storytelling clues and follow where they lead. Clues are pieces of information that raise expectations about how the story will proceed. Sometimes it is useful to fulfill these expectations; sometimes it is better to frustrate them. Either way, a playwright must be aware of what storytelling expectations their play raises—what clues have been dropped—and how that shapes audience perception and engagement. Pay attention to those moments when you have a strong sense of what will happen next or later in the play. Identify what put that thought in your head: that's a clue. As you read the play, do the clues add up? Which ones are dropped? Should they be pursued or discarded? Why? Playwrights are frequently surprised by these observations: certain events in the play can take on more weight than the playwright intended, raising dramatic possibilities that the playwright has no intention of pursuing. These red herrings must be reintegrated or eliminated in order to shape the journey of the play. In other cases, the playwright might feel that a certain clue is obvious when it is not, leaving their collaborators and potential audience floundering when it comes to a narrative turn or a character's decision. Here, it might be necessary for the playwright to emphasize certain information or sharpen a dramatic event.

Be wary of pursuing clarity. In new play development, *clarity* refers to the explication of basic facts, relating to backstory, history, relationships, and setting, in the world of the play. At some point, the play must reveal certain critical facts to ground the storytelling and frame the stakes for the audience. The danger is that potentially rich and fertile contradictions and tensions are eliminated in favour of offering these facts, diminishing the play's power and sacrificing the playwright's vision. How, then, does one determine when to pursue clarity? For me, my guiding question is this: "What facts do I need to know in order to grasp the stakes of the characters' predicament and emotionally invest in this play?" Well-placed facts tether the audience to the play; they provide the clarity the audience requires to stop worrying about whether they can follow the basic story and instead explore the deeper psychological and emotional world of the play.

Describe the play to the playwright. Let's imagine that you have been listening clearly, feeling deeply, remaining mindful, and identifying certain critical components of the play. Based on this information, what is the play about? How does it work? When do you lose track of the plot, story, or characters? What do you think the play wants to communicate to its audience? What does it mean? Based on your experience of the play, describe it to the playwright. You will undoubtedly tell them things they know, do not know, and do not expect to hear about their play. This is really where the work of dramaturgy begins.

Discuss the playwright's vision for the play. Learn what the playwright's vision is for the play. What do they want it to communicate to the audience? Draw out their vision with additional questions of your own. Speak about their initial creative impulses, their formal considerations, their inspirations (for characters, for thematic content, for plot elements), and their research. Compare the playwright's view of the play with your own. Begin to devise a play development path that addresses the gaps between what the playwright thought the play was communicating and what it is, in this draft at least, communicating.

Have your own vision for the play. While I believe that the playwright's vision should lead the play development process, a dramaturge or director supporting play development must have their own vision for the play-text too. Can you get on board with the playwright's goals, and see their potential? What are your hopes for this play and why? What will motivate you to continue doing your work in support of the play development process? Remember that a playwright requires collaborators and that those collaborators are artists. Artists—all artists—have visions for what might be.

EFFECTIVE COLLABORATION IN NEW PLAY DEVELOPMENT

The technical and artistic questions of play creation are made more complex by questions of collaboration. Each of us arrives to a project full of expectations, both positive and negative, of the play and our fellow artists. While there is no perfect formula to guarantee a productive and enjoyable collaboration, each collaborator must enter the creative process willing to do the following things. The first is to articulate your own process and expectations, from your underlying artistic vision, professional history, personal obsessions, and biases, right down to the practical details of how you expect to make work. The second is to pursue honest communication with your collaborators, despite the short- to medium-term discomfort that might entail, for the long-term goal of creating a piece of work in which everyone is invested. Along with the commitment to honesty comes the commitment to listen with—this is crucial—the knowledge that you might be changed by what you hear. The third is to engage in a detailed artistic and philosophical discussion about the play or project, what it is, how it works, and why it is important both to make and to perform.

Here are some of the questions I am particularly interested in asking when I join a project.

How did each collaborator come to be involved in the project? Are any of the collaborators long-term creative partners? Have any of the collaborators been hired by a producing company? Are the artists in question forming new collaborative relationships with one another by choice? These questions reveal individuals' perceived and real obligations to one another, their motivations to take on a new project and/or explore new artistic partnerships. The answers can allow a potential collaborator to gauge how much room and respect there is for their input and how deep their involvement can be in a project.

What is each collaborator's interest in the project? If the creative team is implicated in producing the play, that is significantly different from a situation in which the creative team is contracted by a producing theatre company. No matter how independent people might believe they are, most of us are influenced by the prospect of impressing an artistic director and/or gaining regular contract work at a theatre. What do people stand to gain from working on this project, not simply in the artistic realm but the professional and financial realms as well? Many people are more than capable of acting as reliable collaborators and cultivating future employment prospects at the same time; however, it is wise to consider what is driving potential collaborators in case it seriously diverges from what is driving you.

Why do you want to work with me? What do your fellow collaborators know, or think they know, about you? What interests them in your work, what do they expect from you, and is it accurate to what you know about yourself? This question gives rise to answers that illuminate just as frequently as they baffle!

What are your collaborators' obsessions? Are there ideas and topics your potential collaborators identify as essential to their work? Do they see them at play in the proposed project? Do your own interests overlap and intersect with theirs in a way that is exciting? You do not need to agree on everything, but ideally, friction between collaborators should generate rather than stifle creative exploration and problem solving.

How do your collaborators make work? *For the playwright:* How do they write and revise a script? When and where do they like to write? How quickly can they write? What support do they need to write during a workshop or rehearsal? How long do they expect to be writing during the development or rehearsal process? What production decisions do they want to participate in? When do they expect to attend a workshop and/or rehearsal? How do they propose to offer feedback on what is happening in workshop and/or rehearsal? *For the dramaturge:* How do they frame their role with respect to the playwright? The director? What kind of feedback and support can they provide to the playwright? How will they help support communication between the playwright and director? At which point do they serve the playwright's vision, the director's vision, or their own vision of the project? What is the nature of their involvement in a workshop and/or rehearsal? In case of a dispute between playwright and director, how do they see their role? *For the director:* How do they run a workshop day? A rehearsal day? A rehearsal week? What are their expectations for how the playwright and dramaturge will enter and participate in the rehearsal hall? What are their expectations regarding the frequency and scope of rewrites? Is there a point at which they want the script to become fixed?

What is each collaborator's goal for the workshop or rehearsal process? What does each collaborator hope to explore and discover about the play and performative elements during a workshop or rehearsal process? In each person's estimation, what are the pressing artistic and practical questions that must be addressed during the specified period?

In artistic terms, what attracted each collaborator to the project? From a connection to content to the opportunity to experiment with form, different aspects of a project appeal to different people. Can you find room for your own interests and compulsions alongside those of your potential collaborators?

This is not, by any stretch, an exhaustive list of questions, but it is a healthy start, and the conversation it inspires should open more avenues for discussion.

A director beginning a relationship with a playwright and dramaturge on a specific project must also be mindful of when they enter the process. While some directors are involved in new play creation from inception, many do not begin their work until the play is slated for production. Though there are benefits and drawbacks in each situation, most artists I know prefer the former but are frequently faced with the latter. Early entry into the process means that a director will be familiar with the specific playwright-dramaturge relationship and their working vocabulary; they will often be and/or be perceived to be more informed and invested in the play and its artistic vision. Early involvement also affords the opportunity, with the right resources, for the director's work to become instrumental to the development process. Staging and design concepts can be implemented; the results of these investigations can shape the playwright's conception of their play, expanding its world and presenting new opportunities for formal experimentation and plot and character development. On the other hand, late entry can bring a unique perspective and insight to the project. As long as there is sufficient time prior to production for the director to become immersed in the play, that injection of a new idea or angle can be exciting at a mid-development stage.

Regardless of when the director enters the play development process, once they are collaborating on the project, it is wise for them to connect with the dramaturge as readily as they would connect with the playwright or a designer. Some directors, regarding the dramaturge solely as an advocate for the playwright, fail to do this and it is a missed opportunity. Like any other artist, a dramaturge should advocate for the play. While practically speaking this often means advocating for the playwright insofar as ensuring they are able to do their work effectively, the point is that the dramaturge's loyalty is not to the playwright over the director—far from it.

Indeed, the dramaturge-director relationship can be a very rich one. Throughout the play development and rehearsal processes, a dramaturge can be a great sounding board for a director. The skills they possess are not only essential for reading and developing dramatic texts, but to envisioning staging and design concepts. A dramaturge can see the play text in three dimensions: they can hear its rhythm and pace; they can see the stage and the semblance of a set or playing space; and they can imagine how characters move, time passes, and space transforms. Likewise, a director can provide refreshing perspective on the text during the dramaturgical process. They bring a different but complementary set of concerns and questions to a script as they pursue the physical realization of the play. A director's discussions of and experiments in staging and performance can reveal spatial and temporal relationships that were hitherto unseen or unexplored, cracking open possibilities for plot, character development, and world-building in the script. Theatre-making is at its best when it makes full use of every collaborator's skills to push the play and production forward.

FROM CREATION TO PRODUCTION: THE PLAY DEVELOPMENT PROCESS

The play development process can be overwhelming. Given the prevalence of contests, new work festivals, play development centres, and theatre-specific play development programs, it can be difficult to determine which opportunities are beneficial for a play and playwright, and meaningful in terms of artistic outcome. Prior to taking part in any form of play development, the creative team, particularly the playwright, must seriously consider their artistic goals for the play and how to achieve them. This clarity will help them to determine which opportunities are valuable and why.

Broadly speaking, there are only a handful of play development activities:*

1. One-on-one meetings
2. Play readings
3. Workshops
4. Rehearsal and previews
5. Productions

This list might at first blush appear simplistic, but it belies the myriad of ways these activities can be used.

* Please note that I have left commissions off this list since they are agreements between a playwright and potential producer, buying the playwright time to write. Although they can be complex and bewildering, they usually do not involve the dramaturge or director and are thus outside the scope of this chapter.

One-on-one meetings between the playwright, dramaturge, and sometimes the director take place regularly throughout most play development processes, usually following the delivery of a new draft. They tend to take precedence early in the play development period as the playwright works to discover what they are writing about and why, the general parameters of the plot, and broad character relationships. They are also extremely useful in determining next steps for development, allowing the playwright and collaborators time to articulate goals and formulate a play development plan. Discussions are limited, though: they examine the play as an abstract rather than concrete entity. One can become lost in theoretical ideas about how a play might or should work and miss entirely how the play actually works (or doesn't work). Hence the need for more concrete forms of play exploration.

Play readings allow the playwright to hear their play with distinct voices, speaking with intention and at pace. Typically running from a half-day to a day, they can be helpful in identifying a play's rhythm and storytelling arc, and revealing when the play is dramatically active and when it is not. Furthermore, the addition of professional actors to the play development process fosters fine-tuned character exploration and, often, passionate discussion. Actors can provide valuable feedback from inside their characters, pointing out when background information is missing or overwritten, tracking transitions in character and plot, and pinpointing moments when they, as actors and audience, are most deeply engaged in the play and why. Readings can be immensely useful when a playwright is wrestling with questions of pace, rhythm, voice, story arc, and character development. However, readings can also be immensely seductive. Because they do not have to negotiate space or the practical world, readings can exist almost entirely in the audience's imagination—and it is very easy to enjoy a play this way! While they are good tools for exploring and developing certain aspects of a play, readings are rarely a good gauge of how the play might work in production.

Workshops can begin to reveal the depths of a play and its true capacity to hold meaning in performance. They involve deeper and more detailed explorations of text, staging, and design concepts than readings do, and typically take place over several days or weeks, depending on budget and scope of exploration. Ideally, workshops involve participants from a wide variety of theatrical disciplines—playwriting, dramaturgy, direction, acting, production, and design—to ensure that the play will be thoroughly exercised. Text analysis and improvisation with actors can uncover whether a scene is rich in subtext and storytelling, or simply catchy when read aloud. Experimentation with directorial, staging, and design concepts can determine whether the text is written to be performed: does the addition of performative elements open up possible interpretations of the play, or do they feel redundant because the text leaves no room for them? Observations and input from design and production staff frequently flag significant artistic questions that are otherwise missed by theatre artists working in a more abstract (less practical) capacity. If there is adequate budget and infrastructure, a workshop of several weeks can serve as a "first draft" of a production, allowing every collaborator, not simply the playwright, the opportunity to redraft prior to a planned run.

Rehearsal and previews (if you are lucky enough to have them) comprise play development too and present a magnificent opportunity for growth. However, thanks to a frequently misguided idea that a play needs to "settle" before opening, I have witnessed play development stop in preview or even in mid-rehearsal. This is unfortunate. In my experience, those artists who are the most fearless about pursuing play development—right up to opening night—often see a huge payoff, particularly if they have the benefit of previews. There is no greater test of a play than a performance in front of an audience, and while live audience response can be painful, it often leads to the most surprising and radical insights and revisions.

Productions are often viewed as the end of a play development process—perhaps because so few plays enjoy second runs. I see them as another avenue for development. Witnessing the growth of a play and the variety of audience responses it evokes over the course of a run illuminates how a play might continue to develop and grow. The lessons learned can often be applied to future plays, as well.

In speaking about the benefits of new play development, I am acutely aware that the process has its detractors. Some people are concerned that new play development pushes plays into a one-size-fits-all formula, while others believe that workshopping can become an endless and fruitless cycle. I can only answer those critiques with this: new play development must be structured to suit a specific play and its development needs. Each play development activity should address a specific artistic need or meet a specific artistic goal as determined by the playwright in concert with other members of the creative team. A focus on play-specific artistic criteria ensures that each play is respected as a unique artistic creation, and that each play development activity serves a clearly articulated and agreed-upon purpose. This does not mean that every play development activity will be successful in achieving its goals, but rather that the playwright and collaborators get to determine which artistic terrain they want to explore and how. This is why it is critical for the playwright, dramaturge, and director to prepare carefully for any new play development activities.

CREATING A UNIQUE PLAY DEVELOPMENT PATH

The first play development activity in the life of any play is almost always a meeting with a trusted colleague or collaborator. From there, depending on the playwright's goals, fellow collaborators' input, and available budget, the playwright and collaborators can begin to formulate a play-specific play development process. For this process to be effective, the playwright and collaborators must be clear and explicit in their hopes for the play.

In preparing for a meeting, reading, or workshop, each implicated collaborator should ask: what are the two or three most pressing and far-reaching questions for me with respect to this play right now? It can be tempting to outline every question and criticism when offering feedback, but this is counterproductive for two reasons. The first is that a playwright can only absorb so much information (not to mention criticism!) in a short span of time. The second is that it is wisest to tackle the larger "play-sized" questions first, since how the playwright addresses them will inform the structure of the play and alter scenes, beats, and lines—thus rendering any questions around them moot. Identify where the playwright's questions and needs overlap with those of the dramaturge and director, and thereby set priorities and goals for play development.

Given the questions asked, determine what form the play development activity should take: meeting, reading, or workshop. The playwright almost always has a strong preference for one activity over another, and this should be the starting point for discussion. Does the playwright need to hash out some fundamental ideas about their topic and structure in a private meeting? Or are they hungry to hear the play out loud, in real time, with distinct character voices, in a reading? Are they eager to focus on more detailed work, isolating parts of the play for exploration—that problem scene, that enigmatic character, that staging transition—in a workshop setting? Depending on how the playwright's needs overlap with the dramaturge and director's questions, the team can plan a play development activity (revised draft/reading/workshop) and pursue it with specific questions and goals in mind.

Although this is by no mean always the case, the play development process often follows this cycle: the delivery of a draft, followed by a meeting, followed by the play development activity decided upon in that meeting, such as a new draft, reading, or workshop. Regular discussion and collaborative decision making shape the process as it occurs, ensuring that it is uniquely suited to the play and playwright's needs.

One final note: Budget will always, to some degree or another, dictate how a play will be developed. However, it is stronger to formulate a play development plan based solely on artistic requirements and then make accommodations for budget than to simply pursue what budget will allow. This way of working guarantees that the playwright and each collaborator reflect on what the play is and could be instead of aimlessly undertaking any play development activity simply because it is affordable or readily available.

ON TO REHEARSAL AND PRODUCTION

The goal of play development is production. Fellow collaborators, the director, design team, production, and cast will shift focus towards realizing a polished presentation for the public rather than supporting the playwright's creative journey. Their work, however, will continue to inform the playwright and their script: it is imperative for the playwright, dramaturge, and director to discuss how play development will proceed throughout rehearsal.

Here some questions to consider:

When will the playwright and/or dramaturge attend rehearsal? The playwright and dramaturge should decide with the director when they will attend rehearsal based on what is most useful to them and the play. My recommendation is that the playwright attend table work early in rehearsal and then return only when the cast begins to do runs. The staging will offer the playwright new perspective on the play, and the playwright will offer the director and cast new perspective on the staging. It is often easier on the playwright and cast for the dramaturge to enter rehearsal during the interim to answer questions or convey them to the playwright, but please remember: these are recommendations borne of experience, not hard-and-fast rules.

How will the playwright communicate their questions and concerns to the director? There are many different ways to approach this given the collaborators' temperaments and working styles, and the specific demands of the play. Should feedback be offered in rehearsal during discussion, in front of cast? On breaks, privately? In email form? Should the feedback be conveyed by the playwright, or through the dramaturge? Will this process shift at some point in rehearsal? When in doubt, offer feedback privately, outside of the rehearsal hall—especially if the concerns are serious.

How will feedback from the rehearsal hall be communicated to the playwright? Should all feedback, regardless of its source, be filtered to the playwright through one person, likely the dramaturge? Is it more productive if the playwright and director communicate directly? Is it useful for the playwright, dramaturge, and director to schedule regular check-ins? How will actors' questions be passed to the playwright? Will the dramaturge filter out less-than-useful or contradictory feedback? What are the collaborators' expectations on how quickly the playwright can/should deliver rewrites?

How will rewrites work? How will the playwright, dramaturge, and director determine when rewrites should be delivered to the actors and worked through? How will the rewrites be formatted, printed, and distributed, and who will do that work? Keep in mind that the creative team and cast, especially the stage manager, will have heavily noted scripts with fixed page numbers. Which rewrites take priority? Can rewrites continue to the final rehearsal, or would the director prefer a deadline after which date the script will be "set"? To be clear, I recommend pursuing play development right through to opening night, but I recognize there are a variety of reasons artists might not be comfortable with this.

How will the director's relationship with the dramaturge change throughout rehearsal? A new play dramaturge's primary collaborative relationship during new play development is with the playwright; however, that might change as rehearsal begins and the director more frequently looks to the dramaturge for feedback on staging and design choices. How might the director-dramaturge relationship look independent of the dramaturge-playwright relationship? Does the director want the dramaturge's expertise—on the play, its history, its backstory, and its ideas—to be available to the actors, and if so, how and in what context? Be sure to be transparent with fellow collaborators, especially the playwright, about how the director-dramaturge and dramaturge-actor relationship might evolve in rehearsal.

What are the priority areas of interest for previews? Audience reaction (or non-reaction) is often the most useful feedback. Based on the state of the play and production heading into previews, what are the priorities for further work? Is there time during previews for significant rewrites and follow-up rehearsals?

Ideally, the play should be explored and tested as thoroughly as possible by opening night, providing it with every opportunity to fail and grow before it meets its audience and critical response. While making new plays is notoriously difficult, well-chosen and carefully executed play development activities provide valuable avenues for growth and experimentation, and bring the playwright and collaborators closer to realizing their vision for the play in production.

That said, theatre is tantalizing precisely because we almost never fully realize our aspirations for a play. Theatre is a search—a search for the self, a search for meaning, a search for human connection, a search for beauty. The mysterious is at the heart of the theatre we make, and its power and allure is that it can never be completely contained or understood, but it can be experienced and deeply felt. As much as I hope that my thoughts on new play development will be useful to you, recognize that knowledge, experience, and skills are essential but insufficient in making great art. Throughout your practice, always remember to return to the search that drew you to theatre in the first place, and let that guide you.

BREAKOUT SESSION

How to Speak to Actors

Every year we work with actors in the Lab. We ask a number of the Labbies to rehearse for a short time with the actors using their own techniques or testing out a new one in order to observe directors at work and see how they communicate with the actors. Afterwards, we ask the actors to give the directors feedback on what worked for them and what didn't. We also ask them how they want to collaborate with a director in general and how they want the director to speak to them to allow for a rich and full rehearsal process. These are some of the things they've said:

HOW CAN A DIRECTOR CREATE AN ATMOSPHERE OF PRODUCTIVE CREATIVITY AND PLAY?

- A sense of humour is very important. When it gets too serious, it becomes precious and things can become tense.

- Give the actors the fence, then let them run free.

- The body can't be free until the mind is satisfied. Dramaturgy is very useful. Give us research.

- I want the rules of the game instead of the rules of the task.

- Build the world of the play with the actors.
- Know what you want, then give the actors their freedom to pursue it.
- Use your own life to tell the story to give the actors investment.
- Trust the actors.
- Don't be condescending.

WHAT KIND OF LANGUAGE DO YOU FIND MOST HELPFUL IN REHEARSALS?

- I think it's always about the language you use. I want to know the common vocabulary in the room.
- What's the game of this scene?
- What does each character want? What is their goal?
- What does the play want to say?
- Keep things simple and specific.
- Go for the heartbeat of the play.
- Change the intentions during the scene.
- Know where you want to take the character and make it clear.

- "That was clear" and "that was unclear" are better than "that worked" and "that didn't."

HOW DO YOU FEEL ABOUT EXERCISES OR "GAMES" DURING REHEARSALS?

- Sometimes when you're not given much instruction and you're just thrown into an exercise, it helps you to learn in different ways. Especially when those exercises feel like they can be implemented into the show in some way.

- Exercises help provide reminders during the day, even with a simple exercise, to have awareness of one another.

- I'm always really game to play if I feel invited into it with a playful spirit. That helps me overcome my fear of doing it wrong. So when someone says, "Just do it so wrong," I say, "Okay!" So invitation, humour, playfulness, and a safe space to do everything wrong. This is the place we can do everything wrong as much as possible until opening night. If I feel that I have that permission, then I'm not afraid. I get into a childlike space. If I understand where I'm going with it. Sometimes an exercise that's proposed I may not understand or know and then I'll want to know. Often, I think my fear is about trust. If I trust who's leading me, and I feel like they're gonna get me when I fall, then I feel pretty much like, "Bring it on."

- Sometimes the exercises help me feel connected to my scene partners so I can go into the darker areas we may need to travel into.

- I always think, to do the most dangerous work, you need the safest room. And I don't mean precious, but safe. Because then I know I can go to my extreme edge and go way out there and everyone will get me. That's when I've done my fiercest and most devilish work. But it's not always possible because sometimes I've been shamed in a room. Or people feel like, because I'm a senior artist, they're trying to prove something to me. It's unnecessary and makes me so scared and then I can't let myself out to play.

YOU TALK ABOUT SHAME AND TRUST. I'M CURIOUS ABOUT THOSE TWO WORDS. CAN YOU THINK OF EXAMPLES OF WHAT MAKES YOU TRUST YOUR DIRECTOR THE MOST? SOMETHING THEY'VE SAID OR DONE THAT MADE YOU FEEL EITHER OF THOSE?

- I think it's about vulnerability. As a director, you have to be kind of in a parental role. I also think it's when a director shows me their vulnerability in a playful way, but still has the ability to let us know, "I still have your back."

- I like when a director says in an exercise, "Oh, that's interesting. Go with that." That makes me feel safe and listened to and considered. I find that very nurturing. I also don't mind the "That was not good. Don't do that again," as long as that relationship is there. It's always a balance and it changes every day. Sometimes too, when I'm not getting it, I want the answer so I can move on.

- Some of the times I've felt the most respected and trusted, a director has maybe said something like, "That was really terrible." And some of the times I've felt the least respected were when a director kept telling me how much they respected me. In both those situations, the words those directors said could have been taken completely differently if they were said in a different way. But it was something else, other than the actual content of the words, that made me feel trusted. But I think the big thing about trust—I think I trust directors when I feel they trust me. I feel like I do my best work when there's an understanding of where we are today and where we are now. Which is not to say we're not going to do as much as we can. For me I always feel there are leaps I'm taking as an actor daily and we have to trust that that's going to happen, that the inspiration will come at some point.

- Sometimes I say, "Look, for the first week I'm going to do some really bad acting, but don't freak out, because it's just my way of muddling through until I get to the next place."

IN CONVERSATION

with Playwright-Directors

DANIEL MACIVOR INTERVIEWED BY BRIANA BROWN

This interview took place in June 2017 as part of a session titled the Playwrights Project, and covers Daniel's career as a playwright, director, and performer.

BRIANA: You've worked extensively over your career with Daniel Brooks. How did that frequent collaboration happen?

DANIEL: Daniel Brooks worked with a group that included Don McKellar and Tracy Wright, and when I first came to Toronto we all started out together at the same time. I fell in love with their work and then we became friends. It was a very complex and personal relationship. Then we started working together. I wanted to give him something to work on with me, so that we could spend time together. I mean, this is how we spend our time. Really. We can call it a job, I suppose, and if you can do that, that's wonderful and congratulations, but this is actually my life. And I think for many of us we can understand that. I mean this is it. This is it. So I want to spend time with people I want to spend time with.

BRIANA: And in that relationship did he also act as a dramaturge?

DANIEL: Yes, very much so. In a way, he's the audience, so I present to him and if he's not interested in what I'm presenting, then I'm not following that track. He's my audience and I want to keep him happy. So I take a different track. I won't pursue a particular piece of writing if he's not engaged in it. So it's a very tactile dramaturgy. It's about "I get your attention or I don't get your attention." I want his attention. Then sometimes, of course, sometimes we disagree. And it makes me really clear as to why I'm hanging on to an idea. The worst thing that can happen in that relationship is that someone is wishy-washy about something. Sometimes it's a "maybe this or maybe that," but when we get to the bottom of it, it's a yes or no. It's very clear. But sometimes the "no" projects me to fight, to show him why he's wrong. It's not an argument. It's a show. It's not cerebral. It's not an intellectual argument, I *show* him. And then he sees.

[Laughter.]

Or *I* do. Eventually.

BRIANA: So how does that relationship shift when you become a playwright in a room in which there are actors on the stage and a director?

DANIEL: Yes. Room for the directors.

[Laughter.]

Here in Canada, and sometimes in the United States too, we work within that British tradition. For me the idea that the director leaves on opening night is purely economical. So that seems sad. But when I work with Daniel Brooks he stays with the show. He comes on tour and gives notes. I'm "noted."

BRIANA: So from a writing perspective, I'm curious about how you know that you've found your next play. How do you know that "this is the thing I'm going to write next"?

DANIEL: Wow. Well, my particular process is the word first. So "they" start talking. Then I discover who's talking. Then they talk about something for a while. Then I figure out what they're talking about. Sometimes they talk to no end. So I guess when I'm interested in what they're talking about, it starts to become a play. And also, again it kind of goes back to what I said before—"It's my life"—and it's personal. When I feel that it's costing me something personally, then I know that it's probably the play. When I feel like I'm involved with something that's not just an idea. I do things that are really deeply personal. They don't necessarily look that way, but they are coming from something that's disturbed in me and that needs to be addressed. And I address it by bringing it to the room. I wouldn't say it's purely therapeutic, but I know when I'm disturbed by it that this is "the thing."

BRIANA: But it does come to you from this voice talking as opposed to "This has been in the news lately"?

DANIEL: That doesn't work for me. I tried it. I was trained as an actor, so my training is action through vocalizing. Linklater. The "inner voice." So the impulse of sound is the impulse of creation.

BRIANA: Do you write it down as you are hearing it or do you vocalize?

DANIEL: Both. I talk to myself while I'm writing. I read it and go over and over it, and I perform it quietly to myself while working. Judith Thompson was also trained as an actor. We both had offices here [at Tarragon Theatre] and you could tell when Judith was working because you could hear her.

BRIANA: On that note, something that Judith brought up that struck me—and I'm curious to hear your thoughts—was the notion of commissioned projects as opposed to what she was calling "personal" projects, and the relationship and difference between the two.

DANIEL: For me personally, commissions don't work very well. I've actually turned down commissions because I couldn't always guarantee I was going to find my personal connection to it. If I can't find that, then it's not going to work. I also don't like the psychological economics of it. I like working *for* the money, not *from* the money. I like working *towards* getting paid, not *away* from getting paid. Because after a while that money's all been spent and I'm working for nothing. But if I haven't been paid yet, I'm working *for* something. Feels like there's something to go to, not something that's left.

BRIANA: So you have an idea and people start talking to you . . .

DANIEL: —They're talking to one another, not me.

BRIANA: And who is the first person you show a draft to and when do you know if that's what you want to do?

DANIEL: I try to live by this, and I don't always, but I always try to give this advice: Never talk about a play in a bar. Don't talk about the play until you have something that makes a sound when it hits the table. Because people will tend to have ideas and it will dilute what you're thinking. I usually show it to a trusted friend—an artist but not necessarily an artist of the theatre. Just so I'm not getting their take on it—what they would do, and so on. One of the greatest compliments I ever got was this guy who came up to me after one of my plays and said, "I saw you once do a thing. I don't remember what it was called and I don't remember what it was about, but I remember how I felt." And I thought, "Oh, yeah."

I don't need you to remember what it was called or about; I just like that you remember how you felt.

I guess I look for someone who's going to respond that way. I want someone who's going to respond quickly and succinctly, like, "I really liked it" or " I didn't get it." Those are the most helpful things. I don't really need to know "in the second scene when the daughter says . . ."—that stuff is layer. I don't need that right away. I just need a reason to keep going.

BRIANA: And when you write plays that you won't be performing yourself do you work with a dramaturge prior to rehearsal?

DANIEL: I have. My dramaturge, [Iris Turcott], died last year. I think what I tend to like best is not another body. I like when the person who is the director is also that person. Again, my dramaturge that I had been working with was someone I cared about and wanted to spend time with. What I find that happens with dramaturgy sometimes is that there's this "book." It reminds me a little bit of the film world where there's a kind of schedule of how things need to occur; that there are certain questions that need to be asked, and that sometime feels like there's a box I need to be in and wrestle against. But I love it when the dramaturge is invested in the play because they are directing it. For me, that's the richest conversation I've had around that.

BRIANA: Do you ever direct plays that aren't yours?

DANIEL: I have done. Seldom, but I have. I'm not sure it was my calling.

BRIANA: You've directed two films you've written.

DANIEL: Films are different. That's really like being a dad. The difference in the film world is like apples and cats. It's so different.

BRIANA: Do you make a choice to direct your own work?

DANIEL: I would always. And why do I not?

BRIANA: Yes.

DANIEL: Because people won't let me. I always want to direct my own work. I mean, have I benefited from other people directing my own work? Yeah. I like to be in the room. I just need to be in the room. Especially because I keep changing the play. If there's a problem and something's not working, I can fix it. I can rewrite it. It's okay. Even if it's been published. Someone tweeted, "All great literature is the alphabet reorganized."

BRIANA: So you are in favour of changing things in rehearsal?

DANIEL: It's a living thing. It's not a novel. It's breathing. It's live. The world changes. We change. The play is a living, breathing organism. Some things you can't change.

BRIANA: Can you articulate what that difference is?

DANIEL: If you're having a problem with a moment and I can explain that moment so that you can understand it, then we were just having a miscommunication about the moment. My issue around not changing things is not so much about story but how a line is said or written. There's a way that people speak. It's more about a way that a person constructs their sentence as a character's speaking that—in a way, the insight into a character—might be challenging to an actor. That challenge indicates something about the character that may help you break through something. All the questions about story don't matter, because it's just a story. There's a hero and a journey and this and that happens and then there they are. Unless you're dealing with a caper. But I go to the movies for capers. I go to the theatre because I want to see things "being." Story isn't being, story is doing. Theme is key.

BRIANA: Can you talk about what an ideal relationship with a director looks like, when you only have your playwright hat on in the room?

DANIEL: It wouldn't be a new play. I need that other draft. The first production is another draft, a real draft of the play. Where I've got actors on it full time, in their job, every day, coming in and saying, "I don't get why she says this." And I can say, "I can tell you why." Or I can say, "I don't know either." There's no Moses here. I don't get something handed from the heavens carved in stone. This is just a bunch of letters organized in a different order. And it gets reorganized. I need the challenge of the professionals who are doing their jobs in the room to confront the questions, so that I can understand what is gifted by the universe as essential and what is just my baggage that I haven't been able to work out in therapy.

BRIANA: How do you feel about the workshop process?

DANIEL: I love the workshop process.

BRIANA: And do you do that as a separate thing in rehearsal?

DANIEL: If we can afford it—if it's in the realm of possibility I would always opt for a public presentation or two, even if that's just invited audience.

BRIANA: Are there qualities in your relationship with a director that you would look for?

DANIEL: Depending on the material, I need a director who's going to say, "Okay, you go there on this line, you perch on this line and then sit three words later." I like attaching text to physical movement. I like the rigour in that. Of course, the movement can change but then you stick to that movement.

BRIANA: I think we have time for a question from the Labbies.

LABBIE: I'm curious to hear about that moment when a director has a high conceptual idea that is very strong and very loud for a piece that you wrote that you feel is not high concept. How does that negotiation work?

DANIEL: If I liked it, I would be excited to do my rewriting around that concept.

LABBIE: So if someone says, "This is an underwater show . . . "?

DANIEL: Then I need to filter water as a theme more for me. Then it's not just a directorial concept. I can take that back and understand how it can be part of the action.

LABBIE: So it becomes a sort of proposal and response?

DANIEL: Yes, I've had that relationship with designers in the past where they say, "We're able to do this and this" and I say, "I can write something to support a thing like that." We are allies, comrades. We're a team. Sometimes it becomes like staff and management where the playwright says, "Here it is. Take it and do this to it," but I'm like, "I don't know. I don't know. Do you know?" I think that conversation is really valuable.

[Beat.]

But, of course, sometimes I do know.

JUDITH THOMPSON AND KAT SANDLER INTERVIEWED BY RICHARD BEAUNE

Judith Thompson and Kat Sandler were interviewed at Directors Lab North 2017 in a session titled Writers Directing Their own Work and the Playwright/Director Relationship.

RICHARD: Today we're going to focus primarily on the director/ playwright relationship but will span into other areas as well. As we talk about the process of making a play I think we should consider, "What is a playwright and what is a director and what is it when one person is both of those things?" I'm curious to know from yourselves, how often do you direct your own plays?

KAT: As often as I can. I'm usually my first choice for director for my plays. I have directed every play that Brouhaha [her theatre company] has done and *Mustard* was the first big show that I didn't direct. It was done at the Tarragon last season.

JUDITH: Mostly I direct my own work as well. Occasionally I can't because of time and space. It's very hard for a director when I'm in the room. I have huge respect for directors and the director's vision, and they must have a strong vision, which is, in a sense, writing the play again visually and choreographically and in all those ways, as well as guiding the actors. But I have a very specific vision too, so the director needs to collaborate with me. It only works if there's a protocol set so that I won't keep interrupting or cutting that scene that you just worked on for an hour. We talk at every break for fifteen minutes. It never actually works out like that, but it would be good idea. Then you're not talking directly to the actors and having them just look at the playwright. They need to respond to the director. It has to be the director's room, the director's vision, and that is why I usually do direct. And I'm not necessarily the best director, ultimately I've seen great, beautiful shows of mine in other countries and other cities that I admire, but I like to realize and finish the vision that I have because as a theatre creator, after starting as an actor, director, and a playwright, my vision isn't just what's on the page; it's how people move, where they move, what's on the stage, all that.

KAT: I think of it as: I'm always the best director for the idea but not necessarily the best director for the production. So if I can stay with the idea from inception to allowing it to be seen by a bunch of people, you can curate the experience from idea to production. I don't think of writing and directing (when I'm given opportunity to do them both) as separate. I think of it as one big process of "Here's the thing I want to communicate and here are all the little bits and pieces that I can use to communicate it."

JUDITH: Yeah, that's true, and I often write right up to preview, maybe even more if the actors will allow it. Canadian actors are fantastic with that because so much new work has been done here, so they say, "Yes, give me the new monologue on opening night, that's fine!" Because we all want it to be the best it can be. We're all trying to create something that's much bigger than all of us. Once it comes through us we're all serving the piece and scrambling to serve it. If there's a director there, I feel anxious about saying, "I should cut that line" or "That last line is not right," because they're busy working. They're doing so much, and so there won't be all this interference and this someone in between, so it is best for me to direct first.

RICHARD: I'm curious how the director's responsibility dovetails with the writer's. I know for myself, from collective creation, there has to be a point where I can tell my company that we're not creating new material and that we're using the material we have and making a show of it. And that has to be fairly explicit because we're in the mode of creation. Is that something that comes into your process?

JUDITH: You mean when the writing stops?

RICHARD: Yes. Obviously you're writing right up to the opening night, but you don't want, I imagine, to be rewriting the whole thing?

KAT: I don't think it ever stops. Especially with comedy, the script is always a conversation. The script and the show is a conversation that you're constantly having with the people in the cast and with the audience, so comedy changes vastly night to night. When I get to direct and you have actors that are willing to do this they say, "Oh, this joke hasn't been playing, so I tried this and it worked," and then that gets locked in for future productions and it's much better, so as long as everyone's kind of signed up for the contract that things can happen and be flexible, then the playwright never stops writing.

JUDITH: Yes, that's true. Also, being present for the creature that is created for the audience; every show is different because every audience is different. So being there as much as I can, where I can see it and say, "Oh, that one thing is not quite right," because we are creating a work of literature. Work that will last. A work that should be published, that should be done again and again and again. So every moment, every bit of punctuation, every dot at the end—it has to be right. It's maybe never perfect, because there's no such thing in art and there are different actors that will come, but we're all striving for that. The exception is the show that I just did, *Wildfire*. I created it with six actors with Down syndrome—very bright, brilliant performers and creators. But I couldn't keep rewriting because memory was an issue, as it certainly is with me, so I had to stop at some point, and it worked for me. We had a lot more workshops than we normally would because of the challenges around memory, but that was an example where I had to stop, but I didn't regret it because we had enough workshops.

KAT: I think a huge part of directing is that, when I'm directing, I cast for the writer's room, not for the parts, because I'm writing for people, not characters. So much of the people that I end up casting ends up in the play. So if I cast people that are open and willing to talk, it's like you're casting seven dramaturges. Most of my rehearsal rooms are run like writer's rooms. We do a little bit of talking, talk about it, sharing experience about it, and getting an unwritten contract—actually, I should get a real contract now that I think of it—where people are okay with bits and bobs of stories ending up in the play. I can't make up the stuff that's happened to people that they're willing to share, and if they're willing for those things to appear in the play, then I'd always rather have that, which means that their performances are much more real. I think that actors feel ownership over something that they have helped create as opposed to someone saying, "Here's this monologue about your dead cat." And when you're directing, it actually helps you be less precious about the script and your direction, because they can both change so fluidly.

RICHARD: Judith, you talk about that particular piece having more workshops than normal. Can you describe what normal is and what that difference was?

JUDITH: Well, instead of having about a week of workshop, which would normally be a couple of days, it was maybe six to seven weeks of workshops. We started last summer and workshopped every weekend through the fall, and then two weeks in December and then a five-week rehearsal. It was much longer because of that particular challenge and they mastered it.

RICHARD: Is that a collaborative development in terms of the piece?

JUDITH: In this case I wrote it for them, so I did write it. Although some of that was from their experience in the early parts where they talk about love and such, but then I wrote it knowing each performer really well, what they can handle, and pushing that a bit farther. So I wrote a play for them. I did curate the first RARE. It was all their own experience, and so I brought that to this, but then wrote a play within a play for them—to harness their experiences as activists and advocates for the community of disability. We all became very angry and outraged about what we learned about institutions like Huronia [Regional Centre], where they originally called them idiots and imbeciles. Where people have been thrown—in this province—left in worse than prison because they couldn't get out. So I was very interested in their self-advocacy; writing for them so they don't just say, "Aren't we sweet? Here we are." No. "We're angry and we want to make more change," because although there has been some change, that hasn't been enough. I wanted to serve that.

RICHARD: Well, that leads me into another sort of relationship between roles and responsibilities, and that is of being a theatre creator and an artistic director, because you're both artistic directors of your companies. How does that relationship between sets of responsibilities affect you?

KAT: I think when we first started we were so tiny, so it was really just, "I should have a title and it should be an artistic director because that sounds big." The whole company came about from a botched festival application, and I was like, "Fuck it, I'm gonna make my own company and I'm gonna be the boss of it and that's it—I'm gonna be famous." But I think that now, as I get to work with bigger companies and artistic directors and meet people like Judith who really curate the work of the company much more than I did, I begin to understand what a big job it is when you do other writers' work. With Brouhaha, I think about what that's saying about branding. So for me artistic direction is really about what you're presenting of your company to the world, so it's all about optics.

JUDITH: We are lucky enough to have a general manager, because that's the work I'm not capable of. I wouldn't do grants, marketing, everything to do with administration, board, and all that. I get to just have the vision and I certainly need to bounce it off him. And it is a different stream for my own private writing. I don't think I will ever put on one of my own plays that I wrote just by myself, although for *After the Blackout* I am writing it again but drawn from the experience we had. Weeks of workshop from a company where performers who were blind, deaf, had brain injuries—extraordinary performers and writers—workshop their experiences. Now I'm writing a play and I'm remembering, "Oh, he told the story about the bear in the cabin; I put that in this scene; is it okay if I can use that story here?" So I'm actually in the process now and it's really exciting. It's my writing, but I'm drawing on their experiences. Writers will draw from something someone said ten years ago or a story we heard, but like you say, they will own it because we want actors to own the play. We may be sort of tyrants saying things like, "You have to say this this way or in this way," but please make it yours. Please let it be your own, otherwise it just sounds like something you're reciting.

RICHARD: So over the course of a career of writing a body of work, do you find then that the instigator of a new play has changed in its nature, or are you still drawn to the same reasons of writing plays, and what might those be?

KAT: I think I write more about things that make me angry now. When I first started I was like, "Ooh, that's cool, someone sold their virginity on the Internet. That should be a play people might go see"—that that sounds sexy. Now it's more, "Oh fuck, I don't know how to express anything about this, aside from putting it into other people's mouths, before I freak out and guilt someone about it." I want to say that's more mature, but now that I said it out loud it doesn't sound like that, but I think it is if you read between the lines.

JUDITH: It's similar for me. It's a question I can't answer so it needs to be answered artistically, because I'm very interested in grey areas and a question that really can't be answered with a yes or no. So that when you walk out you think, "Would I have done that?" I'll give you an example. *Palace of the End* is three monologues around the war in Iraq, and the third one is based on a real woman named Nehrja's Al Saffarh. She was a communist and the CIA gave the names of all the communists to Saddam Hussein who was their friend at the time. So they were tortured and captured—they were the only viable opposition at the time. I—it's a true story. Her husband was in hiding. She was caught along with two children, and she would not give up her husband's whereabouts because she felt that millions of lives depended on his being alive. While that was happening, they tortured her youngest son and they tortured him to death. So you have this woman, and as a character I created her as very likable, very witty, lots of fun: and then she launches into the story and you think, "You didn't give up your husband's name while they tortured your son?," But she says,

"You don't understand because you're not in that world I'm in." It's literally millions of lives. Of course, she didn't think they killed her child—they didn't do that yet, they're still trying to win our hearts—but they did. So then you walk out thinking, "I like this woman. This woman's like me, I can identify with her, yet how can that be?" She adored her sons. She's heart-broken. And so I like things we can't wrap our minds around because that provokes autonomous thought. I think as a director, a writer, it's what we want, because the world proselytizes, preaches, is biased, contentious, and if we can make people think only for themselves and get out of the herd, then I think we're actually achieving something. Obviously to do that I have to wrestle with myself first and I don't have an answer, but I'm thinking for myself about that and the actress, of course, and the same for the director. We all have to be on board with that. There's no answer but there's a lot of thought. How do we get out of our zone and actually experience what someone from a completely different culture and circumstance does, and what would we do? But we don't know, of course, that she talks at the beginning of the monologue about the three levels of torture. She says things like, they are pulling out fingernails, teeth, things like that, but she said even before they did that, 99% of people give up everyone they know. That's from a translation from the Arabic that I read. That was shocking because we all think, "never," and she said torture changes everything. I don't judge. I loved hearing that in Arabic and thinking, yeah, pretty much everybody here would think, "I would never give up my friends," and then it comes down to, "Well, I'd never give up my children." I don't know.

KAT: For me that's why I think it's necessary to direct at least the first production because the impetus for talking about this issue came from us. Unless we sat down and I said, "Okay, Judith, will you direct this play? I'm writing about this issue and we both feel really strongly about it and I think we have a good mind meld and it would be great." Because I think people think that a writer's job sometimes is to control what people hear. So they think your job is the script, your job is the text. I think as a creator, it's our job to control what people feel, which is a combination of what they see and what they hear, and from the first moment they see a poster or postcard for the show, how that starts to colour their experience of the whole thing. So it seems strange to me sometimes to filter it through another person's voice or another person's ideology when the impetus for the idea came from a certain place that's very specific and subjective to us.

JUDITH: Also because we come from the theatre, and it's different if someone was a poet or something like that, that isn't in and of the theatre and it's just the script. People always try to insult writers. It is very common in film, they say, "Oh, I'd go see that actor read the phone book." Well, no. And they also think the actor made it up. They say, "I loved it when he said this." Well, actually, he didn't make that up. I do think there's a jealousy about the primary creator. Just like misogyny comes from "Oh, women can have babies and you can't." Because we are in and of the theatre, we have to finish it, which brings me to the subject of commissions. A writer's work is always slightly different when it's commissioned, because I think the act of writing has to be, in a way, an act of revolution.

KAT: I just turned down a commission and they dangled the carrot. They said, "And . . . you can direct it." And I was like, "Ooh" and then, "Oh, no, no, no. I can't, this is awful, it's so boring, it's garbage. I don't want to do it," but I was like, "Oh, I can direct it and I make a lot of money," but it was just something I would never choose to write about. I mean, I don't get as many commission offers as Judith does, but I just can't.

JUDITH: I think that's smart. It's very hard when it's a good payday.

KAT: Well, it wasn't that much money. We'll see what happens later.

[Huge laughter.]

JUDITH: But it's schoolwork in the end. And the director can feel like they're doing schoolwork too. That's why it's very difficult if a director is brought on. Often a theatre won't let the playwright direct—they don't want them to direct for some reason or other—but it can't feel like schoolwork to the director. They have to feel like they're creating it. I know when I direct I'm creating. And it's not a blueprint, it's not a part of it like you said. There's dramaturgy involved when you're the director. It's not like you're commanding, you're not instructing, but you're saying, "What about this do you think works?" It's part of your responsibility, just like film directors. That's just understood. It's part of the responsibility.

RICHARD: If you are in a position where there is a director working on a play you've written, what is it that you as a writer are hoping for in the director?

KAT: For me it's a certain level of collaboration. It's not them receiving the script and saying, "What kind of crazy concept can I put on this to make it mine?" It's, "How do I take my skill as a director that's separate from these people, who are obviously also directors themselves, and make the work that's already there better?"

RICHARD: So you're looking for close collaboration?

KAT: If possible, yes.

JUDITH: Especially in the premiere. That's absolutely essential because you've got to have your vision as a theatre maker fully realized. So it is a collaboration. A lot of directors say, "Come for three days" and that's it, and I understand that—get the playwright out of the room. But in the premiere it's not finished. It needs to be a collaboration. On the other hand I've seen shows of mine in other places where their vision, especially in Quebec, I've noticed this, that their visual sense—directors are very visual everywhere—but there it's really inventive, or maybe their laws are more relaxed, but in one of my plays a whole wall burned down. It was amazing. I didn't understand it but it looked great.

LABBIE: How long was that run?

[Huge laughter.]

KAT: People say all the time, "We don't want you to direct it because you'd be too close." But if I'm not directing it I *want* the director to be too close. I don't want someone to ever direct something of mine that they don't want to get up and fight about and feel passionate about the same way that I would. Understandably I know that they're getting paid, that we all need to eat, but just fucking say no if you don't feel as intensely as I do about something.

JUDITH: I have this one play where there were bits of comedy in it, but ultimately it's a tragedy, and it was directed—it was in London—as a broad comedy and I was not happy about that.

RICHARD: There are some playwrights who don't like to be in the room. Do you understand that? Does that appeal to you?

KAT: A play is my brain and my heart on the stage, so if I can be there, I'd really like to be there.

JUDITH: Especially for the premiere. It's a different kind of directing. If I'm going to direct the premiere then the playwright is going to be there because I will—as a director, I would want the playwright to be there every step of the way. I might say, "Look, I really see this water running through here" or something and try to convince them. But you can't be a servant to them either. It's really important for you to say "I have a really strong vision for your piece. What do you think?" I want it to be perfect right up into the preview.

RICHARD: Does that change much for you if it's a remount or once it's published?

JUDITH: Yeah, then they could do whatever they want. You can't change the words, of course. That's in the Playwrights Guild contract.

RICHARD: You talked about the ideas that spark the beginnings of creating. I wonder, do you ever—in that moment does it ever matter to you, your existence within a cultural ecology? Does your place within a cultural milieu affect your thinking about, "Okay, I have an idea for a play I'm going to pursue, but I live within this cultural milieu"? Does that come into play often?

KAT: Yes! I'm writing a play about cultural appropriation, which is horribly terrifying because I'm fucking white. I just read the copy for it and I thought, "No, I'm just going to get crucified." When I had the idea I had the same thought. I said, "I can't write this play. It could never happen." But I had to. It just kind of tumbled out of me, and I probably should've just sat in it and burned it and never done anything with it, but now it's a thing and I can't fix it. I don't think it's possible nowadays, especially with the buckets of information thrown at us from the Internet, to not be aware of what milieu you're writing in or thinking in. The first thought I had was, "Yes, that thought—it's wrong to think that way." It's just a crazy form of self-censorship. I thought maybe it's wrong to censor myself, but I also thought maybe it's wrong to write it. And this is one where I shouldn't direct it; doesn't mean I don't want to, but I won't.

JUDITH: Right, right, right.

KAT: Judith is scared on my behalf.

JUDITH: Not scared, but it is interesting. What do we have to say, because nobody's appropriating us. I don't know. The appropriation issue is really interesting.

KAT: But how can you not write about something that's so present and so fascinating and affects so many people, and can you do it in a smart and intelligent way?

JUDITH: It has to be a farce, there's no other way. But on the other hand, people are really suffering on both ends. It's a challenge and the pain is very real. I feel that often, seeing things written by men that are all women, about women, and I think, "What do you know?" That doesn't mean we can't write about it. I don't know. That's a discussion that can go on forever. Every writer is an appropriator in a sense. Also, to live in Toronto—and you're a writer. Of course your characters are going to be diverse, because we live in such a great diverse community and our friends are people of many colours and backgrounds. And should we only write about our family? I don't know. You just have to really know of what you write and really know.

LABBIE: I'm from Atlanta and there's a lot of conversation about this, about white playwrights writing Black characters and vice versa. Some people do it very successfully yet some people—you just cringe when you hear it. So from a playwright's perspective, do you have any advice on ways to do it better?

JUDITH: I think you really have to know and to live with the people that you're writing about very, very well and write with the greatest respect. No clichés, no stereotypes, just a real person. When I did Nehrjas Al Saffarh—because it was based on an interview and a neighbour of mine who is Iraqi—I couldn't have possibly have done it without knowing my neighbour, and so I did it really well because I talked to her a lot and she translated for me in Arabic. In every play it's about knowing deeply, deeply. And you never know fully. It's very hard.

KAT: I think it's also just asking, taking the time and doing as much research as you can. I'm not setting out to write ethnic characters; I'm setting out to write characters. I'm not writing accents, I'm just writing people and then I'm reading them and then I'm having other people look at that, and I'm saying, "Where did I go wrong, how can I fix this?" I think it's just about being as open as possible to criticism and to feedback as early on in the process as possible.

JUDITH: And knowing what you want to say about it. *[To Kat.]* Do you know that yet? All about cultural appropriation? What do you feel about it?

KAT: I think I need to stop talking about this now.

[Laughter.]

LABBIE: How do you know when your writing is really working in the room when you're directing it? And how hard is it to make cuts when it's something you really love and want to make it work but, getting it up on its feet, it's just not working? How do you make that work for you?

KAT: You can hear it. You're a smart person; you know when something isn't working. I can feel when something isn't working when I'm desperate to hold onto it. If I'm fighting with my dramaturge, fighting with my actor, then it's not working. It's also surrounding yourself with other people that you trust. I've been working with the same dramaturge my whole career now and he'll call my bullshit immediately, and I surround myself with actors and collaborators who do the same thing. That doesn't mean I don't have things that still sound bad, when I get to opening night and I think, "Why didn't I cut that" or, "Why did no one tell me about that Jesus joke!?"

JUDITH: Or the pace changes because actors are nervous. But I agree with Kat. You feel it in your gut. You just know something is not right. Sometimes you do ignore that because you like it so much, but that little feeling in your gut—just trust it. That's boring, that's cliché, that's too long, whatever, you just know. And do it right away. Don't doubt it.

KAT: And not always, but if an actor continues to stumble on something to the point where you're pretty close to opening and you had time to work it, it's just—sometimes something feels wrong in your mouth as an actor. I think that's usually when you want to change something. And it could be about something bigger in the play.

LABBIE: There's such a stigma with writer-directors. If you're writing and directing, people think you're arrogant and nobody else can touch it, but for me, sometimes I'll have that imposter syndrome thing going on when I'm directing my own work.

I'm thinking people think I'm just smug and that I think I'm the better for it than everyone else. How do you combat those voices?

KAT: I'm 100% confident all the time.

[Huge laughter.]

JUDITH: But you're always going to have that anyways. You're going to get terrible reviews. We know that from the Internet, and before that. We always have haters. You have to do what you believe in, what makes the show better. You're serving the show, not yourself. When you're serving the piece it doesn't matter what other people think. It does matter what the audience feels. You can feel it in the room if it's working or not, but if it's working, don't question it.

KAT: There's a quote that says, "If you take responsibility for everything, then you have the power to change it," and that's always how I look at writing and directing together. Because you're gonna take the fall if it sucks and if it's great you're gonna get the credit, and either way you're gonna get to moderate what's happening constantly. But for the first three years I didn't put "written by" on our posters and now I have "written and directed" like Baz Luhrmann and I think I'm hot shit, because after the first five they were working okay and I was like, "Okay, even if you don't have a body of work, you have the experiences that worked," and then you're moving to something better.

LABBIE: It's interesting that you just mentioned Baz Luhrmann because I was thinking, "Why do we not blink an eye when film directors write and direct their own work? It seems to go hand-in-hand, but in theatre it's something else. I'm curious what that distinction is?

JUDITH: And if they don't write it, they definitely almost co-write it.

KAT: But people think film is a director's medium and theatre as a playwright's medium. And I think it's more okay in films to also have a cool screenwriting talent than it is in theatre. People think of directing as such a different power dynamic than writing.

LABBIE: I'm not sure if both of you direct other people's work, but I'm wondering if there's something that you have learned from directing your own work that you bring into directing other people's work?

KAT: I approach it the same way. If the playwright's alive, I call them and have a really long discussion with them. I don't think it really changes aside from if I'm directing something that is older, I can get a little fancier with the concept. When I direct I think, "What's here already and what am I going to do that will make it better, rather than detract with what's already here." They tell you when you're learning playwriting that everyone's gonna just cross off the stage directions anyway, but like, read them first. Seriously. I'm meticulous with the beats. I do a lot of beats because that's the pace that worked, and I say in the beginning of every play, "Go fucking fast."

JUDITH: Yeah, I approach other people's similar to my own. I usually dramaturge as well, so a big part of the development is to serve their vision and as a director, what music can I bring in? How can I collaborate with the designer on the set? What movement can I bring? Can I bring songs? Anything to enhance the play and serve their vision, which then becomes my vision too.

KAT: You know when you see something and you think, "Ooh, that was directed"? I never want that. You want to leave something and think, "Oh, wow, I felt all the feels and I feel the passion. Something just happened. I don't know what it was." That's a play that works for me, rather than someone who says, "It was raining on stage. I wonder whose idea that was?"

JUDITH: In Germany, though, I understand it really is the director's vision. Playwrights be warned: never let your play be done in Germany. They'll cut the first scene then bring on rain and clowns and things that are not in your script.

LABBIE: *[To Kat.]* I was really interested in what Richard said about your programming re: the Netflix generation. I wonder how that influences both what you write and direct and how you pick your topics?

KAT: We started in 2011. It started as HBO but now we say Netflix. Our whole thing was that our generation was raised on good TV. Really, really, fucking great TV, much more accessible TV than it's ever been. Netflix is insane, so we set out to make something where, well, if we're gonna be competing with TV, then everything has to be fast-paced, funny, high-stakes, short, like, not being more than ninety minutes. I think intermissions are the death of thought. Because why would I want to give someone a chance to think about something else? So I try to make every play hurtle towards something big. And I think we could take a lot from the way that television is marketed. I think that for a long time we thought that, with theatre, we can be a bit more ethereal; but it can be hard, it can be fast, and it could be sexy. So we as a company—the only thing we ever put money into at the beginning was photos. We had a professional photographer, we had beautiful poster design, and it's always an image that grabs you, and a *TV Guide* sentence that you could pitch to an executive in an elevator and have him say, "Ah!" I think theatre's moving towards virtual reality. That's a whole other conversation, but I think even in order to hope to compete with television that we can borrow more from what they're doing.

JUDITH: And, on the other hand, I think we should seek to do what they can't do. What is it that you actually *can* do in the theatre that you can't do and that actually doesn't work on film and TV?

LABBIE: To go back to the question about why the writer-director combo is considered taboo, perhaps it's because there's not a language for it? In comic books you have a writer and illustrator—they're a cartoonist—and everybody understands that you do both. You are this thing. I was really struck with when you both called yourselves creators because that's how I feel. When I'm working as a writer, and if the words are something that I want to live past me in future productions, then I want somebody else to test drive the car so that I can see if somebody else can drive it and direct the piece. How do you feel about that?

KAT: I write in such a panic, honestly, and I write with the threat of a looming production always. Normally I don't have time to think past the initial production. I find it fascinating you mention comics because I don't think anyone who has directed or has a directing gene write without seeing it. You can't hear it; there's no voices. I don't know how to write without directing in my head. So when I'm published and have to write for scary posterity, my editor says, "You added hundreds of stage directions. You have to cut these now." And I think, "Well, I won't be there. What will happen?"

JUDITH: And it's the opposite for me. I don't see it at all when I write. It's just the voices and the internal emotional dynamic. But then I have a great pleasure of visualizing it as a director and, as a director, it is just for that show, those actors, because I also will slightly change the character if I have an actor who is really funny—has really great comic timing—I will make the character funnier. But when I'm writing, it's just the voices, no visuals at all.

KAT: I write in a fury. I write a garbage draft and then I will get my cheapest, booziest friends together and I'll buy them a bunch of booze and we'll read it. And it's not until I hear it read that I know it's a comedy, know it works, know what it sounds like. I need to hear the voices out loud.

JUDITH: The reading does change a lot. I do a lot of revisions.

RICHARD: When you begin rehearsals, do you read the play on the first day?

BOTH: Yes.

JUDITH: Last year before I directed *The Crackwalker* a student of mine asked, "Well, I guess you pre-block everything?" and I thought, "Wow." I would never do that. It's impulse—what is your impulse and then even more. That's a whole school of thought. I experienced that once as an actor. The director would literally say, "You are two feet to the right and then you move your hand that way."

LABBIE: I want to dovetail off of that. I'm with the room in the sense that I'm not a pre-blocker, so know that's where I'm coming from. However, I've been doing a lot of work combining theatre with dance as of late and there is the notion of the dancer's impulse. But I do think that choreography is something specific in that sense and there is room within choreography and technique for interpretation. I guess I'm playing devil's advocate, thinking about the notion that the different ways that we do things leaves room for that. I just decided as I was saying that, that this is not really a question. But writing in a way is predetermining?

KAT: It's funny, I write a lot of the groups talking all at the same time and I think of the first script as a pre-block. So in a way writing is pre-blocking and rehearsal is letting it go.

RICHARD: Let me just go back and perhaps advocate for the possibility that directors might pre-block, because I know Neil Munro was a huge advocate. Everything was planned in advance and his work was brilliant. It's not the way I would choose to work, but everyone's got a different approach and we can accept that.

JUDITH: I just think it negates an actor's impulse. If you want the actors to act on what you create and to really be inside and inhabit a character fully and emotionally, they feel they want to throw themselves into the floor or feel like running this way. It might not work, but try it and let's see it and work on it together.

KAT: I think you have to be flexible. I find that a lot of people who direct musicals and operas do that much more because directing opera is like being the world's most impressive stage manager.

JUDITH: But with choreography it is different because you're not waiting for the impulse. It's how they fill it.

LABBIE: Throughout this week we've been talking a lot about time. For each of you, where do you want more time? Where does time help?

JUDITH: I sometimes feel that if you have a story that's in you that needs to be told, you can basically write as fast as you can type. Then you need to revise it. So someone can give you a year or two years and you write the whole thing the three weeks before, because that's when it's ready to come out. Now I have a sense of what's enough time.

KAT: I find that no matter what, the project expands to fit the time I have. I've gotten a bit cowboy-esque and given myself less and less time. The pressure becomes a bit of a drug. I don't want more time. I want harsher deadlines and I want them to be enforced better. I want a more regimented system for deliverables for how I work, especially in the ending process because I find revising incredibly difficult.

JUDITH: Sometimes it takes time to have a real simple solution.

LABBIE: Do you work with dramaturges and if so when do you bring that person in?

KAT: My dramaturge is also my best friend and my business partner, so I go to him when I have an idea and he'll just ask me questions. So for me, go as early as possible if you're comfortable with that person. But it took me my whole young life to find a person who gelled with me that way. I wouldn't do it with anyone else.

JUDITH: I've had several and I've worked a lot with the great and recently deceased Iris Turcott. She was very powerful and sometimes she'd be so inside it she would phone me at one in the morning and say, "Oh, this and this!" You have to know when to listen and when to say, "No, that's not where I am. That's not what I'm thinking." I've also had some very gentle dramaturges, which is great too because they give you space.

It really is yours, but they're just that guiding hand, instead of someone saying, "Cut the second scene," because it might not be right. Ultimately you know. It is that little gut thing. But an outside eye is always very important because a lot of rehearsal situations become love-ins. We all love one another and everyone is so brilliant. Every Facebook post—everyone's brilliant, it's amazing; and you need someone to come in and say, "That's boring," and put everyone into shock and then they realize, oh, maybe they're right. We've been just so in love with one another—it's an erotic space, with love too, and admiration, but you need someone hard coming in.

KAT: Can you imagine if people wrote real Facebook posts where they were like, "I don't think what Janine did was good today."

RICHARD: When do you bring a dramaturge in to work with you or does it change?

JUDITH: It changes. After first draft, which is really my tenth draft. I really have to be in it and as a dramaturge myself, which I've done several times, I'm wary of imposing my taste instead of respecting this is how *they* write. It's not what you would do, so that's nerve-racking to not make it mine and just ask the questions.

LABBIE: I've a question about your relationship with dramaturges. As a writer and director does what you want or need from them change depending on your role as a writer or director?

JUDITH: I think as a director you have to be the dramaturge. I wouldn't want another dramaturge. I think it's part of your responsibility. That is part of what you do. They might've had one previously, so you might have to make other suggestions.

Some directors are not dramaturges and they will say, "I don't know how to do it."

KAT: Dramaturges end up being assistant directors often. And sometimes you have an assistant director in the room and then it's just a lot of cooks. The ideal relationship of director/writer/dramaturge for me—I write about things that I'm interested in, but I also write about things that will excite an audience—so for me that kind of place where all those jobs intersect is asking, "What is best thing for the play and what is the best thing for the audience?" My dramaturge always says he's the voice of the audience in the room. No matter how many voices are in the room, if you are all working towards the same thing, then it usually works out okay.

LABBIE: I'm curious what you think of how we create theatre for the next generation. Do we move with the new generation or do we try to instill the history of theatre?

JUDITH: We want to reach younger people. I don't want to cater to an audience. I want to write for them in a sense where you read great fiction. It's something where you say, "Oh, I've known this all along but I forgot about it." It's familiar yet strange, and that's what's so wonderful. It's those gray areas that people aren't thinking about.

LABBIE: So do we pull deeper into that next Netflix generation or do we move away from it?

KAT: When I write I think, "What is the last thing people expect to see in a play?" It's about letting an audience see itself on stage.

JUDITH: I gave my students an assignment—I think it was a film class—and it was the question, "Why theatre now?" and one of them gave the most extraordinary answer. They said, "Because film dates and the best theatre is always now." There has to be that grounding to give it weight, to give it gravity so it does last and people are reading and producing it in 100 years, and it's not just of a time that was ten years or five years. I think you do really want to reflect your own culture a lot. That's when theatre is most exciting. We have subtext of ourselves, or ourselves as we can't really see ourselves until it's put on stage. A part of our society we don't see or don't want to see. Our subterranean selves.

RICHARD: Thank you both very much.

THE RULES OF THE GAME/ BREAKING THE RULES: MORRIS PANYCH AND KEN MACDONALD INTERVIEWED BY HEATHER CANT

This interview took place in June 2016 as part of a session titled the Playwrights Project, and covers Morris and Ken's body of work as collaborators in playwrighting, directing, and design.

HEATHER: I want to start by reflecting back just over twenty years to the *Canadian Theatre Review* interview you gave in 1993 where you talked a bit about your "theory" of theatre.

[Morris makes a face; he looks scared about what he might have said. There's laughter from the Labbies.]

You had said at the time that your theory of theatre was to "keep changing, rediscovering, questioning, not only the accepted ideas of theatre, but the reversal of those ideas as well." So that was a long time ago. And I want to ask a two-part question. One: How did that theory inform the work that you chose to do and how you chose to embrace that work, and Two: Has that theory changed now that you're further into your career and you are looking back? Would you agree with your past self?

MORRIS: I'll talk about the second part first. Of course that was twenty-three years ago and one says things. I always find "theories" a little suspect. I love the story about Brecht who only invented his theory because his manager said, "You've gotta come up with a name for this otherwise all these people will be confused and no one will know what it is," so he made up this name. I think that, strangely, my idea that against "accepted ideas" and the reverse being true—I think the reverse has actually become more true for me, because as theories of directing have developed over the last ten years, we've seen a real increase in "auteur" ideas that are big, imagistic, director-driven ideas. I find that now I feel like I'm fighting a battle against "auteurism." I find that a lot of directors now are interested in their idea over and above what's in the text. I think breaking rules is still the most important thing that you can do, but sometimes you end up breaking rules so much that you end up with nothing. Sometimes following rules is just as important. We often talk about how it's okay to fuck around with ideas as long as you understand the idea to begin with. You see great visual artists playing around with form but, by and large, they were also great drawers. They had great skill they could employ before they could start messing around. I think it's important that theatre practitioners have a basis, or a grounding, in the ability to do things—to tell a story—before they start messing around with what that *is*. I've gone back very much to the idea of storytelling because the more I direct, the more I realize there's no other way to talk to actors, unless it's in an arbitrary way. To have a conversation with an actor about what they're doing on stage, the only thing you need or have to refer to is the text you are actually working on, because otherwise the ideas, like, "We're gonna do *Macbeth* and we're all gonna dress like monkeys"—the actor is left with not a lot to work with in terms of the story. So the director has to have the skill and the ability to read the text and go back to the actor and say, "Well, here's the reason you're dressed like a monkey. This is what I'm basing it on." So then the actor can reflect and the designer can deal with it. Sometimes directors give conceptual ideas that don't really make sense. And the only way to find grounding in the interpretation is through the text. So I think that I would stick with what I said.

[Laughter from Labbies.]

But I've already forgotten the first part of your question.

HEATHER: The first part was about how that theory informed your work.

MORRIS: I don't really like to talk about theories because they can be weirdly restrictive. There is a guy in Vancouver who used to write a lot about us, about "metatheatricality" because we were working in this form, and I read recently that all my plays were about loss. So when I sat down to write again I thought, "Is this about loss?" Those definitions are really hard to talk about. That's probably why that theory was so general. Someone asks what your theory is and you're too naïve and narcissistic to think you don't have an answer, so you come up with something and it's that. But to be honest I don't know I have a theory about directing. I mean everything, every project has its own life and its own reality. I think if anything it's what I was talking about—storytelling. About finding the basis of what a thing *is*. Because you can always go back to that. It's the one thing you have. It's like rules of grammar. You can do all this stuff, but that is a *thing* that exists. I love working now in opera because I'm usually giving all these things like, "This is what you're feeling and the colour pink" or whatever the fuck I'm talking about, and the conductor will say, "This is diminuendo." That's it. That defines what that musical passage is. It's not "forte," it's exactly what it says on the page, and I'm very envious of that kind of definitive thing that you're able to communicate with actors. I've started to use those musical terms when communicating with actors because they understand them better. I also think that Stanislavsky and method overaccentuated certain things that are very difficult in certain situations. Even in my plays, certain questions that are brought up can't be answered in method terminology. Sure, you can have subtext and motivation, but there's also a larger picture. You look at someone like Beckett, which I've directed, much to my chagrin, like *Godot*, and have actors come in who are naturalistic "method" actors who nearly lose their minds. And then actors who are basically clowns who just have a whole different approach to it don't have nearly as difficult a time.

HEATHER: I want to ask a little bit about what you've said in terms of directors trying to be "auteurs" and make the work their own. You've directed at Stratford and Shaw where they do classical work, and it seems to me that directors, with text like that, are often trying to embrace risk and not only make it their own, and what does their voice have to say, but to really do something new and push a boundary. What do you think the balance is there between embracing risk and overriding . . . ?

MORRIS: I think it's important to take risks but I don't think *risk* for its own sake. I think risks should illuminate the text—risks to bring out what story is clearer, some way to jar the audiences' minds so in some way the audience can look at it in a different way. Those are risks that are worth taking and they don't necessarily exclude a certain kind of imagistic or conceptual idea, but the conceptual idea should be connected to the story. And I'm just as guilty as anybody, especially when I was just starting out as a younger director. I really wanted to make my imprint because that's what you do; you want to be noticed. "I need to have some kind of style, some kind of *thing*," but then you ask yourself, what are the boundaries? Sometimes it's the actors that train you out of that because, when you direct them as actors and not just as chess pieces and they're good actors, they can really apply rigour that you didn't expect and that you need to answer for. I mean you can wash your hands of it if you want, but that doesn't make for a good atmosphere in the rehearsal room. You need to have a very clear idea of *why* you want to do *what* you want to do, so the actors can get on board. You want actors as allies. They're *the* part of what you're doing. I mean there's design, but actors are selling it.

HEATHER: Can you give us a bit of context in terms of your own work? An example of risk that you took where people got on board or maybe where people didn't?

MORRIS: Well, when I came to Tarragon, my first show I directed was *7 Stories*, which turned into a big hit. When I directed in Vancouver, it was all with people I knew, so everyone just got on board. It was Vancouver and it was the '80s and no one cared. The show is about a man on the ledge of a building who's thinking about jumping . . . or not. And all these people come out of their apartments and they're so not interested. They have their own shit going on and he's trying to figure out the reason why he's not jumping. It's a very absurdist, very existential piece. When I did it in Vancouver, it was just one huge wall of sky with windows in it. He had a bowler hat. We were inspired by a Magritte painting. Then we get here and the first thing someone says to me—we did a reading on the first day and we went for a beer afterwards with the cast, and one of the actors in the Toronto cast had seen it in Vancouver and said, "Oh. That was good. We're gonna do the adult version here." And I was like, "I don't even know what that fucking means." They were so hard on me. They were so distrustful of my process. They did not buy into it at all. And I really didn't know what to do. I went home the first three or four nights and just cried. For like, hours. Just not knowing what to do with these people—and they were really—all of them are now, very well-known, very successful actors. At the time though, I don't know what it was. It was just the mix. But I had to find a way to connect with them that was legitimate. I tried to apply some kind of Stanislavsky, whatever "thing" to imprint it, but the actors in the end said they didn't know what they were doing. It was kind of a disaster rehearsal. And then one day—they all said they had no clue what they were doing in any part of the play—and I was desperate and I said, "Okay, we're going to sit down and we're gonna go through the entire play and go through every line and you're gonna tell me whether or not you know what you're doing." And we went through the whole play, instead of moving forward—I think it was tech rehearsal—I cancelled it. And we sat down and went through the whole script and I'd say, "Do you know what you're doing? You know what you're saying . . . blah blah blah." Fine. We did the whole thing. Next day, we go into rehearsal and one of the first things one of the actors said was, "I don't know what I'm doing." So I just thought . . . "Fuck you. I'm done." And at one point one of the actors was sitting behind me and the other actor on stage said to me, "So you want me to do it like a drag queen?" Just some stupid remark. Normally I'd give some very involved explanation of how the character would blah blah blah. But he says, "So you want me to do it like a drag queen?" and the actor sitting behind me says softly, "Just say yes," and I did, and he says "Okay." And I'm like, "Oh." It was a weird, tough time for me. It ended up being a big fucking success.

[Huge laughter from Labbies.]

And I just wanted to say to all of them . . . "*Fuck you!*" But you can't say that. You have to keep a good atmosphere in the room. I think one of the biggest jobs of a director, to me, now, is being a psychoanalyst. I say to actors all the time, publically and privately, that everything is based on fear. Everything that's happening in the room is based on it; their fear of looking like assholes and not succeeding. So we have to find a way to make them feel not afraid.

HEATHER: I want to talk about the relationship you have with designers, but before I get to that I want to ask you, what is it about other directors' works—when you go to the theatre—what is it about the direction you see from your contemporaries that speaks to you? That excites you? What is it that you see encapsulated in their work that moves you?

MORRIS: The first thing is good acting. Nothing beats good acting. Clear storytelling. It's like, if I get involved, that's all I want. I want to get involved in the storytelling. I don't care about those other bells and whistles. I want there to be an element of thought put into it. I want the director to tell me something through set design or music or costumes, the direction—where I'm supposed to be going with this thing—but other than that, I don't want to be distracted by *stuff.* I just want to get into the storytelling and get involved. That's always the way it is. Even if you go to a movie. I just want to care about this person. It's funny watching Netflix now. It's all kind of retrograde. It's all just good fucking stories. That's what people are interested in. That's what they follow. Design is important but it's all about taking you into that world. So for me, good direction is about *taking* me somewhere that isn't *here.* Not making me think of this or anything, just taking me there. That's part of our job.

HEATHER: It sounds simple, but it's not, as we all know. So when you're directing, whether it's your work or other people's work, you almost exclusively work with Ken. There's, I think, one show you haven't done together?

KEN: We've done close to a hundred shows together.

HEATHER: So that creates quite a working relationship. How do you guys navigate that both for good and for evil? I imagine you can't possibly agree *all* the time?

[Morris laughs loudly, followed by the Labbies.]

MORRIS: We agree on the main points. And that's important. Because we agree about the premise of theatre. We agree about it *being* theatre. About it being a statement about theatre. About it being *not* film. About it being good theatrical storytelling. Taking an audience somewhere they'd normally not go.

KEN: We're married and we've been together for thirty-six years. He has an office above my studio in our house so it's very easy for him to come down while he's writing a play. When we're working on a new play, the design is thought of quite early. I sometimes will say, "Why is your aesthetic better than mine?" but because he is the director, I have to accept a hierarchy, because he doesn't like it. And it goes. We'll argue sometimes, but our concept of what we like in theatre is very similar.

HEATHER: You have a shorthand?

KEN: Yes. Absolutely.

HEATHER: So how do you then, after such a long time working with one designer, try to achieve a similar symbiosis when you're working with another designer?

MORRIS: Well, I work with lighting designers and costume designers, so there's that. It's trickier. I think that working with Ken is different because we travel together. We talk about form a lot. And colour.

KEN: We see theatre everywhere. We travelled years ago on a Canada Council grant and saw eighty-eight plays in four months all over Europe. And we say, "Remember that play we saw in Switzerland, where they had that plastic bag . . ." It was just a fantastic thing for us.

MORRIS: We also share a love of art nouveau, Gaudí, we love Rennie Mackintosh—we went to Glasgow, we looked at all of his things. We'll go and look at all the Frank Lloyd Wright things and talk about them a lot. Sometimes they have nothing to do with what we're doing at all and may never have anything to do with what we're doing at all, but generally they do. Ken never really designs anything that isn't already in our house. I noticed that about three years ago. Everything on stage is weirdly similar . . . . "That's like our back garden."

[Laughter from Labbies.]

HEATHER: Is there a trick of the trade that you can give to us as directors about how to, with ease and some facility and speed, develop a shorthand with a designer that you don't have a relationship with, that can lead to this mutual compatibility?

MORRIS: This is why I go back to this text thing. It's the common denominator. It's the one thing you can actually talk about that has form, that you can look at and say, "It says here . . . blah blah blah.." Now, we can break that rule—it doesn't have to take place in 1910—but there's a reason for that and what's that reason? And once we start breaking those rules then what rules are we now following? So you can have that conversation. This may not sound like shorthand but otherwise you're talking about general concepts floating in mid-air. There's a whole universe of ideas, but you have to nail them down to what specifically you're talking about.

KEN: What a designer has to be aware of is entrances and exits. When you're reading the script for the first time you have to think, "How does someone get on stage and off, quickly. Does it make sense? What is the logic of the pattern of the floor? Where is the kitchen, where is the front garden?" All that kind of stuff. Those things make a huge difference for the blocking. It's a really important thing to talk to a designer about, when you meet—the comings and goings.

MORRIS: There are all these crazy theories like the downstage right is people you like and downstage left is people you don't like. And it may be true, but after a while you instinctively feel, "This is a better place for this person to be." It takes a while to work that out but as Ken says, just looking at the script, practically speaking, how do those people get in and how do they get out in a nice way? When we designed *The Overcoat* we realized we needed to be in many locations quickly and we needed to have a lot of furniture moving on and off the stage. So the first decision, aside from the fact that I wanted everything aesthetically to move in circles, was that everything was on wheels.

KEN: And we've done that so many times since then.

MORRIS: Well, because you learn, "This is the answer to everything!"

[Laughter.]

Everything's on wheels and it goes in and out and if you find a creative choreographic way to move that stuff around, it can not only be good storytelling, but very efficient and very beautiful, because part of what I love doing in the theatre is transitions. Taking people on that journey and watching things move from one thing to another because it's part of what theatre can do. In film you just do jump-cuts or fade-outs. You don't do this kind of stuff where you watch actors or whoever moving stuff in patterns.

KEN: People love to see things fly in or something pushed—that's beautiful. That transition can be just glorious, watching how it moves from one world to another.

MORRIS: I've written plays that are basically based on transitions. *Vigil* is based on transitions. A show I just did here, *Sextet*, is all transitions; moving very quickly from one thing to another so what you're looking at has musicality to it, a choreographic—a musical component that's very satisfying to witness.

HEATHER: I want to talk a little more in depth about *The Overcoat*. It was an incredible Canadian success story, which doesn't happen often in Canadian theatre, where a show goes on to have such an incredible life. This particular show was a non-verbal physical theatre piece that you created with an incredibly large cast that not only did well here in Canada but also went on to tour internationally for quite some time. Can you talk a little bit about the difference in approach for you between working on a production that is text based and one that is not? Where there are no words to speak of involved in the show itself?

MORRIS: Well, when we started *Overcoat*, we mashed Gogol with *Diary of a Madman*. When I started out I wanted to do it with Shostakovich music—I thought it's simpler to do just one composer because it has flow to it. And also Shostakovich was obsessed with certain themes and melodies in his music that I thought I could put into it. So I took the Shostakovich and broke down the story into story elements—like, first scene he wakes up and he's with his landlady. The second scene he's at work and he's getting roughed over by his blah blah blah . . . Then taking pieces of music that I thought would fit each of those scenes, because I thought, "That sounds like a dance," or "That sounds like a violent scene." We just did all that. Then we arrive at rehearsal, and I play everyone all the music and I say, "That's all we've got." And it was like panic stations for everybody—the props people, everybody. But it was awesome. Because I don't think there's a better environment for creativity than not having a clue what you're doing but having to get it done.

KEN: You have the first eight bars and you have to think, "What are we doing?" And then the next eight bars.

MORRIS: It just makes you think. You hear about how relatively easy it was for Shakespeare to write because he had to stick to the score. So it actually created creativity because there was this structure. So when you have something like that where you say to the actors, "Okay, today we have to create ten minutes of this story and this is the music so what happens here? She comes in and it sounds like this and they're moving like . . ." and we just start putting it together the way we did. And we did it all in about three weeks. Luckily, I had worked on that form before at an acting school in Vancouver. It's kind of a funny story. I was supposed to write a play for an acting school and come in and direct it, and I got incredibly lazy over the summer and I didn't write anything. And the head of the school phoned me late August and said, "What are we going to do?" and I said, "Well . . . I have this great idea. I'm going to take the Chopin nocturnes and we're just going to do movement stories to them." And she's like, "Really?" and I'm like, "Yeah." But I couldn't think of anything else and I was lucky because my movement collaborator worked at that school and she came in and worked with me on this thing. Sometimes the pressure of time, the need to get something done, those things create a sort of conduit for creativity that you normally wouldn't have because, you know, in an open space— When I write a play for instance, I make myself write that play in two, two and a half weeks. Once all the patchy things are in and I don't really know what I'm doing— When I sit down and decide to write that play, I have to do it in two and a half weeks. Because if it takes longer, it starts to dissipate. It becomes something else, so I try to discipline myself to make it happen. But that also makes you do things you wouldn't normally do. It makes you get up at eight thirty in the morning when you don't have to, to sit down and start writing again.

HEATHER: You have quite a reputation in this country with regards to your thoughts on—and I'm quoting you—the role of the critic in what we do. One critic said once of you that you can't take a bad review or a good review. Because you have such a clearly encapsulated idea for yourself with regards to your own work, but also the role that the critic plays in our sector, in our environment of creativity, I wanted to get a more one-on-one perspective that isn't filtered through a critic that I read in a paper somewhere about your thoughts on that.

MORRIS: I'll give you one example and this goes way back so I have some perspective on this. The first thing Ken and I did together I wrote was called *Last Call: A Post Nuclear Cabaret*, and it was a very weird, funny, crazy musical about two guys who survived the nuclear holocaust. It was a huge success, I've never—it was unbelievable. Everybody in town had to see it, the critics, just everybody. It was all over the place. We came to Toronto with it and blah blah blah . . . The second musical we wrote, which was far more complex, had way more characters, was musically way more interesting—they just shit on it. And they didn't just shit on it because it wasn't good. They shit on it because we were derivative suddenly, and we weren't very interesting suddenly, we weren't clear. There was no mention in any of that of how we were trying to do a transition from one thing to another. There was no thought about that. It was not that some critic had sat back—one did—but it wasn't like they sat back and asked, "What are they trying to do? I mean, this is the same two guys who gave us this amazing show, so we at least have to give them a pass and ask, "What are they trying to do?" There aren't a lot of critics who ask that question. So you can have a success one year and the next year—same person, same team, same group—they have a failure, and rather than just saying, "This didn't work as well as the last one, but it's interesting what they're trying to do," or, "I'm trying to figure out what they're trying to do . . ." The critic always feels to me that he or she has to be ahead of the game. And instead of following the artist, they're trying to lead the artist. They're saying what kind of diversity should be on the stage. They're saying what kind of plays should be written. I remember when we did *Vigil* in London years ago, one of the main critics in the London paper said, "Where are all the plays about Afghanistan?" and I'm like, "What the fuck are you talking about? I'm not writing about Afghanistan. That's not my thing. I care about it, but I'm not writing about it." It's like they're trying to mold and shape what theatre should be instead of just looking at it and going, "What is this?" and, "This is interesting." It just doesn't happen. I think part of it is they have this imperative for readership, so they have to write things that are compelling or interesting, that they think are modern. Then there's this huge, ugly, personal component to it, which I won't get into. I just hate them. It's not even rational anymore.

HEATHER: They do wield a fair amount of power.

MORRIS: They can make or break a show.

HEATHER: I get the sense, though, from what you've said here, but also because you often reply in the comments sections to the reviews, whether they're good or bad, that you feel the critic actually has a collaborative role to play within our artistic creation.

MORRIS: Yeah.

HEATHER: So can you share with us how you think that should work?

MORRIS: Well, I think the shape of that should be that they support and encourage what artists are trying to do. The last thing they should be doing is applying a number of stars to things. That's a really bad thing to get into because that puts a face value on the artwork as if it's worth a price.

HEATHER: We have time for one question from the Labbies.

LABBIE: I'm wondering, is there some consistent theme or imagery in your work that keeps coming back? Something that you are pursuing? That haunts you?

MORRIS: Lots of things haunt me. Death haunts me. Very early in my life I was confronted by this very weird experience with my grandmother dying, and I think it just made me consumed by the idea of death and the afterlife. I don't know why. I was seven and it was a Ukranian funeral, and it was crazy only in the way those things can be with an open casket and people throwing themselves on the body and just drama and music, and when you're seven you're like, "I have no clue what this is but I love it!"

BRAD FRASER INTERVIEWED BY PETER PASYK

This interview took place in June 2018 as part of a session titled the Playwrights Project, and covers Brad's body of work as a playwright and director.

PETER: What is it you look for in a director?

BRAD: I often look for directors who look for me. Often they turn up that way because they read something and they're interested in meeting me and talking about it. When I see directors whose work I admire, I make that very clear to them. I let them know I admire them. Really good directors are not necessarily always that easy to find, particularly for the kind of work I want to do. I need a director who has a lot of courage and isn't intimidated by me. I've gotten into a couple situations where I was working with a director who was intimidated by me and therefore wasn't talking to me about what they honestly felt about the play. And those things never end very happily. So I find I get a lot of really inexperienced directors with a lot of drive, which I like, or I get a lot of experienced directors who have their own ideas and aren't worried that much about what I think, and I tend to gravitate towards those kind of directors as well. I have very specific ideas about direction in general but particularly the direction about my plays that are structured not to necessarily feel like what we usually see in the theatre, or sound like what we usually see in the theatre, so that is very important to me as well.

PETER: You began directing your plays at a certain point?

BRAD: I *started* directing my own plays. My very first play I got done was called *Mutants* at an amateur theatre in Edmonton. I was twenty-one years old and they asked me to write the play because I'd won the playwriting competition twice and then they asked me to direct it. No one had bothered to read the play and then a week before it opened they read it and said, "Oh my God, you're saying 'cunt' and 'fuck' and people are having sex. We can't do this play. We need a Noël Coward." And I said, "Well, you've had the play for two months. You could have read it. We're going ahead and doing it." Actually, the board voted with me in the room on whether or not they should produce the play and I won by two votes. And I directed the show and it was their bestselling show of the season and unlike anything they'd ever done there. But to be completely honest, I don't really like directing my own work for the first production, particularly. I've done it several times out of necessity, but it's a very lonely place to be. You have absolutely no one to talk to; absolutely no one to share your concerns with, and you have no one to blame it on when it's done in the end. So my preference is to work with someone on the premiere production and then direct the second or third production where I can steal all the good ideas and make none of their mistakes. I work visually as an artist as well and all these things are connected. I can't necessarily pull them apart. But when I work with a director, *they* are the director. I'm the playwright. I'm not there to tell them what to do. I'm not there to do anything but make their job easier. As long as they know what they're doing. I've been in those situations, but for me, it's my play that's going to be up there on that stage and ultimately I'm going to be the one that they're talking about with the play, so I want to know what's going on. I'm not one of those playwrights who goes to every rehearsal and watches everything you do and talks to you about it on every break because they don't understand how the process works. Or that you have to fail repeatedly until something finally works. That kind of thing. So I like to direct my work but not in the initial production.

PETER: Do you invite the director into the dramaturgical process as well, or is it a finished script by the time it goes into rehearsal?

BRAD: That depends. I worked with Iris Turcott for many, many years as a dramaturge long before the show got anywhere near a director. Braham Murray, who's directed more of my shows than anyone, at the Royal Exchange, didn't want to get into the dramaturgy. As far as he was concerned, when I gave him the play, it was done and he is gonna make it work. And I'd say, "No, no. We need to workshop it and I need to hear it." Seeing how the audience responds to things is very much part of my process. In a perfect world, it's a fusion of those things, but it's a different relationship with every director you work with. They all tend to have their own life and their own sort of needs and I let that shape what the experience is going to be.

PETER: You were talking about the Manchester theatre. I'm wondering if you could tell us how that relationship began and developed?

BRAD: Braham called me out of the blue in 1998 and said he saw *Love and Human Remains* at the Traverse Theatre in Edinburgh and he just did it at his theatre, and he read *Poor Superman* and he was doing that too, and that he loved my writing and that if he could support me in any way, he'd be happy to do it. And at that point my career had completely dried up in Canada, so I said, "Yes, I need everything. Do my play." Then he came to Canada and saw *Martin Yesterday* and said, "Yeah, I'll do that." So they started bringing me over. From there they started commissioning me. It was the best thing that ever happened in my life. It was a gift from out of the blue.

PETER: There seems to be controversy that some of your plays will instigate. I read in an interview you once gave, about the controversy over *Poor Superman* culminating in armed guards at the theatre and helicopters circling. How did it get to that point?

BRAD: It was Cincinnati. It was a couple years after the Robert Mapplethorpe controversy. It was a semi-professional theatre, but three months after deciding to do it, they said they weren't because it's too controversial. But the artists in town rose up and said they'd leave the theatre if they decided to cancel the show, so it started this kind of press thing that just kept building upon itself about this horrible play that was going on in Cincinnati that had gay sex and people dying of AIDS and transsexuals, and the police were going to be there. They were going to have the vice squad in the audience to make sure we weren't circumventing any laws. And I walked to the theatre on opening night and, literally, there were helicopters overhead, armed guards at the door, CNN was there, news feeds from across the country, the reviewer from the *New York Times*, *Time Magazine*, and it was the most insane thing I had ever seen. Thankfully, it went really well and it got great notices and it was a huge selling show. But that kind of fuss, which has followed me my whole career, is something I really like in the theatre. I think every theatre event should be like that. Somebody should always be trying to shut down something we are producing in order to keep it vital and important and I'm very proud of the fact that I've produced so many shows that have elicited that kind of response around the world, because it tells me, like it or not, that something important is being said here for people to get so upset about.

PETER: The media has described you in Canada as the "bad boy of Canadian theatre." Over time I know you've embraced that title but also denounced it.

BRAD: I'm fifty-nine years old. If I was a woman and you were calling me a "girl" at fifty-nine . . . It took me a long time. I used to think, "Okay, I'm the bad boy. I'm the rebel. I'm the guy who's doing what everyone else isn't doing." But then I realized that there are a lot of straight writers in Canada who've done very controversial, very challenging work for years and they were never called the "bad boy of Canadian theatre" and what I came to understand is, what they were actually doing in a very subtle, homophobic fashion was minimizing who I was, as if to say, "What he's saying isn't valid because he's just saying it to be bad. He's just saying it to elicit a response." So on the one hand, it's a really great thing to be the bad boy of Canadian theatre when you're young. It's a great title to have. But as you get older it becomes very difficult to carry that title around and to pull it off and eventually you want to stop being a bad boy. Eventually you want to go explore other things and do other things but you're not always given that opportunity.

PETER: It's a fairly reductive term. Like any title.

BRAD: Well, when they're still calling you that at fifty-five? It also says there hasn't been a new "bad boy" or "girl" to come up and take that place that I have. I'm a bit sad about that. I was really hoping there'd be a whole generation of bad boys and girls who were turned on by what I was doing, but I don't see a lot of that.

PETER: What interests you now? How do you say, "This is a play"?

BRAD: It's usually a series of events and images and ideas that come to me cumulatively that start to suggest things to me. Also, the real question I'm asking myself now is, "How do you make theatre immediate to everyone that's involved? How do you make theatre immediate the entire time?" Because it's that thing that—once it starts, it's already disappearing. It's already going away as you're experiencing it. So how can I fuck with that? How can I control that? How can I change that? Keeping things alive, keeping things surprising, keeping things in the here and now, in the present tense is sort of my obsession now. Everything really needs to happen in the present tense. We're living in the past and we're living in the future, but we're not living in the moment right now. And no place but the theatre does that. No place demands as much of your imagination or your attention or your empathy or involvement as the theatre. So I'm interested in opening up some of those elements to directors and actors and designers and saying, "How do we do this?"

[A pause.]

I don't know if that answered your question.

PETER: I think so. Yes. I am intrigued by one of your lectures you give at universities. It's called "Why I hate theatre." I'm curious about this.

BRAD: Well, basically, it's about past tense. It's about how the theatre that we see and that we do so often is past tense. Even if it's a new play, there is something about the acting or the script or direction, there's something about the way we are in the theatre looking at this thing that somehow keeps us distant from it and makes it seem like it's always happening in the past and not right now with us, around us and that's what we're dealing with. So that sense of soullessness that we often see at certain theatres around town—they often do lots of great American plays of the 1940s and '50s and '60s sort of thing, where literally the actors are coming out and just saying lines most of the time and trying to remember their blocking, they're not bringing anything to it. That kind of stuff, when I see it, when I take people to see it, I get homicidal, because it kills the theatre. The new people who want to go to the theatre come and say, "That was so fucking boring, I'm never coming back." That will keep a new audience from coming to the theatre. To keep the theatre vital. I'm absolutely all for reviving these plays and finding a new way of doing them and looking at them, but there is something very WASPy and middle class about the theatre that I've seen. I never saw a play until I was in high school, but I was quickly turned off because they were mostly rich white people standing around rooms talking about paintings. I had no level of recognition.

PETER: What about things you've seen lately that have turned you on, that feel vital?

BRAD: I saw a show at this little storefront theatre that was one of the best nights I've had at the theatre. It was so alive and so vital and so *not* formalized. You felt at any point that the whole thing could fall apart and the fact that it never did was what made it wonderful.

PETER: Your play *Kill Me Now* is also based on something you read in a newspaper. Can you tell us about that?

BRAD: Yes, speaking of where plays come from. I was reading this ethics column about a father of a very badly disabled child who was an adolescent who couldn't use his hands properly; that the son preferred the father to bathe him and do all of that kind of stuff. He was embarrassed by the mother doing it. But he was getting erections and he was making it kind of clear to the father that he'd like some help with these erections. So the father's question was, "When I'm bathing my child, when I'm wiping his ass, when I'm cleaning his foreskin, when I'm cleaning the inside of his mouth, is it stepping over some kind of line if I masturbate him?" And I thought, "Oh, now there's an ethical question." I got uncomfortable just reading about it. What does that do? And I have disabled people in my family and people who are differently abled and I know some of those stories. So that idea—that idea of "Is it an act of abuse or incredible humanity to masturbate your disabled child?" is the kind of question I want to ask in the theatre. And that's where that came from.

[Silence for a moment.]

PETER: Let's end it on a provocative note. Thank you so much, Brad.

MASTER CLASS

Retreating to/Re-treating from "Irreconcilable Space": Canadian Theatre Workers and the Project of Conciliation

BY JILL CARTER

Aaniin. Jill Carter n'dishnikaaz. Chi Kiiwenging / Tkaronto n'doonjibaa.

Anishinaabe ekwa Ashkenazi Kwe n'daaw. I am grateful to my Creator who has placed me here on such beautiful lands, so carefully stewarded over millennia by the Petun, Erie, Neutral, Wendat, Seneca, Cayuga, and Michi Saagiig Anishinaabeg peoples. I am grateful to be here with you on the lands wherein Indigenous life still orders itself around the Dish with One Spoon Treaty that was ratified between the Seneca peoples of the Iroquois Confederacy (the keepers of the Western Door) and the Michi Saagiig Anishinaabeg. I extend my gratitude to Evan Tsitsias who invited me to visit the Directors Lab North today, and I send out greetings, gratitude, and good intentions to you who have travelled here today to listen to a story I was asked to tell and to think about the stories you tell—stories that make, shake, or break worlds.

I thought I would introduce myself and my work with my own current obsessions and preoccupations because, as an Indigenous woman in Canada who works as both theatre practitioner and scholar, I do much of my life in a tight liminal space, picking my way through the tangled wreckage of and moving around or through the little fires produced in the unhappy meeting of two conflicting narratives. We do, indeed, live in "interesting times." And in this fraught historical moment, amid Canada's insistent call for "reconciliation," the work that occupies my brain and body—the work that I am reading, seeing, talking about, and doing—is increasingly bound up in the curation and activation of "irreconcilable" spaces of refusal on the page and on the stage. These "irreconcilable spaces" have been posited by Metis scholar-curator David Garneau as those spaces in which Indigenous people can refute the lie of "reconciliation," which is little more than a limp public relations campaign engineered by a nation that continues to build itself upon a program of theft, duplicity, and violence. This notion of reconciliation between settlers and Indigenous peoples is a dangerous (albeit, attractive) chimera that invokes the promise of safe return to a relationship that never existed, or in David Garneau's words, the "restoration of something lost (that never quite was)."* The pursuit of *reconciliation,* then, is a misguided project that will lead us all down a dangerous path towards division and disillusionment.

A relational shift is required if settlers and Indigenous peoples are to co-develop an alliance in which all of its members—human and other-than-human—are respected and upheld. Reconciliation between Indigenous peoples within our own families and communities and between Indigenous humans and the non-human world (to which we are bound in ancient treaty) is a necessary project. In the meantime, non-Indigenous peoples must reconcile themselves with their ownership of a shameful history and commit themselves to a project of redress and repair before Indigenous peoples and

---

* David Garneau, "Imaginary Spaces of Conciliation and Reconciliation," in *Arts of Engagement: Taking Aesthetic Action in and Beyond the Truth and Reconciliation Commission of Canada*, ed. Dylan Robinson and Keavy Martin (Waterloo: Wilfred Laurier University Press, 2016), 32.

settler-allies can mindfully re-encounter each other to begin to negotiate conciliatory relations, structured within a framework that is upheld by the pillars of respect, responsibility, reciprocity, and trust. Hence, David Garneau's emphasis on the importance of "irreconcilable spaces of Aboriginality" should not be lightly taken. These spaces must be intentionally curated and fiercely protected: "while decolonization and Indigenization is collective work, it sometimes requires occasions of separation—moments where Indigenous people take space and time to work things out among themselves, and parallel moments when allies ought to do the same."*

In 2015, Canada's Truth and Reconciliation Commission (TRC) put out its final report—the conclusion of a rigorous investigation into the truth surrounding Canada's Indian Residential School project. For over a century, Indigenous children were *forcibly* removed from their homes, forbidden to speak their languages, and educated in a spiritual tradition that was far removed from the practices and lifeways into which they had been born. Upon the conclusion of their educational experience, it was hoped, these young people would be so irredeemably alienated from their communities that they would eventually disappear into Canada's body politic, leaving the nations from which they had been torn unpeopled and eventually unviable. After all, there can be no nation without a citizenry. Indigenous nations had to disappear or had to *be disappeared* if Canada was to free itself from its treaty obligations and ravage every corner of these territories unchecked.

When Europe stumbled onto these shores, desperate and starving, the Indigenous peoples who encountered them entered into nation-to-nation treaties with these newcomers. These sacred, enduring agreements between sovereign nations were (and continue to be), for us, alchemical catalysts,

---

* Ibid., 23.

transforming interlopers into relatives within and co-stewards of a shared biota. But these treaties are like a thumbtack on the chair of Canada's politicians. They hurt. Canada doesn't want 90% of the land. *Canada wants it all.* In fact, Canada behaves as if it has always owned it all.

Treaty benefits (medical care, exemption from federal sales tax, etc.) are now seen as gifts by Canadians: "Oh, we're giving you so much! Look at all we have given you. We gave you those beautiful reserves with no running water and no housing on non-arable land, taking you off your traditional territories because we needed them for farming, mining, and hydroelectric projects. We gave you these little bits of land—land we *reserved* for you. We *gave* that to you. We *gave* you commodities—four key staples for survival. Yes, we often delivered these late, so that the lard was rancid and the flour mealy, but you always had sugar and salt to mask the flavor of rot. These we gave you after we drove away your game and poisoned your rivers, so that you could no longer hunt and fish. But who needs to hunt or fish when they have such tasty and convenient subsistence foods?"

They took all of this away and said, "Don't worry; you will always eat." These "benefits," such as certain tax exemptions, education monies, and funded health care, are *treaty obligations*, written into the original agreements negotiated between sovereign nations. This is rent. Simply paying the rent. But if the "landlord" were to disappear . . .

Since the formation of Canada in 1867 as a nation state, Canada has been trying to assimilate our peoples—to eradicate our nations, whether it was literally (through murder), or, more subtly, through legislated assimilation, what the Canadian government terms "enfranchisement." One tactic was to go into our communities, remove the children, and force them into schools where they were abused and told, "You're dirty. The clothes your parents gave you to wear are wrong. Your ceremonies are savage. Your table manners are hideous. Your diet is grotesque.

Your language is bibble-babble. So, you *will* speak our language. You *will* perform our ceremonies. And if you don't do this, you will be punished, punished, punished."

So, when these children "graduated," all they knew was abuse. When these children tried to return to their families, they couldn't speak their parents' languages. There's shame; there's anger; there are abandonment issues. You name it, they had it. Layer upon layer of issues! Many did not feel that they had a home, so they would leave their home communities and go into the mainstream where they were, *and still are*, targeted and mistreated. So, we have had a lot of social problems. Generations. And now we have generations of wounded parents who have hurt their own children. In this generation, we battle to stay safe; we battle to protect the land; we battle to heal our own families: imagine, never having been hugged or kissed by your parents because for them, "all touch is bad touch." Consider a related—and terrifying—lesson that continues to inform the lives of too many survivors of sexual abuse: Bad touch is love.

Four of the calls to action, which the TRC has presented to Canadians in the wake of its investigations, insist upon the repudiation of the Doctrines of Discovery and *terra nullius.* These are doctrines that go right back to those papal bulls, which spoke to the Crusades—the wars between the West and Islam. As Catholic Europe wrestled with ethical questions around the appropriation of others' homelands, the division of the spoils of war, and the enslavement of human beings, the Vatican, with each successive pope, would issue a decree to settle international squabbles and troubled consciences, and these papal bulls, taken together, gradually became the "doctrines" that directed European expansion, acquisition of title, and recognition of sovereignty upon stolen lands. So, *terra nullius* really isn't empty land, although that is the translation from the Latin. Where the Doctrine of Discovery declared that non-Christians (and hence, Indigenous peoples) lost underlying title to their lands once those lands had been "discovered" by agents of a Christian nation,* *terra nullius* strengthened Discovery's foundation and provided a justification for land-theft by asserting that if land and resources were not being utilized in accordance with European custom, and/or if the "discovered" land's original inhabitants "had migratory subsistence patterns," the Europeans who had planted their flag could, with permission from the pope, claim sovereignty over that land.** How convenient! If non-Christians live on this land, you can take it. All their rights to the land have been extinguished. And now, it is yours! The pope sends his blessings and congratulations!

Today, every policy in Canada through which the Canadian government deals with Indigenous people is held in three doctrines: Discovery, *terra nullius,* and Extinguishment. This is particularly ironic, as Canada has for some years considered itself a secular state. These doctrines lie at the base of every land-claims decision, and they are the pillars upon which the Indian Act rests. Tucked right in there with them is the Royal Proclamation of 1763. Authored by King George III, after British victory over the French in the Seven Years War, the proclamation asserts British ownership of and control over all the land from Newfoundland to the Mississippi and from James Bay to Florida. While it also acknowledges that Indigenous presence on these lands predates European arrival, this royal decree is explicit in its claim to absolute title: any territories "reserved" for Indigenous use are the property of the Crown and "reserved" at the Crown's "pleasure."

Now, 1763 was a long time ago; European occupation has expanded; new borders between Canada and the United States of America have been drawn; and the Dominion of Canada is

---

* Jennifer Reid, "The Doctrine of Discovery and Canadian Law," *The Canadian Journal of Native Studies* XXX, no. 2 (2010): 339.

** Ibid., 340.

a sovereign state-player on the international stage—and no longer a British colony. Be that as it may, the spirit and intent of the royal proclamation lives on in the contemporary policies that continue to direct Indigenous life here in Canada: Reserves and all the resources associated with reserve-lands (waters, wildlife, flora, minerals, etc.) are "Canadian lands," held in reserve for the use of Indigenous peoples whose interest in (i.e., longstanding occupation on and stewardship of) these lands is recognized by the state and in treaty. So, while the royal proclamation (and the treaties) recognize that Indigenous presence upon and stewardship of these lands predates British occupation and the Canadian state, and while the proclamation and the treaties (from the Robinson Treaties of 1850 up to and *excluding* the Williams Treaty of 1923) guarantee protections for traditional ways of life (hunting and fishing rights), these protections have only remained in place at the state's "pleasure." If the Minister of the Environment decides that Canadians require another pipeline, another hydroelectric dam, another mine, or another shopping mall, those hunting grounds are disrupted and despoiled; habitats are flooded; watersheds are poisoned; treaties are violated; and Indigenous rights are swept aside to clear-cut the pathways towards economic growth.

Terra nullius—works for some of us. But not for all of us. And not if you're Indigenous!

That is quite a bellyful of history to swallow in one afternoon—especially if it is new information for you. While my intent this afternoon was to enter into conversation with you about *refusal*—about the spaces of refusal that are being carved out on- and offstage and about their affect, we need to understand this history to understand the spirit and intent that undergirds the myriad expressions of Indigenous refusal upon myriad "stages" across these lands. And if this history is new information for many of you today, we can begin to apprehend the scope of the problem that confronts us here on these lands we now call "Canada."

Every person here is an accomplished storyteller—a builder of nations, an architect of possible worlds, a myth-maker, a truth-teller . . . So, if you—the Canadian artists—have not been made aware of this history, have not been educated as "treaty people," how can you re-story the badly damaged relationships that exist between Indigenous people and settler-Canadians? How will you be able to curate those spaces in which the work of conciliation might be activated? As Stó:lō scholar Dylan Robinson points out, conciliation between our peoples will not be possible until all Canadians "acknowledge their *intergenerational accountability*," meeting their "civic responsibility" by intervening upon their own "miseducation" and educating themselves.* So, when I refer to the TRC, I am also invoking its calls to action that pertain to education: more Indigenous educators should be recruited at every stage of the pedagogical journey. Pedagogical praxis should be informed by and infused with Indigenous knowledge systems. All Canadians should understand the history and the current legacy of the Indian residential school system.

All Canadians should know about the treaties: what are their treaty responsibilities? What treaties (nation-to-nation and human-to-biota) govern the areas in which they live and do their work? What personal responsibilities does each citizen bear to those treaties, to that history, to the lands that sustain us, to those who stewarded those lands for millennia? This is not a job for governments, alone. *This must be personal.* Ignorance may be bliss, but it is criminal bliss, engendered by

* Dylan Robinson, "Intergenerational Sense, Intergenerational Responsibility," in *Arts of Engagement: Taking Aesthetic Action in and Beyond the Truth and Reconciliation Commission of Canada*, ed. Dylan Robinson and Keavy Martin (Waterloo: Wilfred Laurier University Press, 2016), 63.

active choice. It is, as Dylan Robinson calls it, an act of "intergenerational perpetration."*

Today, in the wake of the TRC's 2015 release of its comprehensive and freely accessible final report about the residential school system (which was but one arm of Canada's campaign to eradicate Indigenous presence), claims of ignorance issued by settler-Canadians can only be received as disingenuous posturing. Our own artists, scholars, and activists with mounting urgency call upon us to refuse such state-administered soporifics as acceptance and apology and to arouse ourselves from the lull of their enchantments. From David Garneau's concept of "irreconcilable spaces of Aboriginality," to Tara Beagan's *Deer Woman*, to the Water Protectors at Standing Rock who refused to be moved by state violence, to Anishinaabe scholar Leanne Simpson's Radical Resurgence Project, an ever-intensifying alarum rushes at Indigenous peoples from all directions, urging us to take action before the final harvest—before our bodies, knowledge systems, and the biotas under our stewardship have been utterly consumed.

I do not overstate the urgency here. My intention here is to communicate this urgency and to ignite in you the conviction that a drastic shift is required and that to you falls the responsibility for activating this shift. I am here because you are the storytellers who inspirit the present moment and who will spin your stories into future worlds. In this moment, we occupy a liminal space—the space between now and then, the space between now and later. We hover at the edge. In the moment just before creation was activated and the skies blazed with light. In the moment just before the last visible sliver of sun sinks below the horizon. At the beginning of a beginning? At the beginning of an end? So, I ask you, "With what intentions

* Ibid., 63.

did you enter this liminal moment? With what intentions do you listen to my words?"

Indigenous protocols globally have required us to pause in a liminal space, never touching that place where water kisses land, never venturing into the clearing beyond the dense forest, never stepping off the tarmac until we have sent out the call announcing our presence and intentions and until we have received a response—an invitation to step into the territory of another. Today, I invite you to *refuse the role of occupier*, to meet us not as ones who would push your way onto these territories, who would extract Indigenous knowledge for your own purposes, but as ones who come with good intentions to con-*verse* with us, to shoulder your share of the responsibility, and to fully invest yourselves in the creation of a new treaty relationship.

This is an incredibly complex task in this historical moment. You do not stand, as if for the first time, at the "edge of the woods." Your people have stood there before; treaties were ratified then violated; promised, uttered, then broken. The original peoples of these territories have been subjected to centuries of attempted erasure through extermination or assimilation. *Yet evicted from our homelands and driven into the margins—onto this edge—we continue to assert our existence as Indigenous bodies. And so, for this political act, we continue to be targeted.* Consider, for instance, the thousands of missing and murdered Indigenous girls, women, and two-spirited people. Consider, also, that while the last residential school closed its doors in 1996 and that the Sixties Scoop (the removal of Indigenous children from their families, so that they could be adopted into white families) has seemingly ended, our children are still being spirited away from their communities to be brought up "in care" as wards of the state. On their women and children rest the continuance of our nations. They are our hope. They are our future. That hope and future have been targeted for extermination.

Just as these lands are targeted for resource extraction and blighted for development, the Indigenous body is targeted for extraction and consumption. We are exoticized in life and on stage; we are researched, and our knowledge is appropriated and patented by corporate interests; our ceremonial items are displayed in museums; our sacred sites are tourist attractions; and even our tragedies, the injustices we have suffered, when they are not swept away on a tide of erasure and wilful forgetting, are produced as fodder for the edification and titillation of Canadian audiences. As performing "others"—facing the Canadian Army at Oka, facing the water cannons at Standing Rock, facing the Canadian public at the TRC hearings, facing an audience in a national theatre—how do we negotiate this "edge" between invisibility and hypervisibility? How do we realize ourselves, as corporeal articulations of resistance to a hegemonic entity that has been built upon theft of Indigenous land and unconscionable acts of violence perpetrated upon Indigenous bodies and minds, without being utterly consumed by what Monique Mojica terms "the pornographic gaze"? Our elders tell us to unashamedly wear our teachings, to embody the words and ideals that we espouse. Still, as Guna-Rappahannock playwright-performer Monique Mojica articulates it, "it's like dancing on razor blades."*

Are the narratives raging in our blood and nesting in our cells rendered visible through our performance? What processes and aesthetic strategies must we perfect to refuse consumption by the voyeur and to, instead, engage settler viewers as witnesses? How do we ensure that we are not up there on stage, laying ourselves bare, while invisible whiteness sits there nice and neutral and safe—feeling pity, perhaps, without fear, without the sting of *anagnorisis*? The voyeur remains apart and bodily disengaged

---

* Monique Mojica, Personal Conversation, 20 January 2017, L'Espresso Café, Toronto.

from the "spectacle" he consumes, collecting new experiences and new knowledge for titillation, for personal edification—for the sheer pleasure of *acquisition*. Witnessing, by contrast, is not a recreational activity. Today as in the past, Indigenous witnesses are charged with the responsibility of carrying the entire bundle of what has been given, of stewarding that bundle, and of delivering it or any part thereof intact at any time back to the community for its edification and empowerment.* The witness embodies communal Story in that she offers her body as the vessel upon which that Story is written, her mind as the surface upon which its details are imprinted, and her voice as the vehicle through which it is transmitted, passed back to those who may have forgotten, and passed forward to those who will have to remember.

Canadians have long become accustomed to "learning" about Indigenous people through settler-written plays that unfold as *peep shows*—with a social conscience. These spectacles foreground the bleeding, degraded Indigenous body—a cathartic on- and offstage for settler rage—and then invite their audiences to "care." Take, for instance, George Ryga's hugely successful—indeed, canonical—*The Ecstasy of Rita Joe.* With his 1967 hit, the Ukrainian-Canadian playwright thrust Indigenous experience onto the national stage for the first time. He did so with the best intentions, indicting Canada for the Indigenous failure to thrive and condemning this nation's legal, religious, educational, and social assistance arms for their failure to properly serve Indigenous peoples within its borders. But good intentions can lead to devastating consequences. In Ryga's story—the story with which he introduces us and our concerns

* Qwul'sih'yah'maht (Robina Anne Thomas), "Honouring the Oral Traditions of the Ta't Mustimuxw (Ancestors) through Storytelling," in *Research as Resistance: Revisiting Critical, Indigenous, and Anti-Oppressive Approaches*, ed. Susan Strega and Leslie Brown (Toronto: Canadian Scholars Press, 2015), 185.

to Canadians—we are a special interest group whose members *require* appropriate and well-intentioned intervention from Canadian lawmakers, religious leaders, educators, and social workers to survive. We are not, as he presents us, sovereign peoples resisting colonial violence. We are a "forgotten people" unable to help ourselves, unable to withstand modernity, and unable to adapt: Rita Joe, Ryga's Shuswap protagonist, and her lover move to the city, fall into a bad life, and die violently and horribly. Ryga's stated aim with this work was to "throw open the protective shutters of [Canadian] civilization and make Canadians *look* . . . "*

Look they did, and look they still do—at "important," "powerful" performances that appeal to settler sympathy for an abject other. In her preface to the published script of *Pig Girl* (2015), settler playwright Colleen Murphy tells us that she has no wish to "exploit" the murdered and missing "or to feed off the pain" of those who mourn their loss.** Then, she invites her audiences into an *abattoir*, where they can "witness" the torture and murder of an Indigenous female suspended from a meat hook, so that they will, perhaps, "care enough for a woman they never knew and *perhaps would not want to know.*"*** But witnessing demands total care for and an absolute offering of self to a community that the witness has intimately come to know and in which the witness is absolutely invested. The type of "care" that Murphy calls for demeans all of us. And the only reasonable response Indigenous artists and activists can offer to such orchestrated expressions of settler sympathy is *refusal.*

* George Ryga, "Program Notes," in *The Ecstasy of Rita Joe* program, National Arts Centre, Ottawa, 2–14 June 1969.

** Colleen Murphy, *Pig Girl* (Toronto: Playwrights Canada Press, 2015). Kindle Edition.

*** Ibid.

I want to conclude today with a brief introduction to the indigestible Indigenous body that refuses to be consumed. It refuses to disappear and forcefully pushes back against the consumption of its suffering and against the dismissal of its resistance. A body that offers itself as a palpable articulation of Indigenous rage. And in giving form to that rage, it carves out, on stage, a space for the Indigenous witness—an *irreconcilable space* of aboriginality. An interior antechamber in which to commune with our angry spirits and to release them. A space in which Indigenous viewers may experience catharsis. Outside of and apart from this antechamber, our artists carve out a separate space where nothing is offered up for consumption or comfort: in these spaces, Indigenous flesh-made-rage is rendered indigestible.

The phenomenon of dual reception—the frontier that separates the witness from the voyeur—is a central technical question into which Indigenous artists have begun to dig with increasing urgency. Jaime Black's *REDress Project*, Christi Belcourt's *Walking With Our Sisters*, and Tara Beagan's companion pieces *In Spirit* and *Deer Woman refuse* to show the Indigenous body—broken, mangled, subjected to countless indignities. Instead, their indictment of Canada and its ongoing campaign of genocide is communicated through the "voice" of the discarnate. Each artist curates a discrete, irreconcilable space in which to remember our missing and murdered and from which to issue a collective call for address and redress.

REDress Project *(Jaime Black). 2017 Installation, University of Toronto. Photo: Jill Carter.*

Jaime Black's *REDress* performs a hauntological intervention, re-*presenting* the missing and murdered within two-dimensional folds of red fabric. Once painstakingly cut and stitched to both conceal and showcase the female form, they swing bodiless, alternately animated by gentle breezes or swept into a sudden frenzy by gusting winds. Implacably still, by contrast, Christi Belcourt's serene arrangement of moccasin vamps (moccasin tops)—each lovingly shaped and beaded to adorn a precious and unique female foot—achieves a similar affect. As Indigenous audiences travel through these spaces of love and care, the "material witness" communicates a detailed and lengthening account of Indigenous loss in each unfinished shoe that awaits a foot—in each dress that awaits her wearer. But here, too, in the waiting, we may experience some hope. Some now missing may be found. Some of these vamps may be collected and made into moccasins; some of these dresses may yet be worn in celebration by the women for whom they wait. At the same time, a separate psycho-spiritual space has been inscribed—a space into which the settler is invited—not to contemplate the mutilation and degradation of the human form, not to "care" for the Indigenous "victims" but, instead, to perceive the monstrous *monstra* [signs and portents] of the colonial machine at which breast she has been nourished, with which she has colluded, and of which she has become a part.

In her 2013 production of *In Spirit,* Tara Beagan calls into service a discarnate, subtly forestalling settler-sympathy by placing her audience into relationship with the corporeal manifestation of an exuberant girl-child on the eve of her thirteenth birthday. As the play progresses, we and she slowly realize that this birthday will never arrive. For more than three decades, this girl has been and will forever remain on the threshold of womanhood. One of countless Indigenous murdered and missing, this *forever-'tween* is (like many, perhaps, who await their lost girls) eternally locked within a temporal stutter, cycling endlessly through irreconcilable space as she re-members and re-members the moments of her undoing, only to be undone again and again—forever to repeat the process. Like its more recent and less subtle sister work *Deer Woman*, *In Spirit* is a play that subverts all expectation, carrying us into the chaos where monsters lurk even as it refuses to display the carnage—broken Indigenous bodies or the broken survivors who mourn them—they have wrought.

I have neither time on the "stage" nor space on this page to enumerate in any detail further examples of the myriad performances of Indigenous refusal—on the land, in the courts, in the theatres, in the public commons, in the lecture halls, across this continent. Our peoples face one another at the "edge of [a clear-cut] woods" on lands that have borne witness to centuries of massacre, deceit, child-theft, biological warfare, desecration, enslavement, re-education, and relocation. And for too long now, there have been no songs of welcome, no words of condolence, no mechanisms to carry us beyond the tangled history of settlement, so that future conciliation might be operationalized. So, again, I ask: as settlers, or temporary visitors, on Indigenous lands, how will *you* curate your own "irreconcilable spaces," so that you may activate your own refusals, your own acknowledgements, your own strategies of redress, and your own practices of condolence? What aesthetic strategies will you employ to intervene upon an ongoing cycle of "intergenerational perpetration" and to inspirit settler-audiences with the courage and the will to rigorously and unflinchingly examine their own accountability? What is the work that we (Indigenous peoples and settlers) must do for ourselves—*apart*? What is the work that calls us together?

When you are presented with the opportunity to work on an Indigenous production or with a group of Indigenous individuals, what will this entail? You will need Indigenous people in the room—designers, production crew. You will require an understanding of Indigenous methodologies. You will need to study with masters like Columpa Bobb, Sid Bobb, Penny Couchie, Floyd Favel, Michael Greyeyes, Margo Kane, Jani Lauzon, Ange Loft, Lee Maracle, Muriel Miguel, Monique Mojica, Marrie Mumford, Santee Smith—and so many more! You will need to understand (with reference to the peoples with whom you are working) the mechanics of Indigenous storytelling, the structure of Indigenous languages, lifeways, cosmology, aesthetic principles . . .

The stories we tell can lift our neighbours up, or they can silence, denigrate, and destroy. The stories we tell can open up spaces of fruitful encounter between Indigenous and non-Indigenous peoples, or they can engender disaffection, distrust, and disengagement. As Indigenous artists ignite activations that lend voice and give body to Indigenous resistance, I invite you to consider the ways in which you might curate fluid spaces in which to address yourselves and your audiences to the question of what it means "to rebel against the permanence of settler colonial reality," to "dream alternative realities," and finally through story-ing together to create both the "context and event"* out of which a process of re-worlding might begin.

* Leanne Simpson, "Land as Pedagogy: Nishnaabeg Intelligence and Rebellious Transformation," *Decolonization: Indigeneity, Education & Society* 3, no. 3 (2014): 8–9, https://jps.library.utoronto.ca/index.php/des/issue/view/1584.

BREAKOUT SESSION

A Lesson in Creative Disruption: A Note for Directors from a BIPOC Creator

BY JOSEPH RECINOS

So my talented and fearless director, you're helming the project. The team has assembled and it's the first day of rehearsals/creations.

Let's pretend for a moment that you're a director/creator who is really about inclusivity and accessibility. You've done all the homework and your team is diverse as fuck! No tokens, 100% equal representation throughout (cast, creative, technical crew). Congratulations to you! If this is true you may want to take a second to skip this part OR read on because there still may be some facts to learn!

The truth of the matter is that as hard as we try, having a 100% truly diverse cast/creative/technical crew on the job probably won't be realistic for most of us. Especially true for those of us who are directing/creating in more rural areas but is still true for those of us of the urban diaspora. The reality of the performing arts industry in North America is that we're still deconstructing and relearning. We are fortunate to be working in the arts where we can talk about and act on decolonization, inclusivity, accessibility, safe/brave spaces, and so on, to practice in our workplace. Most lay people who work outside of the creative sector can't and as a result, society is playing catch-up and many of our organizational structures aren't ready to legally/societally take on the challenges of decolonizing, of being transparent and equitable. We are up against a system, circles operating in a square, so to speak.

We live and operate in a systemically oppressive system. Colonization, patriarchy, capitalism have created huge gaps in who has access to power, creation, support, and sustainability in the performing arts. The institutions that distribute funds, support, sustain, or create space for artists tend to favour fair-skinned Eurocentric peoples and stories while often tokenizing the "marginalized" creative voices also seeking support.

To invite a marginalized voice in the room is to immediately create a crack to the foundation of this system. This within itself is an act of *disruption*.

DISRUPTION

To begin, I'd like to acknowledge that my lived experience as a "diverse," "minority," "priority," or BIPOC (Black, Indigenous, Persons of Colour) artist is unique to myself and that I don't speak for any other marginalized voice. However, my contribution stems from close to a decade of working in the performing arts in a myriad of positions and titles.

Throughout my artistic career I have been and in many cases continue to be a marginalized voice. In some cases very much the token in the room. The difference? How I am acknowledged, perceived, accepted, and used in the room.

The times when I have felt tokenized have left me feeling crazy, alone, full of doubt, anxious, stupid, afraid, angry. It left me in a position of wanting to lash out and stay silent for fear of "acting up," being portrayed as difficult or problematic.

So if I am perceived as being problematic or difficult, it means that there is a larger, unseen elephant in the room that really needs to be addressed. I've always tried to use my voice in the room to inform or stand up against any and all injustices no matter how small. Microaggressions or ignorance is hurtful, especially when it goes unchecked and becomes commonplace.

With that said, let's get started. To decolonize is to reframe our individual thinking. To question our relationship to the land and the original peoples and stewards of these lands, and how one can then create space for these cultures and customs to once again thrive and become "normal" within these structures. That is, to coexist and operate within colonized structures/cultures that leads to a new way of existence for all. To create space in our brain to unlearn then relearn in ways that go against how we have been educated and taught to learn, to create, to grow. How we assess and look at the world, how we are guided through it and act in it has been grossly tainted by colonization, patriarchy, and capitalism.

Once we are able to decolonize ourselves the work can then begin. We can then apply this new mindset of decolonizing in our everyday lives through small actions. These small actions lead to indigenization.

To indigenize is to disrupt the system by taking intentional actions to implement other methods of living, cohabitating, existing, working, and creating that are inclusive, equitable, accessible, transparent, and truthful.

I mentioned earlier that inviting a marginalized voice in the room is to immediately create a crack in the foundation of this system and disrupt it. At first this may look and sound like "problematic" behaviour but let's paint the whole picture here.

No matter the intention, the fact of the matter is that this marginalized voice will be just that: marginalized, a token, until equity and diversity (in every respect) is completely balanced in any room, organization, or practice.

This puts the marginalized voice in the room in a very precarious position: to speak out or stay silent. Those who do speak out are often seen as problematic. In a creative setting this can lead to whistleblower mentality and victim shaming. However, how we acknowledge this marginalized voice is really the difference between tokenizing this voice or supporting it.

This is where you, my fearless *activator,* come in.

An activator is a person who is consistently doing the work. Listening, engaging, reflecting, growing. An activator does just that, activates their truest potential, and in so doing inspires others to activate theirs. An activator is often a leader who puts the needs of their community first.

A director has this power to *activate* everyone in the room and to influence whether this marginalized voice is merely a token OR a gatekeeper.

Acknowledging and supporting this marginalized voice: checking in, being transparent, and acknowledging truths, no matter the size, and providing and accommodating space and needs will greatly impact how this person will navigate their marginalization. If this marginalized voice in the room feels respected, acknowledged, and supported, then they will begin to take steps to feel like themselves. They will begin to get comfortable, speak, and act more freely.

SUPPORT

Performance, for me, is one of utilizing and channeling energies, the goal of which is to tell a story. Truthfulness, transparency, and transformation are the three stages through which any serious performer will try to move to adequately play their part in this narrative.

Speaking from experience, when a marginalized voice feels tokenized, it inhibits their ability to be truthful, which blocks their vessel from becoming transparent, which effects their ability to transform, that is, to play.

Being the only one in the room, a minority (in any respect), isn't usually the best feeling. Often times this marginalized voice conforms to the status quo. They often act and change their behaviour to fit in, so as not to stand out any more than they already do, and trust me, they do stand out. Our tactics of survival in this realm vary from person to person and room to room, and can change moment to moment.

The adage "it's not you, it's me" definitely fits the bill here. Being the minority in the room activates all sorts of FEARs (False Expectations Appearing Real). And our defences are up. Always. Trust me.

As such, any grievances or insights, comments or suggestions can be seen as disruptive or problematic behaviour. What this marginalized voice needs is support and validation.

Allies or accomplices in the room can provide some of this support, but what is really needed are more diverse voices in the room. We need people like ourselves with our shared experiences and cultures. This is how a token can become a gatekeeper. With proper acknowledgement, support, and validation, this token can become a door that allows for more diversity in the room. This not only adds to the creative content being explored and played with, but most importantly supports and validates the minority voices.

Remember, to invite one marginalized voice in the room is to create a crack in the colonial structure. Having one voice that is acknowledged and supported creates a fissure. It emboldens this marginalized voice to embrace what would make them different or exotic as unique and beautiful. This creates an inclusive space, one that makes minority voices feel safe and brave enough to be themselves.

Can you begin to see what happens?

This inclusive space will then be filled with more marginalized voices, creating more cracks that lead to more fissures.

Soon the space will be filled with myriad diverse voices, cracks in the structure, which will ultimately break the foundation.

Thus a new structure, a new foundation, way of living, cohabitating, existing, working, and creating begins. The arts really can change the world and my suggestion on how to begin is a small and simple thing: check-ins.

THE CHECK-IN

Check-ins are commonplace in most BIPOC circles. Generally they take place before rehearsal begins. Often the group circles up on the floor. Check-ins can be super-quick or lengthy. I've been part of some check-ins that lasted five minutes and others forty-five minutes. Check-ins really depend on the group, size, time, intentions, and so on. They are a great exercise in team building. In my experience, once the team gets accustomed to them, check-ins become the reason most get to the rehearsal room on time, and the work has always benefitted.

The intention of a check-in is to do just that: check-in with your group about where they are sitting mentally, emotionally, physically, and spiritually. It allows everyone in the room to be present and heard in whichever way best suits them—a word, action, story, picture—whatever is agreed upon on how check-ins will be run.

The trouble that can come from check-ins occurs if they turn into social hour or become a therapy session. Remaining vigilant about what the goals of the check-in are and keeping the group on track will be incredibly beneficial through the creation/rehearsal process. Having a second to let us know where each person is sitting in the moment is key.

We are circles operating inside of a square. To check-in is to speak with one's heart wide open, to share our feelings with our peers, which should allow us to delve into the work with minimal anxieties and stress. Sure, stress will come up, but to check in is to breathe, to connect, to listen, and to share. It allows our vessel to be clear so that our creative energies can flow through us.

This kind of time is not something most in this colonial world are used to. Countless times have I been told in rehearsal by stage managers or directors that we just don't have the time to check-in.

In my experience, most creators outside of BIPOC circles do not truly understand or practice check-ins. The importance of these cannot be understated, *especially* when there is a visible minority in the room.

I'd like to address this notion of time. Firstly, as creators in the performing arts industry of North America, we have positioned ourselves to think and act in *scarcity*. That is, if we are not busy, running, creating, doing something, anything, then we are not being productive. We view time as a finite resource that resets itself every twenty-four hours, then back to the grind we go. We congratulate ourselves and others on keeping busy and warn ourselves not to crash. We remind ourselves of self-care but seldom do we actually take the time to do it. Then we do crash and wonder why it's so hard to get out of bed, why we feel depressed or anxious.

This notion of not having enough time is nonsense and couldn't be further from the truth. If we begin to think in *abundance,* we will be doing ourselves a greater service, as many of the stresses and pressures we feel will be eliminated and the results will be the same, if not greater.

I liken us creators to a garden; only our fruits are artistic. Think of a garden, of planting a seed, nurturing it with sunlight and water, tending it while it grows, reaping the harvest, digestion. Repeat this cycle. That's us—creatives. We start with a seed—the impetus to create. We nurture it and tend to it while it grows—write it out, paint it, practice, rehearse—then we harvest and share our fruits of creation—finished work, presentation—then we digest, take time to enjoy the fruits of our labour before we go off and create again, though many of us skip this part.

Does a garden say to its flowers, "Sorry, no time for your roots to dig deep, to ground; we need you to start budding"? Or does a garden ever tell the sun to hurry up and quicken its cycle?

Our days aren't going anywhere. It's our notion of time and our thinking in scarcity that has us rushing and stressing. But if we accept that time isn't going anywhere, that in fact we have as much of it as we're ever going to need, we can begin to breathe and work from a more grounded pace.

If we are asking creatives to be truthful and transparent, that is, vulnerable, checking in with these creatives to see how they are feeling before delving into the work is crucial. It allows you, director, an insight on how to engage your team. For example: "Oh, Jermaine isn't feeling physically good today. Perhaps fight call won't be so long."

Check-ins are extremely important and can help facilitate a smooth process when dealing with sensitive/triggering subjects and stories. For example, you are directing a piece about migration and immigration in North America. Your lighting designer, Juana, is of Latinx descent and the piece is triggering for them as their lived experience resonates with much of what is currently going on. A check-in provides a space for Juana to speak, or not, about how this may be affecting them mentally, emotionally, physically, or spiritually. The check-in puts everyone on the same page.

It is important to remember that *the work* is the important thing. Check-ins should nurture the work through creating a space that is truthful and transparent. Truthfulness and transparency adds to a productive work environment as it allows space for any tensions or drama in the room to be acknowledged and respected.

A proper check-in allows for all the egos and feelings in the room to be present and acknowledged. It gives you, the director, the ability to listen to your team and then activate, lead, or facilitate the room in a way that, at the very least, acknowledges every team member.

I think of a chessboard, and check-ins let me know where all my pieces are and who the knight is that day. This allows the director to work within their team's boundaries and acknowledges how to move and interact with their team. For example, a knight can only move in an L: "Carlos isn't emotionally stable today. Better give him a little space and not push him as hard." Or it changes the director's tactics on how to engage their team as a whole.

Well, that's it for me, my small anecdote in creative disruption. Our artists and cultural activators are creating spaces and changes to an already fractured and crumbling structure. Whether this is your intention or not, my fearless director, the stage is set and the players are ready. Lights up.

IN CONVERSATION

with Artistic Directors

CURATING FESTIVALS: JOSEPHINE RIDGE AND NAOMI CAMPBELL INTERVIEWED BY ALLEGRA FULTON AND HEATHER CANT

This interview took place in June 2017 as part of a session titled Artistic Direction and Curating Festivals. At the time Josephine was the artistic director of the Luminato festival, and Naomi was a producer with the festival. In 2018 Josephine stepped down as artistic director, and Naomi was promoted to that role.

ALLEGRA: My first question to you both is: How do you begin? What is your departure point for curating each year's festival in terms of deciding your theme or mandate?

JOSEPHINE: I don't actually start with a theme. And I don't think there is a singular theme to this year's festival. And the reason I don't start with a theme is they become straitjackets. You then have to start to look for work that fits into that. It doesn't help you be expansive and it doesn't help you really be explorative and investigate what that particular year's presentations might be. But having said that, there are ideas. And the ideas come from the first question we always ask ourselves which is: What is the point of the festival? And the point of any festival, to me, is relevance and engagement and being part of the conversation, and if possible, provoking the conversation. So the next question is: What are the conversations? What's in the air? What are people thinking about? What are they concerned about? You have, with any festival, the unique opportunity to make the connection between what artists are doing and saying with their work and what is out there in the world. You know, turning on our radios and listening in our living rooms. Those conversations. And festivals can beautifully connect those worlds and just say very clearly that art is life and not something tangential to life. Artists can say so many things so much better than so many people and festivals can provide that opportunity. So it looks like a theme now, but it started with those questions: What is relevant now? What are people interested in and how can we further these discussions? And that's where we begin.

ALLEGRA: And is it instinctive at some level? How then do you craft, with the knowledge that some of these artists are booked somewhere else at the time?

JOSEPHINE: Yes, and things fall out and shift around. That happens and there are all sorts of reasons why things fall in and out of a program, and when one does, you have to look at it all and think about how to recalibrate, because it all needs to feel cohesive. I'd say one of the things that is really rewarding for us this year is that people are making connections with the ideas that are driving the festival, so it has achieved, I think, that level of cohesiveness. The issues that we are exploring this year are with human rights: the justice system, the status of women and gender equality. All of these are issues that are manifesting in everyday news, and some of them are, sadly, getting more currency since we decided to explore those questions. It sort of, quite neatly from a curatorial point of view—it started forming into the areas of status of women, gender inequality—what does all that mean now anyway? And the expression of how do we discuss human rights really started because of the works that were presenting themselves, and it started to become very much about "artists as activists" and art as activism. Not just as a vehicle for discussion but artists who exist to change things. Art can do that.

NAOMI: Why it looks like a theme from the outside is due to things we insert to sew the program together: the conversations. Some of the smaller works are added later alongside the larger ones at the beginning, so how do you connect those? Sometimes you connect them through conversations, through musical works that are sometimes more nimble with scheduling and complement the theatre shows, and address some of the same issues. And that's what turns it into what appears to be a theme. But it wasn't like at the beginning of the year we said, "Okay, let's find shows that do this." These are the shows that are speaking to the issues of the day, and we fill it in with that.

ALLEGRA: I'm curious about how you made the synthesis between the international offerings and the community that exists here.

NAOMI: What's been really great is that Josephine, when she arrived in Toronto, wanted to know who was creating interesting work and to meet people right away. We did pitch sessions with an astounding array of artists. You could curate a festival just out of those works. It was very inspiring. I've also been lucky to travel to a lot of festivals around Canada and get to see the breadth of work across the country. I spent a lot of time putting together a list of artists from around the country for Josephine.

JOSEPHINE: You can't be a festival and be engaged unless you're working with the artists that are here. And our ability to bring in visiting producers and presenters from elsewhere in Canada as well as overseas is about doing that *other* thing—which as an international arts festival we can do—which is to bring that work not just to the attention of the audiences here, but also the potential for touring elsewhere so they can have their work seen by audiences elsewhere. And that's again something that a festival is very uniquely placed to be able to do. And it's all part of that commitment to being part of the fabric of the place. International work is also something I'd like to address. The work that we're trying to look at to bring here is because their ideas are already embedded in what the festival is doing. So it's bringing a global dimension to a local discussion.

ALLEGRA: It's a big job and big world, and there are a lot of people who are going, "Me, me, me" so it's a lot of threads you follow.

JOSEPHINE: Yes, and it also comes down to connections and relationships either here or in the world. If you're part of the city, it's about celebration and pride in the place.

HEATHER: I'd like to talk about the nature and the difference between producing and presenting and particularly in the context of Luminato where you're commissioning or premiering new work. What is the level of involvement in that? When you are starting to participate in new work what does that relationship look like?

JOSEPHINE: Two things to start to frame it. The conversations start to get serious because you are interested in and have faith in the artist that you are talking to in front of you. Then, of course, you are interested in the idea. If one is commissioning that artist or company to create that work, we ask for what they need. There's a clarity because of who the artist is and where they are in their career that it becomes more of a mentoring role, which is something Naomi has done exceptionally well her whole career and I have also done. Other times, there are artists that don't need us to sit in the room. So in many instances, the commissioning process for many festivals is a bit removed from the artistic development process, and we will be invited into that when they are comfortable having an outsider come in and be an outside eye. So it's like I said, it's about having faith in the artist and the idea and supporting that and giving them the opportunity. The other thing about commissioning within any environment is that it's a high-risk game. And I have never regretted a cent of commissioning a project, even when we didn't end up presenting it. And that's because an artist has to have the opportunity to play and to develop, and not even the most accomplished artist is going to fire on all cylinders all the time, but it will be fed into another work. So I think it's really beholden onto us as a festival to recognize there is risk involved in the supporting of new work and to not be frightened of that and follow the work on its own trajectory. And then at the very other end of the scale is the straight presenting, which is when there's a work that's completely finished and you've seen it and you think that would fit beautifully within and then you get to the curation and it would fit beautifully into the fabric of the program for that year. And then there's when we'd act as the producer, where there's an idea, where we're the ones who are actually having the idea and bringing together the team.

HEATHER: Can we talk about the curation aspect? In terms of where you want to see the organization grow? How do you know it's the right time for that work and how do you know it's the right work?

JOSEPHINE: There's a bit of instinct working. The first thing about curating a festival is that we are not making a festival for ourselves. We are not the audience. The audience is all of you, and multiply the diversity and multiply the ages and multiply the demographics on every sort of measure. And one of the big challenges is you often hear that a festival is for everyone. The whole city is our audience. Well, that's nonsense, of course. You can't get six million people to come to the festival. But the trick is to try and make sense of that and say, "What are the characteristics and the personality of the city and the people who make up that six million?" And think about the city from that perspective. So you're not literally trying to touch everybody, but what you are trying to do is respond to and reflect that breadth and that depth in a way, not necessarily all in one year but that over time there really begins to be a comprehensive engagement by the festival with the place. So in starting to think about what work might go into a program, there is that layer of, "Is it relevant? Is it about this place? Is it speaking to urgent conversation, or is it responding to an interest that is in the air or in discussion or is it something which should be?" Can we use this work as a provocation to focus a public debate about something? Perhaps be a catalyst because there should be a type of leadership role in what we are doing. So there are these filters, if you like, that are going on all the time. It's a puzzle. And then it's the idea that we really want to engage with local artists, with national artists and find out who is making interesting work and where does that work fit, looking through those filters. And perhaps you're asking when. There can be very deliberate decisions that something can work much better next year because it would sit well with that show, and those two works together will help frame that discussion. So you think across time frames like that as well. And in terms of commissioning, the question becomes, "Where can we make a difference?" We think about the artists and ask, "What can we do to help you achieve what you can't achieve otherwise?" A lot of what we can do as a festival is lift up projects that can't do it on their own. And it is a lot of "Realize your own dreams" moments; looking where there's potential and an artist and idea where we can help it come to fruition. When it comes to international work, I think it's equally important to keep hold of those filters and think about the work that might be relevant here because of the issues the artist is talking about or because of the way they are working or the vocabulary they have or their approach, and where those things can find either a parallel or contrast here, that we can help frame that perspective. Or there is just an amazing artist whose work should just be seen here because it will be an inspiration to everybody who sees it. And that in itself provides a legacy, because we all take that away with us. There will always be those examples where this artist hasn't been seen here, and this way the audience can develop a relationship with them and follow that through. So it might be as simple as, "This work is great. It should be seen."

NAOMI: There's been a certain kind of work that's been available to Toronto audiences over the years. One of the important things that an international festival can offer is that we need to engage in exchange and be delighted and disgusted and angered and pleased and influenced.

HEATHER: You've talked about curating for the city and serving the people, but how do you think the curation impacts the arts community here, and is there an inherent responsibility on behalf of the festival to think about that?

JOSEPHINE: Absolutely. If all we do is present a lot of terrific shows and then at the end of that it's just gone, then there's no value. So we think about it a lot—what is the contribution we make—and we're constantly looking for opportunities to ensure that we are helping people make work, but also the exposure that the artists get. It's about the artists working here to have those connections.

HEATHER: Noami, can you talk about the timelines? When you find an idea that speaks to you as individuals or the festival, can you talk about the necessity for that, whether it relates to programming or the artistic development?

NAOMI: You have to let the project lead the timeline. You can't say, "Great idea. How much time do you need?" and they say, "Two years," and you say, "Well, we have to do it next year."

That's just not fair to the project. The policy I try to adhere to is that there's a dramaturgical process around the process itself that is lead by the needs of the project and the needs of the artists involved. Sometimes the most important aspect of a show is its timeliness, and in order to really make a mark it has to happen in six months, and sometimes it requires years of engagement. It's not up to us to decide.

JOSEPHINE: We've also put the brakes on an artist and said, "You're trying to fit into the fact that there's going to be a festival in June, but the work will need longer than that. Take the time." The work itself will dictate the time frame.

ALLEGRA: Let's open this up to the Labbies.

LABBIE: What's different from working with a smaller independent organization to a larger one like you both do?

NAOMI: Not much actually. There's more money. And for me, coming in from a producing background, I wasn't responsible anymore for raising all the money. And I didn't have to do all the marketing or the accounting. Suddenly I was liberated. I was working on much larger projects so the other details, I had the time for. So in some ways it's easier but you're also responsible to more people and more answerable to more.

LABBIE: What is the most challenging aspect of creating festivals?

NAOMI: Building audience. You try to get somebody that's interested in music, or dance, or a conversation, to read the brochure or look at the website and recognize that these things are connected and, hopefully, over time, build an audience that's actually interested in going to the festival regardless of knowing what they're going to get. If you travel internationally to other festivals you see what's there when you get there. You have the choices that are in the program and you look at your schedule and try to see as much as you can. But the trick is to get the local audience to look at the festival the same way. People will go to a three-day music festival with fifteen bands and there might be one or two that they really know or care about, but then they get exposed to all of the others. Our challenge is to try and do the same thing with our various audiences to get them to be more integrated and to speak to one another.

JOSEPHINE: It's one of the things we have to do. I was a bit shocked how little crossover we had here and how few shows festival attendees go to. And there are two reasons, I think. One is curatorial. It has to come from creating pathways for people. Shows that connect, one with another, and people can see that. But it's also just a marketing thing. By putting very loudly, "Buy three and save." It's a scheduling thing. You can go to two shows a night. Three shows on a Saturday. Providing there is communication and a pathway for people to go. That's how you create a festival. People go to the Toronto International Film Festival and they go to six movies a day. That's something that we're really attacking now as a concept, because you can't say you've been to the festival if you've seen one or two shows. Part of the problem there too is that we would love to have a family program and work with kids. And I'd love to have a visual arts program. Again, this is about resources and capacity. And you have to make choices and use it as a building exercise to get where you want. One of the things that we haven't had effectively is that we haven't got that social hub, that honey pot that everyone is drawn to. We nearly had it this year, but it was just out of reach. If you have that, it's incredible how the energy from that encourages people to really be in the festival in every way a lot more. So there are curatorial mechanisms and structural mechanisms, in terms of the way the festival is structured.

LABBIE: What are the advantages and disadvantages of having a festival in one building as opposed to spread around the city?

JOSEPHINE: There are lots of advantages in having a place that is identifiable to the festival. But I think you can also do a virtual hub or precinct by having all venues walkable with a central hub. And you have all the natural restaurants and so on around it, so you actually create that. There needs to be a central focus point.

NAOMI: It's also nice to go around the city and see that something's going on in all these different places and see the Luminato flag. Creating things that people come across by mistake is also exciting.

LABBIE: What are your goals and dreams of the festival?

JOSEPHINE: From a curatorial point of view, I'd really like us to connect with those missing bits. I want the visual arts. I miss them. And to have a much more robust music program. And to really work more with digital media. We are multiform arts festival and you can't have blank bits in that. And it's not to say you have to say everything every year, but you can't also go several years without it at all. I want to really explore the arts and use it all to connect with one another and the issues.

NAOMI: Mine is to continue to be embedded in Toronto. For people to look forward to it. For people to want to see what's going on in the festival. For people to care about it in a real, genuine way. And the more relevant we are the more it feels right to me. It's crucial.

JOSEPHINE: To be a much loved and anticipated event on the calendar.

RICHARD ROSE INTERVIEWED BY ALLEGRA FULTON

This interview took place in June 2017 as part of a session titled Artistic Direction and the State of Theatre. It covers Richard's career as an artistic director, director, and theatre creator.

ALLEGRA: Why directing? How did that come on your radar? When did your soul say, "Yup, that's what I want to do"?

RICHARD: I think like most young people I was interested in being an actor. I was also a great reader. As a child I disappeared into books. I was an only child and so I spent a long time in books. And I don't know why the act of reading a novel made me interested in creating whole worlds. It's always intrigued me. Then my high school teacher sort of cornered me in the last year of high school to direct a play. I chose this play set in a New York subway station in 1960s Harlem, I think. I had no idea what I was doing. I grew up in Sudbury, Ontario. But I was very successful with it and I got the larger bug to go to university for directing. It turned out they cancelled the directing program at the university so I went to Europe. Then I followed this mentor of mine—a lighting designer—to Saskatchewan. She didn't just teach me about lighting design, she taught me about making art, and that bridge between your own life—your own subconscious, your deeper experiences—and the play or the show, and creating something that melded that bridge and the bridge of the text, and trying to find something between them that made *your* version of *West Side Story*. Very creative approach and I still use it to today, with less rigour if you like, but more thoughtful. She was the technical director of a dance company and I followed her out there and I made enough money after a few months to go to Europe. And I saw plays in the West End, but I wasn't really following anyone at that point.

ALLEGRA: What inspired you in England? What theatre did you see that you loved, or what was exciting to you at that time?

RICHARD: *Equus*, because I was on stage right there with the horses. It was a very unusual staging at the time. Now it's very common but at that point in time, the experience of being on stage as the audience was quite memorable to me. I don't remember much else. I was quite poor and didn't go to a lot of theatre. I spent a lot of time going to more art museums—that kind of experience. I went to Epidaurus, which kind of amazed me as a performance space. I stood centre stage. I whispered and my girlfriend heard me at the back. The fact it was empty behind you, nothing, no back wall, how does that work? And so I had those kind of experiences there. Being among Greek ruins was probably more influential to me than anything. That kind of experience. The Parthenon. I just went to museums basically, but that was more the substance of my experience than theatre going.

ALLEGRA: So you really educated yourself by immersing yourself in culture as a human being?

RICHARD: Yes, I needed to expand my mind. It was only when I went back to Europe years later that I realized I should go see the Royal Shakespeare Company or the National or the West End or this avant-garde company, those kinds of companies.

ALLEGRA: The time that you were in Europe—the first time—I'm thinking there's a lot of new stuff going on there, like *Equus*, like people sitting on the stage, and I'm just now thinking about how you've pushed a lot of boundaries when you came back to Canada and created your company. *Tamara* was a big show for those of you who know it. Richard created that show and it was kind of the first "site-specific" play where you can follow different characters. It was about Tamara de Lempicka, the great artist and fascist of Europe. So you followed a different story every night. You could go every night and get a different play. Then that play went all over the world. So these influences, was that part of what cracked you open as an artist, or the things that you pursued?

RICHARD: Well, a lot of my actual theatrical experience from other countries actually came from reading about them. The early days, of course, I read *Empty Space*. Follow that up with the work of Robert Wilson and Wooster Group. There were people writing about that stuff that were five—ten years older than me. I never actually really experienced it, but reading about it was actually in a way better, in an odd kind of sense, because I could imagine it. Maybe it goes back to my earlier days where I was imagining novels. Imagining the experiences was a better task for me then actually going to see the play. Reading about it was fascinating. The play that really stood out to me when I was very young was a play here [Tarragon] called *The Donnellys*, which was a trilogy. It was illuminating to me about what theatre could be. How you could do it and how simple it could be with so little. And that led me to tour around Saskatchewan with another play, which was an adaptation of *Woyzeck*. We went from space to space, high school auditoriums, community halls, simple halls not much bigger than this, all sorts of weird auditoriums, theatres, giant theatres, nothing, room, that kind of thing. And we had to keep on adapting it spatially, and it was something about adapting a space and orienting it to the actors differently that kept telling me that the play is changing every time we do it. Because the space keeps changing and the relationship between the actors and the audience keeps changing. I had a play prior to that—*Elektra*—which told three stories simultaneously. So the audience could go back and forth. I guess I was trying to evoke that sense of inevitability somehow, that all these people were linked. So that was very influential, which led to the idea of trying to do simultaneous stories in *Tamara*. Changing spaces is what intrigued me and how I had to adjust the play for the different spaces. So we went up to Casa Loma. We were going to do the play simply in one room—the main room—it has a big fireplace, a balcony, a stairwell, double doors to the dining room. We weren't going to move, we were just going to sit like this. Set of chairs in a ring. And then we started to walk around the billiard room, the conservatory, the patio that looks over the city of Toronto, the swimming pool in the basement, the giant washroom, and we thought we could do a scene here and a scene here. Originally we were going to break it up into three parts and the audience would see it in a different order, and I guess we were drinking gin and tonics, and I believe it was me who said this, but, "We need to let the audience choose whatever path they want to choose and go where they want to go. You have one rule—you must always follow one character." The play falls apart if you don't do that. You must follow a character and make up your own story. So that required a huge amount of simultaneity.

ALLEGRA: And this is thirty years ago. It's so interesting to hear how you find text kind of viscerally in the experience of 3-D. It's actually a very super-modern idea right now that's really starting to be what audiences crave. And it's kind of interesting that you already explore this because one of my questions—I don't want to jump around too much—about the idea now that we have so much technology in our theatre. Is it helping us? What are the ways that we can get people in the theatre? What is actually drawing young people? And I do think this kind of "I'm in the play, I'm part of the play, the play is different because of me" is a very *now* idea. Can you speak on that?

RICHARD: I was just reading an old play by Marshall McLuhan and he talked about the content of the TV through the content of the viewer. No one ever remembers the wonderful scenes he wrote. They kind of remember it, remember the scenes or the writing, they remember following the character through the house, they don't actually remember his Lear-on-the-Heath scene. The content of the play is gone and I think maybe the idea of doing plays on a stage is gone. In that the content of the audience is what's going to be the content of the show.

ALLEGRA: Richard did a version of *Enemy of the People* from the Schaubühne in Berlin. There was a scene in a town hall and suddenly people from the audience—the lights came up—and usually if you ask an audience to participate we cower away, but it was incredible the night that I was there. People were suddenly in a town hall meeting to say things—it was just prior to our election and the American election—and, boy, did they have so many things to say. That was fascinating. Suddenly they were invested in the play. Invested in a way that they were owning it, and I was so struck by that.

RICHARD: Again, that event in the play kept stealing the play. It became about that and not about what was actually being said about politics. People went away with that experience as "the thing" that they remembered and talked about. That was part of the genius of the people at the Schaubühne that came up with that. It didn't really matter what the actors did. I'm gonna dare say this. I think what's going to happen is that it doesn't matter what the writers write, it doesn't matter what the actors do on stage, that virtuosity, it becomes about the viewer more so. It's a kind of interesting theatrical time, whether we believe in that or not. I may not choose to go in that direction like I did in 1981. I'm trying to weigh how I proceed in the next few years as an artist because I might say, "Oh, yeah, I want people on stage voicing opinions on the content and challenging the current aesthetic of the whole culture." The thing about the town hall of the Schaubühne was it was kind of amazing how angry—to the point of being irrational—people were about the politicians. After a while I thought, this is disturbing about the nature of democracy. The Tarragon is a CBC Radio One audience. They are upper-middle-class, they have an education, they're left wing, so it was them, the old people—it wasn't the young people—but the old people that got animated. They were furious. They had felt so betrayed over time about other politicians. They had seen it time and time again and they went at that character with a fury, and I thought, "Oh, this is not dialogue. This is acting on a feeling." So it was interesting that the character couldn't be heard, and it was the old people stepping up and really raging.

ALLEGRA: If this is where your thoughts are about theatre right now, what would be the three most important qualities to impart on directors? What are the things to sharpen up inside yourself to help you become a great director?

RICHARD: I wasn't really taught directing. I had to assimilate after watching shows and assisting a couple of people, and, like all assistant directors, learning what *not* to do. Not saying anything was a very common thing in Canada in my day. In Canada directors didn't talk, they just said, "Let's run that again a couple of times." They couldn't speak to the actor, so that was the real big tell for me as a director. I could talk to the actors, but what I talked to them about when I was younger was just bullshit. It was all in my brain; it was all intellectual, all philosophical, high aesthetics, which was very important for me so

I could come up with conceptual conceit or imagery, all that kind of stuff, but it wasn't really collaborating with the actors in a sense. So I wasn't able to really talk to actors. I needed the brainwork for my own conceptual development as an artist, because really being a director is working in your head. But you need to get it onto the floor. How to get it into the room is the key to working with younger artists. So I began to work on my own processes about "what does a director actually create?" Then I began teaching and by teaching I began to understand my own work, because as you start teaching you have to articulate and as you articulate you start to think, "Oh, okay that's what it's about." And then a friend of mine went to U of A to get an MFA and had this sheet that his professor gave him and it was kind of useful to me. I would track, in terms of—these things are the kind of things I have to check as I go through my process. But even then I kept evolving from that piece of paper as I looked at my own work and how to get clear about what I was saying to my fellow theatre artists. I began to realize what the director creates. I open my class with that: "What does the director create?" Some answer, "A good place for people to work." Who gives a fuck? That's irrelevant. I don't care; they don't care. What does that mean? Why do you create a good place? That's not important. When people make you feel good that's not important. What is important is how do you make everybody feel good? But it's not your job to make everyone feel good. To cut to the chase what I say is: "A director creates action in time and space." And so the action of the story evolves over the time and space of the story. It moves through time and changes spaces and what you do is create the action of the story. You don't write the play, you don't act the play, you don't design the play, you create this thing, the thought upon which everybody can participate in the way they do participate. I understood that. The evolution of time and space and how the action moves through time and how the action moves through space and the coordinance of those two. I can look at what a climax is, or what an inciting incident is, what exposition is, when the action starts and what is the action in terms of a skeletal examination of the text or the skeletal examination of the improv. Or you could do a whole show based on improvisation that you come up with as a collective. Then the examination happens at the end of that process. I use this as a dramaturgical tool. I just try to follow action in time and space and then determine genre and determine style, which is manipulations of time and space by the author or whoever's creating the show. And that's become my guiding handrail. It's very ABC work. I call it the combustion engine of the play. What's driving the car through the whole play and where everyone else can jump in and participate in their disciplines in the theatre if they understand how the action is developing in time and space.

ALLEGRA: Do you do a table read?

RICHARD: Yes, I do. I do tend to do text work because I was very interested in content. I'm afraid of content now. I am actually afraid of it because no one is interested in content. They're interested in a sensual experience. A sensory experience, not a rational experience, and that's the whole world, it's not just theatre.

ALLEGRA: Do you think that's because we don't have enough time to think anymore? Long critical thought?

RICHARD: I think it's because of this *[holds up a cellphone]*. We're not reading a book or newspaper. The experience is through the cellphone, which is a different kind of medium. This is the message. The content isn't about what's happening out there, it's about how I'm feeling about it. All audiences are diminishing. That's everywhere. And I think there's been—this is what I say, take it with a grain of salt—but post-Shakespeare there was the rise of the Puritans and they closed and wiped out the theatres. But they can only have done that if there was a cultural shift that was in part imposed by them through their violence but also supported by the people through some kind of cultural shift that embraced Puritanism and allowed that to be closed for many years. And I think what we may be experiencing right now is a post-Jacobean cultural shift that has changed the way people want to see the world. Trying to understand that as an artist is important. One of the things about *Tamara* that was a tell for me was after watching audience members, I began to figure out who would follow who, or at least guess. Trying to guess what kind of person would follow this kind of person. Who would follow Tamara who's interested in glamour, or who would follow the maid who had a sexual life, or who would follow the fascists and very few people followed the fascists. I just watched people make choices.

ALLEGRA: I'm curious about working with technology, with projections now. What are your feelings about that, also as an adjunct to connecting to younger audiences and the emotional or visceral experience of theatre.

RICHARD: I can't tell you why projections succeed. When they have been too representative they seem to fail. When they try to recreate reality on stage they fail. When they speak versus trying to recreate reality they seem to succeed. I don't use them much. When it does happen I think that live ones are better for me. It's not my medium. Light is my medium. I always think in light. I like not putting much on stage except for light.

ALLEGRA: That's an interesting way in. And I know quite a lot of directors who look at great art as a way in to the lighting or the mood of the piece.

RICHARD: I just did a piece here called *The Realistic Joneses* by Will Eno. I have this folder of Edward Hopper paintings, something that just is on the shelf, and so I brought them to show the designer, which I sometimes do and sometimes don't do. Sometimes it's too narrowing, but there was something about the stillness of these characters that reminded me of the Hopper painting. Something else going on in the picture and you can't put your finger on it and this sense of blackness that he puts into his painting. There's that famous one of two people kissing on the porch. But it's black all around and we worked with that and we just said, "This kind of quality in the piece," because death is also looming in the play and there were these oases of light.

ALLEGRA: Let's open it up to questions.

LABBIE: You've been talking about simulation—audiences going in to feel like they're experiencing something like the town hall. And I see what you're saying that this might be the future of theatre and my question is: Do we make that choice to make that the future of theatre or do we try to settle the audience down into the quiet world and say to them, "You will experience something astounding by hearing the writer's words and experiencing it that way," instead of making them the storyteller?

RICHARD: Theatre is fashion, right? As a director you have to cope with changing fashions throughout the course of time. When I first did *Tamara* I couldn't get any professional work and I was a big hit. I went to Los Angeles, it was a big hit there. Angelica Houston and Karen Black were in it. But when I got back to Canada nobody would hire me. It took me another three or four years of doing theatre to get hired, because that [*Tamara*] was fashionable and unique, but people in theatre thought, "He can't direct a play." And in a way I couldn't direct a play because I still didn't know how to direct actors or how to talk to them. And then it took me three to four or five years to figure how to actually do plays on stages. And now it's come back to this kind of theatre. The thing about *Tamara* is that it was so expensive that nobody would pick it up. The stuff that's being done now is very cheap. People aren't getting paid properly. People are using non-actors to perform their shows. They're not virtuosic. They don't have to command language. Virtuosity doesn't seem to be what people are using. It seems to be more about community to do that simulation, to do that engagement of the audience, and that's the fashion right now. So you as a director have to operate with some principles, but the world changes.

LABBIE: So could you do *Tamara* on stage with an audience in chairs now and make that statement? What would it be like?

RICHARD: It would be chaos.

[Huge laughter.]

LABBIE: How do you choose which plays to do in a season and who directs them and why?

RICHARD: All of you will be directing next season at the Tarragon.

[Huge laughter.]

I try to have as clear a head as possible when I choose, without being influenced by friendships, cultural relationships, or politics. If I read something and it surprises me. It could be an old story told again, like the old story itself can be a surprise after a certain period of time. I'm looking to be surprised, so that's the key factor. And I don't even know what "surprised" means. I think, "Oh, I never thought of that." At the same time

I'm looking at new plays and I'm hoping that I'll be surprised at something I hadn't thought of. And it could be something where two people fall in love and stay in love and somehow, in their process to love one another, they stay in love. That can be surprising. Same old classic story but how they got to that spot is sometimes where the surprise lives. Typically, with most of the plays, I discuss with the playwright who they're interested in working with. Because they do have relationships and you want the playwright to be working in the best conditions possible for them to develop the play.

ALLEGRA: Because they have their own ecosystem that you possibly invite in?

RICHARD: At times I will say I don't need directors just yet. Let's work dramaturgically for a length of time and then bringing in a director at the end is more suitable. Sometimes a director is attached in the beginning. Sometimes I want to just get to know the playwright without a director involved in order to just develop the course of the play dramaturgically. There are some playwrights that won't let anybody else direct their play but themselves. And, of course, not just surprise but also plays that speak about what's going on today. One of the problems I have as an artistic director is I'm choosing plays so far in advance that sometimes the topicality of the play goes past you. Sometimes people have exhausted the topic and they don't want to hear anything about it. It's too current.

LABBIE: I'm curious about your relationship with directors you invite into your "house" and your process for setting expectations with them when they come in to make sure you're on the same page in terms of making sure there's an understanding of what the Tarragon vision is and their personal vision of the play—when you give notes, how often you're in rehearsal—just your relationship with them.

RICHARD: It's the hardest part of my job. I try to talk ahead of time about what's going to happen. What you want us to do, how we can help you make that step. Dramaturgical discussions of the play. But once we get into rehearsal it gets very sensitive. I try to talk about when I'm coming in to a dress rehearsal or I'm gonna be coming to the rehearsal hall and I'm gonna sit and they ask me questions. I ask them to create the agenda of what they need and what they need to hear. They're usually in the middle of it, there's no finality to it, so you don't want to influence them but you also want to encourage them. Try to have a relationship with the director and writer because they're usually a team so you try to encourage them. I try to get them to ask me questions so I can respond to them, but it's an odd thing because they become like independent bodies and they get into a room and they're working together. The room closes off and that's the world they are in, this cocoon, and you realize, "I'm the stranger in this room."

ALLEGRA: I was just thinking you have a double duty. You want to give people autonomy to do their thing, but you're also responsible for the bottom line to keep the theatre alive.

RICHARD: Yes, and box office is very important.

ALLEGRA: Richard, thank you so much for your time.

MASTER CLASS

Collaborating and Co-directing from the World Wide Lab

It started off as an experiment. What transpired was a decade-long pilgrimage to a theatrical utopia. An epic journey of negotiations, collaborations, experimentation, and mitigations. It is a project called the World Wide Lab. We were all members of the 2010 Lincoln Center Directors Lab. A German/Taiwanese director named Chang Nai Wen had the idea to continue our connections past the lab. With the help of Anne Cattaneo and the Lincoln Center's new connection with Robert Wilson's Watermill Center in the Hamptons, thirteen directors from around the globe met for a residency that year to explore a way to continue these global connections. After a week of experimentation, instigation, communal cooking, and plenty of sharing around the dinner table, the Directors Feast was born. We began with a question:

How could we create a common theatrical language that transcends cultures, borders, theatrical trainings and techniques, pedagogy, and the most difficult of all . . . personalities?

While exploring this question, more emerged. How could we unify the group and consider all these voices while maintaining our own unique directorial vision among the myriad ideas and voices? We strived for a type of theatrical socialism where each voice is equal, balanced, and relevant. It turned into our very own political system. It was a microcosm of politics around the world. We quickly realized why politics are so complicated and why socialism is ideal in theory but difficult in execution.

The main negotiations were within ourselves. Fighting the ego was a Herculean effort. Fighting the urge to have our voice be heard and validated. This was all accomplished by trial and error. We had to learn to hold back unless our voice was contributing to the piece or the discussions, as opposed to the need for a thought to be applauded.

This chapter will explore the art of collaboration, which can also be called the art of negotiation. That is what lies underneath. My colleagues from the WWL, Chang Nai Wen and Annie G. Levy, will share their experience with the group for us all.

GREAT THINGS HAPPEN WHEN YOU LEAST EXPECT

BY CHANG NAI WEN

1. Who we are: The World Wide Lab is an international directors' collective, with eleven members from seven countries (Canada, Germany, India, Israel, Italy, Taiwan, and the US), who are creating dynamic, diverse, and engaging work in every corner of the globe.

2. What we are: Using our geographic and cultural diversity as inspiration in our work, we create an international model of storytelling by engaging with the unique ecology of each individual community of our hosting country.

3. The Core of the WWL—Co-directing: We endeavour to experiment with different models of co-directing by harnessing and synthesizing our personal techniques and expertises in order to foster new and innovative methodologies.

Excerpts of the World Wide Lab Manifesto 2017.

Whenever I tell people about our international directors' collective, the World Wide Lab (WWL), I am often greeted with a look of astonishment and a lasting question: *But how . . . ?*

How do eleven directors based on three continents create a theatrical event together? How do you find your hosting theatre partners, an acting ensemble, and production and design teams in different countries? How do you finance your production, including all the travelling? How do you work with actors whose languages you don't speak? How do two, or three, or six directors co-direct a piece? How have you sustained your working relationship since 2011? How do you even come to a decision you can all agree on to begin with?

These are all valid questions when it comes to international cooperation as well as collective collaboration. As a matter of fact, even with nearly a decade of collaborative experience, every year we have to answer these questions anew based on learned lessons as well as new circumstances. However, if we had only co-founded the WWL once these questions were answered, there would have been no tale of the WWL to tell.

Back in the year 2010, on a summer night in New York City, I was out for the last time with a bunch of directors in a bar before I left for Berlin. We met among a group of seventy directors who gathered from across the globe at the Lincoln Center Theater Directors Lab (LCT Directors Lab) and spent three intensive weeks learning from one another, sharing ideas and directorial approaches. It felt very surreal to me that such a once-in-a-lifetime experience was about to end. In the heat of the moment, I proposed to New York City–based director Jay Stern, "Let's do a directors lab festival together!" Jay: "Okay." Me: "Really?" Jay: "Sure." In the same night, I emailed seventy directors from sixteen countries: "When saying goodbye is so hard, let's talk German: Auf Wiedersehen!" Tons of positive replies came back; a spontaneous meeting was scheduled the next day before my departure; and directors Jocelyn Yuchia Chang (Taiwan) and Yveyi Yi (South Korea/USA) joined us. Jay's meeting minutes arrived as soon as I landed in Berlin, and lively email discussions about what such a festival would be exploded around the world.

I was not alone in wishing our shared experience would somehow go on. Many of us wanted to continue collaborating with one another in a way that would draw on the best elements of our Lab experience: learning about traditions other than our own, collaborating on new ideas and techniques, and working on projects and methods outside of our normal practice. We began to ask: *Can we find a way to keep the spirit of sharing among directors alive? Can we take this approach to experimenting together and bring it to actual productions? Can directors really collaborate together, and if so, what would that look like?* (excerpt of the WWL 2012 evening program) After months of communication, mostly online and some in person, we came to agree upon the idea of creating an annual festival with three integral elements: each director is required to attempt a project that otherwise is a risk, outside our own comfort zone; an element of international or cross-cultural collaboration would be required of each participant; different from the Lab, the project would push past the idea stage (a rehearsed scene, or a reading) to partially or fully-realized production. It had also become clear to us that we needed to find a way to get back to the essence of theatre: meet in person and rehearse "this thing" to see what it could be in practice.

Some of the New York–based directors continued the conversation in person and contacted Anne Cattaneo, the creator and head of the LCT Directors Lab, about our idea and asked for advice. Coincidentally, the LCT Directors Lab and the Watermill Center had just begun developing a partnership, and the idea of LCT Directors Lab alumni coming together to plan a festival that extended our Lab experience interested both parties.

A proposal for a collaborative retreat was sent out requesting input from any member of the 2010 Lab who had a desire to participate. Our primary objective of this residency was to define the structure, format, themes, and goals for our intended "International Directors Lab Festival," not only for an inaugural one in 2012, but also for a repeatable one that would grow, change, and become stronger over many subsequent years. In October 2011, with this inaugural residency as part of the

Watermill Center/Lincoln Center Directors Lab Partnership, thirteen directors managed to come together in person for a one-week residency at the Watermill Center on Long Island: Laura Caparrotti (Italy/USA), Jocelyn Yuchia Chang (Taiwan), Evan T. Cummings (USA), Patrick G. Hughes (North Ireland), Esther Jun (Canada), Annie G. Levy (USA), Orly Noa Rabinyan (Israel), Vidhu Singh (India / USA), Jay Stern (USA), Laura Tesman Gillette (USA), Evan Tsitsias (Canada/USA), Calla Videt (USA), and me (Taiwan/Germany).

Going from acquaintances to intensive one-week communal living and working companions was quite a challenge. It forced thirteen different minds to find ways to communicate with one another so that we could move forward with the idea of creating work together. We were negotiating and collaborating on every level: from sleeping, shopping, and cooking arrangements to working schedule, content, and methods. Different expectations triggered an explosionon our very first night together. Not until we got on our feet to do what we set out for—to co-create by sharing one another's techniques—did we start to listen and allow a real dialogue to emerge. This dialogue enabled us to turn the corner, making our differences our strength. Every day we had group meetings, shared sessions, and rehearsals based on individual proposals while continuing to adjust our schedule and content according to our daily discovery and new-found insights. Out of different working groups, in which we were both actors and directors, we created a thirty-minute showcase portraying our different ways of working as a whole. A small crowd was led through different stations from site-specific solo shorts to a Beckett reading from London on a video call, from rehearsed movement and a vocal piece to interactive ensemble work, that ended with a talkback facilitated by Sherry Dobbin, director of the Watermill Center. Our audiences gave us a lot of positive feedback. One mentioned how rare it is to find leaders in general who come together for the sole purpose of collaboration, even though our global reality demands such cooperation. But having lived through the ups and downs of finding a common ground as a group, we knew why it's so rare—"How do you collaborate without compromising?" That being said, our Watermill experience strengthened not only our artistic vision, but also our trust in our ability to collaborate with one another respectfully and to function as a collective entity. It helped us make a leap forward as a group: together we founded the international directors' collective "the World Wide Lab," committing to produce collaborative, director-driven work!

Once we founded ourselves, things started to fall into place. Inspired by our communal meals, reflecting the flavours of our different cultural backgrounds, we wanted our festival to be a "Directors Feast," using the metaphor of food to create a menu of entertainment options from which to choose. Our desire was to create an immersive and sumptuous theatrical experience: to invite audiences into our kitchen, our creative home, and to entertain them with a variety of globally inspired "dishes." In order to have the in-depth exchange we experienced and desired, we all agreed that, as convenient as online communication tools are, we'd need to commit ourselves to coming together in one place. We could move from city to city but to start off, it made sense to be in New York City. Some creative online solution could still be an option if one of our members could not make it in person.

In 2012 at our new-found home, the Irondale Center in Brooklyn, we invited an acting ensemble and a bare-bones design team to be part of our dialogue while we carefully stepped into the new and raw terrain of "co-directing." Twelve projects were brought in—five of which had co-directorial teams while the others continuously received input from directors visiting at their rehearsals. Every day was like a blind date, entering a new rehearsal excitedly, leading an exercise and giving feedback carefully at somebody else's rehearsal. It was incredibly inspiring. We successfully showed an evening of "Directors Feast" with twelve shorts, leading our invite-only audience from one corner to another at the vast space of Irondale, each with a very different style. Our audiences congratulated us, with great excitement and interest in our international collaboration. This collective achievement made us even more hopeful and we were ready to dream bigger. Going forward, we decided on a model of co-artistic directing with two members rotating each year to help instigate a collective artistic vision throughout the whole process.

We were invited back to Irondale Center the next year with financial support from the Theatre Communications Group from the US, the Stavros Niarchos Foundation from Greece, the Taiwanese Ministry of Culture—Taipei Cultural Center of TECO in New York, and our crowdfunding supporters around the world. We had grown! And part of the growing-up deal is "no pain, no gain." We aimed high and struggled even harder this time to come together as a group that shared both artistic vision as well as production responsibilities. It was definitely helpful to have two co-artistic directors this time. But it was still extremely challenging to constantly negotiate different ideas about co-directing and co-producing among twelve directors under high pressure to "succeed" in producing public-compatible work. Dialogues that had helped us as a group in critical situations like our time at the Watermill or had helped us make a collective step were somehow more and more difficult to sustain. That said, we did what directors do best in spite of all the challenges—we got things done. But inside the shining suit of success, tensions were high. We realized theatre-making alone, which could be done anywhere and possibly under better conditions, is not what WWL meant. It is the intercultural and interpersonal communication through theatre-making as common ground that makes all the efforts for WWL worthwhile. The proposal for WWL 2014 in Rome was already on the table but how could we resume our communication that brought us together in the first place and move forward as a collective?

We couldn't answer this question as a group after WWL 2013 came to an end. Each of us left our last group meeting in New York City with a decision to make alone—whether or not to join WWL at our next stop, Rome, a collaboration with our Italian director Laura Caparrotti and her company KIT—Kairos Italy Theater and Teatro Due. I couldn't stop wondering what happened to our dialogue. What inspired me for this whole lab festival idea after our Lincoln Center lab experience was dialogue. And what made one idea brew was dialogue as well. But only when all the different dialogues came together and became a forum had we committed ourselves to create WWL as a collective. So how could each of us make the decision about our collective future alone? It felt so weird and wrong to me. However, one of the many things I have learned out of the WWL experience is to fight for a "yes" that crumbles walls and opens doors. Oftentimes making all the efforts to squeeze that "yes" out of myself feels like going against all my better judgment. But then WWL wouldn't have come into being at all if it weren't for that "yes" to begin with. In an exchange on a video call, each of us shared personal achievements and failures with WWL in general and in 2013. This helped us remind one another of what brought us together in the first place and how much we had grown since then. With some distance, we were able to be constructive again when talking about mistakes, from which we could learn for the future. This discussion probably didn't really help us resolve concrete issues, but it did help us touch base with one another again. We were learning how integral honest, open dialogue was in the collaboration process. After all, there is no model for what we are doing. The only way to figure it out is to remind ourselves of our strength as a group and fight for a "yes" that helps us make a step forward, even though we don't always know where it leads us yet.

In 2014, WWL entered the European continent for the first time, followed by many more "firsts." In Rome, the hometown of our Italian fellow director Laura Caparrotti, it was a first for most of the native English speakers of our group to work in a completely foreign environment and for all of us to work with actors who performed in a language we don't speak and to be equally foreign wherever we went. Out of all the fresh experiences, what had changed the whole dynamic of the group most was that we could finally embrace the creative process fully without having to attend to local producing responsibilities. There was more time between rehearsals since we were sharing one rehearsal space. It also slowed us down a bit so we could have a moment to take in all that history and culture the city has to offer and be inspired. Even though the leftover conflicts from the previous lab stayed unresolved, the dialogues that used to bring us forth, and that I so longed for, took place only in small groups, and our involvement in one anothers' rehearsals remained scarce, somehow being where we were and doing what we did slowly paved our way to one another. At our final group meeting in Rome, we talked about what we had achieved and what we had missed while everyone was sipping cocktails through straws made of pasta. It was magically effortless to come to a group consensus: let's find our way back to one another again, something similar to our one-week residency at the Watermill. As usual, we didn't know how, but that collective consensus was enough for a gentle step forward.

The universe obviously had overheard our request. On Christmas Eve of 2014, our Greek fellow director, Ioli Andreadi, brought us some surprising news: Apollon Theatre on the island of Syros would like to host us and we could use the Syros Institute, the former monastery, as our residency, where we could all live and work. Exactly what we said we needed at our meeting in Rome and better, with an amazing theatre space, where we would have all the technical support to put on our shows.

In August 2015, we kicked off WWL on Syros by doing exactly what we did at the Watermill on Long Island—we presented our different ways of working as directors by taking turns leading an exercise or giving directions at our first ensemble warm-up. Actions speak louder than words. After experiencing what it meant to work with eight different directors, our cast and designers who we'd just met appeared relieved and ready to embark on a new journey with us. The uneasiness and anxiety that were in the air started to fade away. What continued to unfold in the following days of communal working and living in a monastery with eight directors, ten actors, and two designers was something I have been having such a hard time putting my finger on. It was again less about us, more about the place and the people we met that stirred something in us. Our co-designers who we met for the first time showed us inspirational pictures that completely spoke to us. Our actors, whom we worried that we exhausted, couldn't stop rehearsing after a long day of rehearsal. They continued to rehearse on their own in the kitchen, in the hallway, in different corners of the monastery, and at the beach. When they couldn't figure out a scene, some stayed overnight to work alone; some grabbed us in the middle of the night to discuss it. At our technical rehearsal, the nature of which is normally stress, our lighting designer who barely spoke English never lost her cool, patiently suggested what worked better in Greek, waited for translation, and provided us what we asked for. Everyone in the space was ready to jump in whenever a translator was needed. These people, who worked to such a selfless extent with the single goal in mind of producing a wonderful evening together, humbled us and made us want to be better with one another whenever ego should get in our way. It was not about any individual or WWL. It was about a utopia that we all believed in.

Our Greek experience had prepared us for strong ensemble-driven work in Taiwan. In 2016, we collaborated with the company of our Taiwanese fellow director, Jocelyn Yuchia Chang, ESP-I Performing Arts Group. Seven directors and twenty-six actors from ten countries co-created the site-specific piece *In Transit* at 435 Art Zone in New Taipei City. WWL's Asian debut was born!

After not having worked in my own home country for fourteen years, I undertook the task of co-artistic directing with Jocelyn, juggling with many firsts within the WWL: first time in Asia, first time sewing three proposals into one piece co-directed by all, devising the first ensemble-driven site-specific performance, and the first time bringing together multicultural and -lingual actors from previous labs with local Taiwanese actors. How could our geographic, cultural, and theatrical diversity be the inspiration of our work? How does such work relate to the people of our host country?

In 2016, Taiwan had just undergone a major political transfer of power, which many people celebrated. Some others, however, felt uncertain and endangered. To top it off, a terrible natural catastrophe occurred, causing the loss of many lives one day before the traditional family gathering event—the eve of the Lunar New Year. How do people move forward in the face of what happened? How do people from different cultures deal with their traumas? Could they relate to one another's traumatic experiences? All the directors weighed in with their personal artistic entries to WWL 2016's themes, "trauma" and "healing." Based on different angles, three directorial teams were formed fluidly. The creative process had focused on three specific questions: How do we deal with trauma? How do we talk about it? How is trauma passed on from one generation to another? With the goal of presenting a unified piece out of three proposals, Jocelyn and I made sure the artistic exchanges among participating directors took place regularly in the conception phase and daily during the rehearsal process. We wanted such exchanges to go beyond us as well. Apart from having an ensemble coordinator, who led an hour-long training session before each rehearsal, we had workshop sessions, each of which was co-run by a pair of actors. A diversity of voices melted into our site-specific piece, *In Transit*, which incorporated the history of Taiwanese society, some very personal memories, and the landscape and background of 435 Art Zone and led our audiences through a universal tale of trauma.

What we had achieved in Taiwan was quite a milestone artistically and production-wise within our WWL history. It felt like we had arrived somewhere new and exciting, which would not have been possible without our history together, our tireless striving for this thing called the WWL. But how did we get here? We had been learning by doing throughout the years. It was time for us to take a step inward. As quite often happened, we made up our collective mind and things started to fall into place. In summer 2017, the Directors Lab North in Toronto, founded and run by our Canadian fellow directors Evan Tsitsias, Esther Jun, and Elif Işıközlü invited us to share our WWL experience with their participants. A one-week residency at their partner institution, Tarragon Theatre, followed. With five of us being physically present, we live streamed our daily meetings so that other WWL directors could chime in whenever they could. Based on our past experiences, as well as our vision for our future together, we co-wrote a manifesto that included sixteen guidelines of what and who we are, as well as how we want to work with one another and other partners. During our residency, we also met up with Donna Marie Baratta, the artistic director of the Superior Theatre Festival, to brainstorm a possible cooperation in 2018.

Over the past eight years, there had been conversations within the WWL about the possibility of going beyond our duo or trio models of co-directing. Our communal creative process on Syros had strengthened our bond; our multi-layered, site-specific piece in New Taipei City in Taiwan in 2016 had prepared us to tell a diverse yet unified story; and our digestive and reflective residency at Tarragon Theatre in Toronto in 2017 had helped us substantiate our vision with our experiences of growth. It felt like we were no longer chasing after a vision for home. In 2018, we came together as a collective of six at the Superior Theatre Festival, exploring what home meant to our eight diverse ensemble members who call Thunder Bay their home.

Some of them were born and raised there. Some came from somewhere else to make their home there. Others had once left but decided to go back, and another was thinking of leaving. For us six out of eleven WWL members, who left Berlin, Houston, New York City, Taipei, Toronto, and Tuscaloosa to make Thunder Bay our temporary artistic haven for three weeks, home was where we chose to come together to create. Even though we hadn't seen one another for one or even two years, we'd come together at our communal kitchen table every day during the first two weeks, planning our rehearsal, writing our script, sipping our coffee, making our silly jokes . . . as if this were the most natural thing to do in the world. What we and our ensemble had in common was that there was no doubt about what we chose our home to be at that very moment. And this alone was an incredible achievement. Questions and doubts I've often had in past years about the essence and values of the WWL as an artistic collective had not taken any brain space in 2018. There was a consensus among us six that we'd come together for a collective vision, which we trusted wholeheartedly even though, as usual, we didn't know what it was to begin with and how we would get there. But we knew it was there in us and among us. The question was how could we each be present for ourselves and for the others so that we could live it?

Our lives in other parts of the world continued to catch up with us in Thunder Bay. We would catch ourselves trailing off from our present, from each other. Our egos still got in our way sometimes, preventing us from listening to one another. We would disagree, argue, shut down, and wish we could just go back to our individual islands. But somehow our committed decision to live in that collective artistic home had so far always brought us back to look each other in the eyes and speak our minds as truly as we could—even though it sometimes felt like it was the hardest thing to do in the world. Convictions are never convenient. As always with the WWL, we are in constant negotiation—artistically, personally, and culturally. But what I have certainly learned from our eight years together is that no single voice alone can represent the World Wide Lab, and owning one's voice is as important as giving space to someone else's voice. In fact, the more I travel with the WWL to work with different theatre communities around the world, the more I realize how our voice is not just ours alone. As individual stories of our ensemble were weaving into one theatrical piece, *Between Two Breaths*, their stories about finding, fixing, or owning their "home" in Thunder Bay had echoed our WWL experience.

As I am writing this article, my company Sisyphos, der Flugelefant in Berlin is planning to collaborate with the WWL in the summer of 2019. So the tale of the WWL shall continue. We never know how but we will. As Steve Jobs put it, "You can't connect the dots looking forward; you can only connect them looking backwards. So you have to trust that the dots will somehow connect in the future." (2005 Stanford Commencement Address)

THE PEDAGOGY OF CO-DIRECTING: TRAINING THE NEXT GENERATION OF THEATRE DIRECTORS USING THE WORLD WIDE LAB (WWL) MODEL

BY ANNIE G. LEVY

Since its establishment in 2010, the World Wide Lab (WWL) has served as an incubator for experimenting with different models of co-direction, that is to say when more than one director is at the helm of a production. The focus of this chapter will be on investigating this model of creating, working, and collaborating and how this model could transfer pedagogically in training the next generation of theatre directors.

INTRODUCTION: ON TRADITIONAL DIRECTING AND AMERICAN DIRECTING TRAINING

In North America, unlike in other parts of the globe, there does not exist a single unified technique for training directors. Director training in many German schools is built on a foundation of the theories of Brecht and Reinhardt. In England, directing training often relies on the apprenticeship model. Training in Moscow or St. Petersburg both begin with Stanislavsky, but includes his full evolution as a director and pragmatist and places great importance on his proteges and detractors, such as Meyerhold. Many formalized directing training programs in Europe emphasize the director/actor relationship going so far as to include the actors' training as a tenant of the directors training program.

While Stanislavski's system continues to dominate formal acting training of every level and calibre, no single methodology wholly dominates directing training. Instead, directors are trained in a series of common objectives (but not industry standards) such as the fundamentals of staging and methods of script analysis, with many of the skills needed to direct being taught through a laboratory manner versus a lecture hall style (such as directing scenes in a classroom setting). Most programs feature some opportunity for directors in training to see their production concept through to fruition and thus will need to learn to communicate and collaborate with designers as well as actors. Other times, directors may need to flesh out a full concept for a theoretical production, which would include considering and making decisions regarding all of the various design elements. Above all, the director-in-training hopes that all the various approaches and methodologies that exist support them with the task of understanding how they approach the director's primary responsibility: of achieving a sense of unity in a production and making sure all elements come together to tell a cohesive story and create an aesthetic whole.

When directing training programs are not able to offer students multiple opportunities to see a project through to its completion, a solution is often to focus the training around theoretical productions, where a student might complete a thorough "Director's Book," following the practice of early twentieth century pioneer director, Max Reinhardt. In keeping with Reinhardt's original intention, this book would include a "moment-by-moment placing of the actors, their moves, gestures . . . noted on ground-plans of the stage setting, together with the detailed notes on the lighting changes, music, and sound effects, in addition to the three-dimensional sketches of each scene.* Indeed, Reinhardt with his director books seemed to be making all of the creative choices and decisions needed for the entire production, earning him, along with pioneer director Gordon Craig and contemporary master Robert Wilson, the designation of auteur director.

The auteur director, as the name implies, is one whose singular vision is manifested in every aspect of the execution of the piece: not only in the directing of the actor and creating of the design, but also in crafting the text being used, either by writing it or sculpting it to fit the needs of the vision. Due to a limited number of opportunities for full productions, many directors experience some portion of their training that is in line with the philosophy of auteur directing. That is to say, they are being trained to solve every aspect of the production rather than being exposed to the experience of collaborating with as many other theatre artists as possible and working together to create the production.

While there is great value in auteur-ship as a directorial model, it is problematic in that it is contradictory to the collaborative spirit of making theatre. It should not be the only lens through which a director receives their training. An emphasis on auteur-ship bypasses the development of collaboration as a skill and does not prepare directors for any sort of theatre-making that emphasizes collaboration as a process. And by not preparing directors for collaboration as a process, auteur-ship fails to prepare young directors for the very model the theatre seems to be progressing towards.

In the past decade, there has been a significant uptick in the number of new theatre pieces being presented in professional houses in cultural hubs across North America by companies that strongly deviate from the auteur-ship model. The preferred

* Christopher Innes and Maria Shevtsova, *The Cambridge Introduction to Theatre Directing* (Cambridge: Cambridge University Press, 2013), 151.

hierarchical model of these companies is often one of a group of theatre makers, rather than actor, playwright, director, dramaturge, and so on since, in order to create collaboratively, the needs of the piece and the process require a fluidity of responsibility.

A benefit of a collaborative ensemble is the potential for diverse experiences with and expertise in different theatrical traditions. In the effort of creating theatre that says something truthful about what it is to be alive today—perhaps the medium's highest goal—being able to draw from a variety of life experiences and methodology is integral to expressing those experiences.

While the level of collaboration among theatre makers aspires for the highest heights, often one member of the collective must step outside the action to provide the necessary pair of outside eyes: the director. More often, the director fulfills a solitary position and is responsible for maintaining the vision and the unity for the production. While theatre existed without an individual in the role of the director for hundreds of years, the variety of different elements trying to achieve harmony in production requires that pair of outside eyes. The questions is, what might be gained by experimenting with a model that includes more than one individual in the role of the director, a model of co-directing?

WHAT IS CO-DIRECTING?

Co-directing is perhaps, philosophically and practically, as far from auteur-ship as two different approaches can be, emphasizing collaboration as strongly as auteur-ship emphasizes a single vision. It is the practice of having two (or more) directors working together, as artistic equals, not as director and associate director or assistant director. Since a single director is the norm, having two directors remains radical and is regarded by most professionals with some suspicion. However, not only is co-directing a worthwhile model for theatre-making, but there is a precedent for co-directing that exists in some of the most well-known forms of theatre. Anne Cattaneo, literary manager at Lincoln Center Theater and head of the LCT Directors Lab, who first introduced the idea of co-directing to me and many of my collaborators at the Lincoln Center Theater's 2010 Director's Lab said, "if you went back to any theatre that was made before directing was [formalized], it was all co-directed . . . with *commedia dell'arte* or Goldoni, you could see how co-directing might work, whether co-directing or redirecting by a group."

Starting in the earliest days of project selection and pre-production (in order to form and agree on a vision) co-directing invites complete engagement with a partner throughout the process. In order to envision this partnership in practice, it is best to remember that the collaboration covers highly subjective areas of art making, including not only the vision of the piece but also how the vision progresses through the rehearsal process. This also includes being a united front throughout the technical period, where all creative and technical aspects come together during a highly concentrated period, where a decision needs to be made quickly.

How is such a partnership possible? In order to fully engage in a co-directing partnership, each director must surrender a sense of ownership of a project and honour someone else's impulses, even if they differ. Obviously this necessitates a strong sense of trust between collaborating directors and a belief that both partners are invested in the shared success of the piece. In other words, not only does the partnership as an entity need to mature, but also each participating director needs to believe in the validity of the partnership. The potentiality of this partnership, indeed what the co-directing collaboration even looks like, was birthed and has been enveloping through the existence of a collective called the World Wide Lab (WWL).

WHAT IS THE WWL?

The World Wide Lab is an international directors' collective that experiments with different models of co-directing. The concept of the lab is that each year, members engage creatively with the artists and community of our host country around a theme that we think will resonate with the assembled community (both artists and spectators). Each member director is tasked to work intensively in a co-directing partnership with a different member director on a collaboratively determined project while also observing and contributing to the work of other teams. The laboratory setting allows for focused attention and true engagement with local artists and community members. Many creative confluences emerge as a result of this concentrated format: themes, ideas, questions, and images reverberate across a variety of contexts, cultures, languages, styles, and approaches.

In 2012 and 2013, the WWL produced the lab at the Irondale Center in Brooklyn, New York, receiving a residency fellowship from Irondale in the first year, and a Theatre Communications Group Global Connections "In the Lab" grant to support the second year. In September and October 2014, the WWL was hosted by KIT—Kairos Italy Theater and Teatro Due in Rome, Italy, as a part of the international festival collaborAZIONE (Collaboration in Action). In 2015, the WWL was hosted by the Syros Institute, housed in a refurbished sixteenth-century Jesuit monastery in Ano Syros, and the Apollon Theatre of Ermoupolis in Syros, Greece. In 2016, the WWL was hosted by Taiwan's ESP-1 Performing Arts Group and the 435 Art Zone in New Taipei CIty, in a site-specific exploration around the thematic and methodological focuses of trauma and healing. Most recently, in 2018, WWL created a verbatim-style piece about Thunder Bay and its residents as part of the Superior Theatre Festival in Ontario.

Through these performance residencies and over the last eight years, the WWL has collaborated on more than thirty projects, ranging from provocative excerpts of full-length plays to vigorous reimaginings of classic works, from lively adaptations of literature to wholly original devised works. Oftentimes the work developed as a part of WWL has found continued life in productions in New York, San Francisco, Taipei, Berlin, Toronto, Tel Aviv, and Milan, to name a few examples. But perhaps more importantly, we are developing a dynamic working methodology, a practice of civic, global engagement that embraces our geographic and cultural diversity and seeks ways to connect in the act of storytelling.

The WWL member directors hail from seven countries: Laura Caparrotti (Rome/New York), Jocelyn Yuchia Chang (Taipei), Chang Nai Wen (Berlin/Taiwan), Evan T. Cummings (New York), Esther Jun (Toronto), Annie G. Levy (Boston/New York), Orly Noa Rabinyan (Tel Aviv), Vidhu Singh (New Dehli/ San Francisco), Jay Stern (New York), Laura Tesman (New York), and Evan Tsitsias (Toronto/Houston).

WHAT IS CO-DIRECTING IN THE WWL?

The World Wide Lab is dedicated to cross-cultural collaboration through experimenting with different models of co-directing. Over the past eight years, the variety of those different models has yet to settle into a set definition of what exactly co-directing is or which model can be viewed as more successful. However, in asking fellow members of WWL to reflect on the evolution of our methodology, several key tenets emerge. The first is, as one WWL member put it "building an idea together," in that our co-directing collaborations now begin with a conversation that leads to the inception of the idea, whether text-based or not. The second key tenet that has evolved over the WWL's existence is the opportunity to, as another WWL member put it, explore "the collaboration between directors in a cross-cultural context," which allows for dynamic exploration that is not "merely theatrical, but rather it uses theatre to create a cultural exchange." This aspect of co-directing under the WWL's evolving definition is very specific to the WWL and is only possible in an organization with international membership and participation. As the WWL continues to come together to create work, we have discovered a vital need to "consciously bring our culture's rituals, language, and collective memory into the process when directing." This means we must carefully consider concepts and material that will allow for dynamic practice of this key tenet. It also means that by participating in this type of collaboration, WWL directors' co-directing has become a way to create, as another WWL member put it, "a common language of theatre while expanding your own toolkit. [It's] a constant evolution of techniques and practices and your own aesthetic."

The third key tenet is an understanding that nothing is fully formed in the most nascent stages of a piece, but that through the back and forth between directors, the germ of the idea will begin to take shape into something more solid. In order to fully participate in that conversation, there needs to be a sincere dedication to, as another WWL member articulated, "trying to find something beyond and larger than my own ideas through openness and trusting [the process of] creating something bigger than ourselves." This translates into a dedication to remaining open even as the initial conversation between co-directors may move the concepts for the piece in surprising directions. During the WWL's 2018 performance residency where we were commissioned to create a new piece for a theatre festival in Thunder Bay, Ontario, the direction of the piece went through consistent rethinking and retooling based on impulses each director had while watching the work happening in the rehearsal room. With a commitment to the idea that each director had something unique to add to creating a universal piece, directors had to communicate their visions in the effort to see where the individual visions were in powerful conversation with one another's visions.

It is often pointed out among WWL members that co-directing is like a marriage, where both parties must be invested in the health of the partnership. While there is truth in this metaphor, if it is a marriage, it is a temporary one, with the partnership ending with the closing of the co-directed show. More importantly, there is room (and also the responsibility) to revisit the very reason for the partnership's existence before re-engage as co-directors on a different project; being honest in self-reflection and in acknowledging that past experience allows each director to bring a separate combination of skills to the rehearsal room. In turn, this energy spent self-assessing one's skills allows each director the opportunity to grow as an artist through the collaboration with other directors.

The question becomes, then, how can co-directing become a part of regular director training, enabling student directors' evolution to actively co-occur with their colleagues' in a training program?

While WWL is not the only entity experimenting with co-directing. Joseph Haj, producing artistic director of PlayMakers Repertory Company in Chapel Hill, North Carolina, published about his experience bringing co-directing to his theatre in *American Theatre* magazine in 2014, and the Hawaii Shakespeare Festival regularly experiments with this model. However, rather than seeing co-directing as an opportunity to get more work done in less time by having each director work separately on different moments or scenes, under the WWL definition of co-directing, the two or more collaborating directors are always in the same rehearsal room working together with the actors.

WHAT (AND HOW) COULD INCLUDING CO-DIRECTING (AS IT EXISTS UNDER THE WWL MODEL) CONTRIBUTE TO TRAINING THE NEXT GENERATION OF THEATRE DIRECTORS

The way directing, as a discipline and as an art form, is taught in North American colleges and universities is, like directing, a relatively young field. The question becomes what could be created if artists with past experiences in various methodologies collaborated? Would new ways of telling stories emerge? Naturally, with so many different approaches to the craft of directing and the art of making theatre, the question becomes, which way is the right or best way. Forward thinkers conclude that "a multiplicity of approaches is necessary to facilitate the unique nature of contemporary theatrical creation."* In other words, as theatre (as an art form and a discipline) continues to reflect what it means to be alive in the world right now, we need artists who are able to utilize a variety of approaches and styles in order to be truly part of the ongoing dialogue between story, play, and audience. But being able to collaborate between styles takes consideration and practice; collaboration in and of itself is a muscle that needs to be built and developed. This is where co-directing should enter the conversation as an effective aspect of training the next generation of North American

* Peter Benjamin Welch, *Art and Craft: Contemporary Directing Pedagogy in Colleges and Universities in the United States* (Tempe: Arizona State University, 2010), 20. Thesis.

directors and the WWL's work on establishing a working model of co-directing is a good place to start.

What could be gained through the WWL's model of co-directing that makes it a worthwhile reason to shake up the model of one director steering one production? What has been gained by directors engaging in a co-directing partnership? For WWL, there are several key benefits to co-directing that have become apparent over the years of the company's existence. These benefits would also have a positive impact if introduced in a directing training program.

The first benefit is that co-directing forces the co-directors to remain communicative and to stay out of our own heads. In the WWL model, co-directors collaborate at the most nascent steps in pre-production. This means that no concept or idea can live in the ether of creation. It must be articulated, shared, and discussed between co-directors. Through co-directing, collaborating directors are accountable to each other and the process so far. This way when a new idea doesn't fully add up or violates the system that has already been established in the piece being made, it is quickly apparent through dialogue and can either be finessed or discarded. As student directors learn how to communicate visions with their professors, designers, and actors, being held accountable to another director who is as equally invested in the final outcome would help strengthen communication skills within the safety of training.

Another advantage that has served WWL is that through the partnership of co-directing, the work being made would avoid the trap of self-indulgence that often plagues young directors. Having a co-director means having an accountability partner in sound script analysis: understanding the facts established by the text; coming up with meaningful questions suggested by the texts; and answering those questions with comprehensive research, supported by the text. Too often, student directors are tempted to apply a slapdash "concept" in place of a thorough understanding of the play they are working on. By working with a co-director, the student director who has yet to grasp the rules before breaking them learns that the process must truly become about serving the text instead of their personal whims.

Co-directing also becomes a way of either finding or testing the universality of the story being told. In the WWL, many of our member directors come from different countries and different cultural backgrounds and when we think about partnering up for a co-directing collaboration, we take into account which partnership will contain the most variety. In a university setting, student directors may come from a variety of backgrounds, even if they share the same state or country of origin. As every director will naturally possess a different subjective life experience, the challenge for the co-directors will be actively trying to harness their differences with the understanding that it is in the best interest of the piece.

Co-directing is not a shortcut—it is considerably more time consuming and requires a deeper level of directorial preparation before the actors enter into the rehearsal picture. But, one of the major benefits of co-directing, especially cross-culturally, is that directors gain exposure to different working styles that stem from different training experience. Space is given to discover how training and methodologies differ and, instead of this leading to a spirit of competitiveness among a cohort, it would encourage directors to view the previous training and experience of each of them as resources for future collaboration.

In the WWL, member directors have wildly different background training (from Theatre of the Oppressed to Viewpoints and Moment Work to Suzuki to film directing), but we have learned to see our various trainings and expertise as tools in a collective toolbox for the work that we make. While we do not suggest that an entire training program be dedicated to co-directing, the question might still remain of how directors, both practicing and students, can mind their own aesthetic, their own voice, while engaging in co-directing collaboration. From the experience of working as part of the World Wide Lab, it is through co-directing that many of us have become more aware of how we differ as directors and what our individual aesthetic is through our work actively engaging with someone else.

CONCLUSION

No matter what direction a student director's career may go in, whether it be the professional director path, the academic/educational director path, or the community theatre director path, directors will benefit from practicing as much active collaboration as possible. While there is a benefit in practicing the skills of auteur-ship in directing, in terms of fully fleshing out the vision of a production or a piece, there is an equal benefit in engaging in all the various partnerships that a director would engage in while creating work. Following the WWL's model of co-directing, directors in training would benefit from careful consideration how a different director interprets the same material while still in process (versus solely through watching the production), thus understanding their own impulses and aesthetic through the necessity of discussing it openly with another director. With an increase of devised theatre, ensemble theatre, and collaborative theatre at major theatres across North America, being able to create beyond the hierarchy is a skill that is incumbent upon directors in training to master.

IN CONVERSATION

with Musical Theatre Directors

THE REVOLUTION OF MUSICAL THEATRE: VINCENT DE TOURDONNET INTERVIEWED BY SHELLY MEICHENBAUM AND TRACY MICHAILIDIS

This interview took place in 2018. Part One of this interview is Vincent's session with the Directors Lab North titled Musical Theatre. Part Two is taken from another session with Vincent moderated by Tracy Michailidis as part of a Musical Theatre Lab created for Eclipse Theatre Company in Toronto. The Labbies for the first part of this interview were Aaron Jensen, Jill Gollick, Mark Weatherley, Kieren Macmillan, Emily Dallas, Colleen Dauncey, Akiva Romer-Segal, Trevor Copp, Julia Appleton, Murray Foster, and Alex Sandoval.

PART ONE

SHELLY: Let me start with directing musicals. How can we, as directors, facilitate the process of new musical collaboration? You're in a room full of many collaborators. How can you best navigate that room with so many voices? As a creator, what do you need from a director?

VINCENT: I need to create alignment with a director. If I can't create alignment from the get-go in some way—and new musicals are often flawed in some way, my work, everyone's works are, especially if they haven't gone through a large development process—then there's a problem. So if you can't as a director say, "I can align myself with the central thrust." If you can't go, "I can take this piece of crap and turn it in a direction that may work," then you are going to get in trouble for yourself too, because you're fighting against something as opposed to going with it. I would say don't take that gig. That's what I've learned as a creator.

SHELLY: So what is that in real practical terms? What is that conversation? You're saying for many months, for years before, you're sharing your vision? What, practically, is that director doing?

VINCENT: It's just them working and talking about it with the creative team and feeling that they genuinely like and support where it's coming from. And if they have real hesitations about the thrust of the work, that's maybe not a good fit because they will be struggling against it. And musicals are hard. You have to see where that alignment can happen. And maybe things can shift, become a conversation that goes, "This show is about X. But is it also about Y, because I'm interested in this in the story." And the creators might say yes and there can be change that can happen, but you must be able to be connected. Life is too short to feel like you're on a train that's not headed in the same direction.

LABBIE: I think it's about finding your collaborators.

VINCENT: Yes. It's another collaborator. And the thing that musical theatre directors need to keep in mind, I think, is that we as creators work on the piece for years. Then the director comes along and they are the public face of the piece and their direction defines the piece for that time. And that production can hugely influence the trajectory of that piece so it's really important to bear that in mind as a director.

SHELLY: So, in your opinion, what is a musical?

VINCENT: Well, I'm glad you asked "in my opinion" because we all probably have a different opinion on this. I think that for us, here in North America, musical theatre often gets defined in relation to the commercial American Broadway musical. And I think that a lot of our creators in Canada almost can't escape the influence of it. It's a very sublime form, a very popular form. But I find that a lot of people's work repeats the same patterns and tropes based on what we already know. I'm curious to know, for people from England or other countries, does Broadway and the traditional standard great classic musical have great influence on you?

LABBIE: In Bucharest there is the longest running Jewish theatre in the world. It was running during the Second World War and they produced musicals as part of the Yiddish tradition. I think musicals came out of the Yiddish traditions. Folkloric traditions and storytelling.

VINCENT: You're absolutely right that the Yiddish theatre and the Yiddish musical is probably one of the single biggest influences. There are others but that's a huge one. So we struggle with this in Canada. We struggle with it and we're blessed with it because it's a commercial form. It's this thing that people are willing to pay for, which is very important to us as artists because we all struggle to make a living. So when people are willing to pay good money that's a compelling thing, especially because the reason that people are willing to pay for it is because they love it. Because when it's well done it's hugely compelling and powerful.

SHELLY: So do you think the art form has changed at all recently?

VINCENT: Not enough is what I would answer. The patterns repeat themselves far too often. There was a time when the other major influence on Broadway, in addition to the Yiddish, was jazz. Klezmer was also related to jazz. Jazz came along in the 1920s but certainly in the '30s on Broadway. And it was this hugely exciting form of popular music that had people going, "Whoa! That is new. That is fresh. That's exciting." And that's what turned the Broadway musical to what we still know it as today. And with the close exception with a few things like *Hamilton* and some other things, they didn't have the impact that we thought they'd have. The Broadway musical has remained staid within some level, for my taste at least. I'm interested in musicals because they have the power to break through our intellect.

LABBIE: Why do you think the form has—"resisted" isn't the right word—but why has hip hop not found a larger place in the popular Broadway musical? It seems as though it would have a much bigger space within my culture.

VINCENT: I think that the milieu remains conservative in commercial musical theatre because people are putting up a lot of money and they're afraid to risk it. That's a problem. But it's a commercial industry and it influences what we all do. It doesn't have to. But your question is very valid. It's valid for hip hop and other forms of music that are hugely relevant to our culture and what people respond to viscerally, and yet the music in the shows we see commercially produced tends to be more old-fashioned and filled with tropes we recognize. I don't know how it's going to change. *Hamilton* has probably opened the door though.

LABBIE: My question might sound stereotypical because musicals from North America are a new idea for my country, Greece. They're not part of our culture. Maybe that's because of the inaccessibility for the audience because it's expensive and there's no tradition of it there. So there's an immediate demand for the audience. So if the audience doesn't feel connected to the form or the themes, then maybe that's why things are being repeated?

VINCENT: It could be.

LABBIE: Musical theatre used to be that we used popular music to put in the theatre. Then musical theatre became it's own genre. And now it's gone off on its own.

SHELLY: I was wondering if you wanted to talk about—since we're talking about audience—to speak about your latest musical that employs electronica sound and what drew you to that and perhaps drawing in a new audience?

VINCENT: Well, drawing in myself, and the dissatisfaction that I've had with the Broadway musical. I was looking for some music to tell this story about a visionary scientist from the nineteenth century. It seemed to make sense to use a very, very scientific sounding music, which was electronica. It allowed the history to become surreal. It gives the narrative a unique quality I've not seen in a musical before.

LABBIE: You felt the story would work better as a musical, so you pursued it that way? Which brings me to my question: What comes first? The music or the story?

VINCENT: With this project, the story came first.

SHELLY: Which brings us back to the question, "Why musicalize?"

VINCENT: I always ask myself about the great Broadway musicals: what constraints or barriers are they smashing or breaking down or causing to no longer exist? If you can find big themes in the story, then it gives it a reason to sing. We were talking about the Greek chorus and the idea of the collective. That's why musical theatre matters or is useful. And when something can be transformed socially, when themes are huge, they can sing. And if it doesn't, you might get into trouble, or you might end up with a play with music, which is a valid form.

LABBIE: I'm wondering if you can expand on what the difference is between musical theatre and a play with music. I think of *Threepenny Opera* as an example of something that can swing both ways, though I think of it as more of a musical. Which category would you think that falls under?

VINCENT: *The Threepenny Opera* is my departure point into the musical theatre. It's what drew me into musical theatre. You're right to say that it's pretty much a musical. Though some of the songs do function more like songs that are in a play; some of them don't come out of the plot. The basic definition is that in a musical, the most important stuff happens in song or in movement or in feeling on music or in a moment that's musical in some way. That's what a musical is. A play with music will be the play and songs are interjected. But it's not a hard and fast separation. Shakespeare put a lot of songs in his plays, but they don't generally have a transformative moment of realization. I think that's the difference.

LABBIE: This begs the question, why do I need to see these musical adaptations of films that capitalize on the success of movies and safe choices? But then people support these shows. They see them over and over.

VINCENT: Yes. There always has been and always will be commercial art. Most of the most popular plays from the nineteenth century are long forgotten because they were huge commercial schmaltzy romances. That's the reality that we're faced with. But we need to ask, if some of these shows are not an important topic, then why bother?

LABBIE: Then there's this whole slew of musicals adapted from albums.

LABBIE: And the jukebox musical.

VINCENT: The jukebox musical is easier in a way because there's this tremendous advantage of songs the audience already knows. There's some strength developing around the jukebox musical partly because of this commercial imperative that we talk about. We've got a saleable entity already there.

LABBIE: Isn't that the problem? We're doing these shows because there is a built-in audience. We're asking them to pay $180 a ticket. The audience wants to see their money on that stage. We're pricing ourselves out of our own art form. We're fighting against our own art to come up with something new.

LABBIE: Well, we've been talking a lot about failure this week. And the audience won't accept failure, because they've paid a lot for their ticket. And their parking. And dinner.

LABBIE: Plus the plane ticket to New York!

LABBIE: Yes! So there's less room for failure, unfortunately, which is a disservice to the art.

LABBIE: I've got a genuine block. If we're talking about changing form—we've defined musical theatre around its form—how do we shake musical theatre up when essentially it *is* the form that defines musical theatre?

VINCENT: That's a fantastic question. I think that there's a thousand ways of doing music and narrative. We're born into this world and we make noises. The fact that musical tropes and lyrical tropes repeat themselves as much as they do is, for me, a pattern of a genre gone stale. And there's a world of music out there. So my question is, in a world where hip hop is so explosively popular, why is musical theatre still using old-fashioned music? That's my interest.

PART TWO

VINCENT: Part of what I wanted to chat about today was the idea of musical theatre as an act of revolution. Take for example *The Threepenny Opera*. That was revolutionary. It mocked authority. It mocked militarism. It mocked fascism. It mocked control in a way that was revolutionary in Europe and the Weimar Republic of Germany when fascism was rising. And it was this *huge* hit in Europe. So that's what I want us to consider here today as well: How can musical theatre be revolutionary? I'm drawn to that particular musical because social change is something, as artists, we're excited about that some of us share. There are other kinds of musical theatre, but it's also valuable to consider these ones as well. What's a musical that people can think of that has that kind of story?

LABBIE: *West Side Story*. Everyone is trapped by their circumstances in that show, these kids that don't really see a future for themselves. And there are also the racial and political messages in that show. Intercultural relationships.

VINCENT: I'm drawn to big musicals. And I ask myself what the connection between big commercial musicals and these revolutionary shows are. I'm wondering whether, when there's a big group of people on stage, if it's like a community is breaking through. It's like a culture is smashing through something that was holding it back. I guess I'm speaking to why I'm drawn to large-scale musicals. Then there's the question, "Why musicalize?" So this is one myth. What other stories or musicals are you aware of that share that breaking through or breaking down of barriers or myth?

LABBIE: *King and I. South Pacific*. There were a whole bunch of those shows created in the mid-twentieth century where the creators were hoping a breakthrough would happen.

VINCENT: Right. And, of course, Rodgers and Hammerstein wrote *The Sound of Music*. What's the theme of that show?

LABBIE: The whole Nazi story in the background.

VINCENT: In the background, yes, but in the foreground it's also reflected in the father character. So it's like the father has one foot in the Nazi world and the pseudo-mother character draws them out of it through the power of love and music. So that's exactly what that myth is about. And what role does the music play?

LABBIE: Resistance?

VINCENT: Absolutely. Resistance to what?

LABBIE: Fascism.

VINCENT: Yes. So it's about the power of music to transform or to melt the heart of the fascist father who's tempted by fascism. These are the kind of questions I like to ask of the story. What other ones?

LABBIE: *Fun Home* and *Dear Evan Hansen*, which don't have big ensembles necessarily, are dealing with pretty big issues that are prevalent now, and it feels like a new kind of show.

LABBIE: Also *Next to Normal*. They also seem to choose to put them in a family unit, a microcosm to reflect the macro.

LABBIE: *Hamilton* is breaking barriers in many ways—casting and the music, and so on.

VINCENT: Yes. And even our own National Arts Centre is trying its best to decolonize theatre. I think the reason this topic is so important is because musical theatre can be a really conventional form in some ways. Not that there's anything wrong with that for those who want to do that kind of work. But part of the reason for that is that there's a commercial aspect to it. And there's money to be made. And producers tend to go for things that are already known.

LABBIE: One of the most subversive things about *Hamilton* is how conventional it actually is. Even though everyone thinks it breaks all these barriers, the forms that he uses—and I'm not saying this cynically, he's just so educated—are conventional. But it's not that radical.

VINCENT: I don't think it's even as radical as *Jesus Christ Superstar*.

[General agreement.]

LABBIE: I think it's the fact that he's put those songs on the Broadway stage that's radical. All the kids that are growing up seeing that on stage and thinking theatre is "cool" is radical.

VINCENT: How about *Fiddler on the Roof*? Talk to me about the context of the topics in it that relate to today.

LABBIE: The fact that you have this patriarch that is of the old world. He has these daughters that break the tradition. The opening number establishes what those traditions are and the rest of the show breaks down those traditions. Whether it's the daughter not marrying the butcher or the other daughter running away with the Russian, it's about the loss of a way of life.

LABBIE: *In the Heights* lends itself heavily to *Fiddler*. It's about a neighbourhood trying desperately to retain its identity.

VINCENT: Yes. And they all share these story elements of breaking of constraints, patriarchy and arranged marriage, and all these patterns, which is why the show was a global success. There were so many other cultures that had recently experienced that shift away from arranged marriage to a marriage that you chose; the patriarchal imposition of authority on a daughter's choices. I would posit—because it's kind of considered the granddaddy of the great book musical—that is because of its structure. It starts off with *Tradition* which actually defines the theme of the that show. And then, piece by piece, those traditions are broken or challenged. It's incredibly transformative. It was huge in Japan.

LABBIE: Like *Anne of Green Gables*. It was huge in Japan as well. There's a balance of feeling tied to your family, but she also goes off and gets an education, but still stays home with Marilla. It was progressive, but still there is a respect of values. And I feel that *Fiddler* does that as well.

LABBIE: There's a new balance coming in.

VINCENT: Yes. And I would suggest the reason why *Anne of Green Gables* stands as Canada's longest standing classic hit—probably the only one we have from the '60s—is because it's about breaking through. About an incredibly powerful preteen who is so incredibly smart and interesting and commands respect, despite being a girl and an orphan. And it's wonderful that that exists. What about *Hair*? It was revolutionary in that it dispensed with plot. But what themes—in what way was that show—it came out in 1967, a very conservative culture—in what way was it breaking barriers?

LABBIE: Everyone took their clothes off!

[Laughter.]

LABBIE: I think that the looseness of the narrative was trying to address a counterculture that was trying to move away from structure. The loss of structure as a statement.

VINCENT: I also don't know any show that embodied a counterculture, then announced it to an audience that was oftentimes only vaguely familiar with it. And that celebrated sexuality and body in a culture that mostly just despised those things and kept them private. That celebrated open interracial relations. There was also a transgender person who was standing up with great pride in that show in '67. So it was radical. And again, my point here, getting you all as artists to consider these things, is that, as conservative a form as musical theatre can sometimes be, some of the greatest successes and reaching of powerful transformational feelings in an audience are actually super radical. And that's valuable to think about—that we as artists think about—what needs to be, and what can be transformed; what stories can transform what.

LABBIE: And from a musical standpoint, I think that *Hair* was significant because from the '20s to the '50s, pop standards coming from Broadway shows were being recorded, but the sound of Broadway froze. Everyone was still writing in the style of the '20s to the '50s so that became what Broadway sounded like, even though it was meant to be a pop medium. But *Hair* said the songs you hear on the radio can still tell the story and further the character. So *Hamilton* wouldn't have happened if *Hair* hadn't happened. Every few years, audiences need to be reminded that musicals don't need to be stuck in the last thing you heard. It can reflect what we listen to as audiences outside of the theatre.

VINCENT: How about *My Fair Lady*? What's radical about that?

LABBIE: Well, it's all about class. And can you fake class through language? Is a person's external appearance what constrains them in society? Is class intrinsic?

VINCENT: And Higgins's own constraint was his lack of emotional connection or intelligence, which Eliza already had, that he taught her to perform as a high-class person. So class is a performance that you put on.

LABBIE: The story is about a man who's very misogynistic and he's going to "fix" the woman. But I think it's a very level playing ground for the two of them and they have this battle. By the end there's this meeting point.

LABBIE: I think the way we're seeing these shows now, these revivals, is different. The lens in which we tackle these pieces changes. The times are informing these shows.

LABBIE: Talking about specificity, and issues—one of the easiest pits to fall into is trying to tackle an issue with a piece of art that then allows the audience to pat themselves on the back and say, "Yeah, racism is bad." We reaffirm what we already know, then go back to our lives. As opposed to art that makes us feel uncomfortable; that we talk about afterwards. I think it's very easy on the surface to deal with an issue that we all can understand like, "Gender should be more equal"—these kind of pat answers.

VINCENT: That's great. What's a musical that makes us feel uncomfortable?

[No one can think of one.]

I can think of one. *Cabaret.*

[General agreements and "Why didn't I think of that?"]

There are some very challenging things around race and there are some very challenging things around sexuality and connections to fascism that are intense. What I'm inviting us to talk about is how to socially transform. We can't just take what people already know and then tell a sweet little story.

LABBIE: Can we talk about why we musicalize? Why make something a musical? If we adhere to the theory that once we can't speak it, we sing it and once we can't sing it, we dance it, that doesn't necessarily seem to be the case anymore. When do we need to sing in musical theatre now? Has it changed?

VINCENT: I don't know if it's changed. I think that the reason we need to sing is because we need to transcend the intellectual. How do we reach beyond the constraints that we've had. We need to sing because if we just say it, it's not as powerful as if we sing it or dance it. It's all connected. It's a full-body proclamation of social transformation. That's how I see it.

TRACY: There are things like the "I am" songs or the "I want" songs—things that are embedded in musical theatre structure. Do you think in terms of musicals, that there are musical theatre structures that need to be adhered to?

VINCENT: I don't know. But in terms of what we've been talking about, I think the perfect example of the "I am" song is from *La Cage aux Folles*—"I Am What I Am" which is an anthem about someone asserting their identity as a gay man in a world that it was sometimes difficult to be in at that time. And that remains anthemic for exactly the reasons that we're talking about. But I don't know. Formal? What do people think about that?

TRACY: Look at the Greeks and their way of storytelling and the way that audiences latch on. If we don't have an understanding of character it's going to be hard for us to care. You talked about transcending the intellectual—it feels like some of these intimate shows we've talked about, we're getting to know characters more and in a different way.

LABBIE: Coming from the opera side, the classical side, I've always had difficulty where two people are just waiting for the subway. I don't want to hear you sing that. And I think it's related—the error is that, I think, to sync or musicalize everything as if it is worthy of musicalization has an analogue in the history of musical theatre, in that at what point in the story you are telling do we get to the point where we need a full-body proclamation, to use your phrase? And I think the rules are wide open. A certain story—even someone reading the paper—two different versions of it might be totally different. To one character, that article might mean so much that they have to sing in order to be that character's most successful self. And the other one would have to read it. So I think the context makes the difference of when you need to musicalize.

VINCENT: Things are changing so much too. Things you see on television, there's such a postmodern radicalization of form that there's a lot of room for inventiveness, of shifting in time and space and place and using music to take us to places that we don't normally go, that I think to be too formally strict will limit what musical theatre can do.

LABBIE: I think that we've consumed more story than in any other time in history. When *Teletubbies* came in, it was the first time anyone made television for babies. Before that we had *Sesame Street*, which completely revolutionized the way kids learned the alphabet. You used to have to go to school to learn that. Now kids start watching television as babies and they consume so much story that the patterns are so inherent. Everyone knows exactly which turn the story is supposed to take. So you really wake up your audience when you don't take that turn. And that's why breaking rules in storytelling is so powerful right now.

LABBIE: So does that mean that there is something intrinsic in storytelling that we need to hear? Are we programmed to react to storytelling in a certain way?

LABBIE: An opening number or an "I want" song is just good storytelling and tells us who's there. In the absence of that, the audience is out to sea. They need that basic information before you start telling the story. I'm not saying there's not any other way of conveying the information but there's a reason those are a standard—the fundamentals of storytelling.

LABBIE: I don't think it's just musical theatre. Every genre has its structure. Any movie, I can break down the story. No matter how experimental it seems, you can pick out the structure.

LABBIE: But you can take those elements and put them in a different order as long as you keep the audience saying, "What's going to happen next?"

VINCENT: One way that I'm committed to breaking rules—I've always been told by senior artists that you have to use true rhyme and I quite deliberately and consciously don't because of my aesthetic—I grew up listening to popular music—but there are people who staunchly insist that you are hurting the craft of musical theatre by not using straight rhymes. To my ear, that's just old-fashioned.

TRACY: We're talking about whether there are certain rules for lack of a better word, in terms of being a collaborator—you've worked with different composers—how do you collaborate with one another? Is that something that happens with the work? You get to know each other through the collaboration? And if one person has a more formal approach? How do you approach that?

VINCENT: Collaboration can be challenging. Hopefully, you're on the same page thematically—what the thrust or soul of the story you're trying to tell is—then you're going to have more alignment. I've learned that there's so much value to deeply listening to someone else's perspective even when you totally disagree with them. Ultimately you may not do exactly what they've insisted on, but we may be inspired by that thing that really matters to them. And the "two heads are better than one" or the three heads is better, is really true. And if I can get over my own ego to deeply listen to, "Why do you keep coming back to this thing?" then I'm going to have something special happen.

THE MANUAL

The only thing I am certain of after all these years of the Lab, is that there is no singular, absolute formula to directing. When I started directing, I read every book I could find on the subject. I quickly realized that because each book was written through the lens of that one director who wrote it, it felt so definitive. I found myself feeling a bit handcuffed by their specific process and unsure how to recalibrate it to make it my own. And although they were terrific manuals with tremendous insight, it also, at times, felt like a paint-by-numbers approach to directing. This is what I love about this section of the book. Just as in the actual Lab, there are no definitive answers. We spend a lot of time discussing our personal approaches and listening for nuggets that we can incorporate into our future practice.

The following is a compilation of questions and responses from directors or Labbies over the past ten years from Directors Lab North, Lincoln Center Theater Directors Lab, and Chicago Directors Lab that they have discussed with one another, as well as the guest artists and master teachers. These directors range from recent MFA directing graduates, to working mid-career directors, Broadway directors, to renowned established directors from around the globe.

There are so many individual perspectives on how to direct and on the rehearsal process itself. This is reflected in these varied responses that often enhance and complement, but sometimes collide or conflict with one another. I wanted to include all these differing perspectives so that you can choose the ones that resonate with you. Pick and choose, or put them all in your toolbox. They will come in handy when you least expect it. I have asked questions from incubation, preparation, and rehearsals to post-opening night techniques and philosophies. Some answers you will know and have already done. Others will be entirely new. My hope is that they will spark exploration and experimentation within your own process. Off we go!

1. INSPIRATION

HOW DO YOU CHOOSE YOUR PROJECTS OR DO THEY CHOOSE YOU?

- They choose me, usually. I don't believe certain plays or projects come into your life by accident. If I'm choosing a play or project, most of the time I think about the community in which I'm directing and go from there. I try to suit the needs of the community while doing a project that challenges me.

- Ideally, they choose me. I get inspired by a story or a new item, or I become aware of something I knew nothing about before and I use the project as a way to learn about the thing.

- I ask, what issues are in the air? How might an audience identify with that? It's usually very personal.

- At this point I'm only interested in investing my time and energy in stories that position female, POC, and/or transgender characters at the centre. These folks should also represent the majority of the cast. I'm interested in flooding the canon with stories that are not present in classic texts.

- I'm lucky in that I have been working with a writing/producing partner for over twenty-five years. We started a theatre company together, and we started to write our own shows due to limited funds. But as the years passed, the audiences came to our original shows more than when we did licensed shows, so we focused on only original work. I have also done outside work, but I mainly get my creative juices going best when I collaborate with my partner. My main advice is that if you are fortunate enough to find people you creatively click with, by all means keep them around and nurture that.

- I always seem to magically gravitate towards material that I need to investigate in my own life, something I'm trying to figure out that might be solved through this particular show.

- I need a personal connection to my life. Something that I read stimulated my imagination; the stimulus or identification moment must be rich.

- I am always looking for an identifiable thing.

- A play will say something that I know to be true, but I never understood it, but the play articulates it.

- When I read something and it resonates deeply inside me and I say, "Yes, I can taste this. I can picture this. I know this world. I can relate to this. My brother was like this. My mother was like that. I can see it. I can visualize it," then I know it's for me.

HOW DO YOU SEEK OUT INSPIRATION?

- Inspiration comes from everywhere and if it feels like an omen of inspiration, don't ignore it. If you aren't sure where it goes yet, take a picture, write it down, whatever. Create a scrapbook of potential ideas.

- I am always responding to things that have impacted my life—through theatre I express my response in that time. I translate my work and hopefully touch other people. That is woven into the fabric of creating my work.

- Inspiration is all around us every day. We just have to open our eyes to see it. I don't necessarily seek out inspiration. It's more like . . . I open my eyes to it. I try to be present and to see beauty and revolution in the everyday. Nature. Graffiti. People on the street. Urban sounds. Changing natural light. The creative ways that individuals avoid direct eye contact. I'm always storing these experiences. I'm always listening and watching. So when I have a project in front of me, I already have a font of information to pull from.

- Inspiration can come from anywhere. I find a lot visiting art galleries, reading newspaper articles, and seeing other shows. Nothing like someone else's art to inspire your own.

- Everything can be inspiration for me, but seeking inspiration from outside always gets me into trouble. I often come back to my heart to scan what really touches me at the moment. It could be someone's speech, a scene that happened in my dream, a moment I see on the street. I let that touching moment stay with me, and meditate until it reveals the next step to me.

- I find inspiration in travelling and in nature. I think you have to be sensitive to what really turns you on creatively. That could be *anything*. Do what you love. Eat the foods you love. Spend time with the people that feed your soul. This is a great recipe for feeding your soul, which in turn will keep you creative.

- I find that free time or time to think and ponder always yields great results. The ability to free your mind from the task at hand will allow room in your mind to wander. I find that when I bike ride or exercise without the pressure of coming up with a great idea is exactly when the inspiration or idea comes.

- I first got into theatre through writing and my love of literature, so there's a lot of reading that goes on in my life. I try to keep this reading crossing as many segments of human thought as is possible: from classical literature to video games, hip hop to opera, my nerdish obsession with post-dramatic theatre and the works of Kane, Churchill, and Barker to my deep appreciation of Shakespeare. And then, of course, there's the world outside all of these works and mediums, and the thinking and the processing of how all these works intersect and communicate with life. Which of course works on inspiration in marvellous ways. I don't think of inspiration as a kind of revelatory flash—it's something to be worked on, continuously, a muscle that needs training to be able to see what holds all this material together in the scope of the human experience. There are however, always multiple projects that I keep filed away in my head, rethinking and reworking how and when any of them could occur. The longer I think about them and carry them with me, the more I know they matter. Inspiration and ideas come like fire—some are small and burn out fast and are forgotten, while others are fed over time and become massive things, taking on the shape of signals or rituals. So the problem isn't so much finding inspiration, it's figuring out which inspirations to keep lit.

- I spend a lot of time (and too much money) acquiring art books. I often find a painting that expresses the mood or tone of the play but using the different medium of painting.

I find this can be a helpful way to start a conversation with a designer and keep me generally inspired when the process gets to be a process.

HOW DO YOU GET YOURSELF EXCITED ABOUT A PIECE THAT YOU ARE HIRED TO DIRECT AS OPPOSED TO ONE THAT YOU FEEL COMPELLED TO PURSUE?

- There's always something to connect with. I focus on that. Look for my "in" and expand from there.

- Find the little nuggets of joy in the piece and hold onto those as tight as possible.

- I try to find something inside the piece that resonates with me, whether it's a theme, a character, an idea . . . something. If there isn't, then it will be a losing battle. If it doesn't ignite a spark in you, then I would do yourself a favour and let someone else do it.

- I read the play and decide what I can bring to it.

- Not every project is gold and has amazing people. This is rare, actually. So these days I really am just appreciative of any kind of directing, performing, or teaching work I get. I still try and choose projects I have some heart connection to, but if I find myself "stuck" in a gig I try and focus only on the "good" things I love to do and lessen the focus on the negative. I try and not bitch about it with the other people in the project. I treat myself to fun things I like to do outside of the project so I can bring that good energy to work.

- Lots of research. I also try to find a team of actors and designers that I know will make the project fun and as fulfilling as possible.

- I have certain affinities in plays (mythology, historical turning points, and scientific breakthroughs). So when hired to direct a play I did not choose, I look for where these affinities might be in the script as a way in.

- I must identify with it in some way—a part of the human experience—otherwise I can't direct it.

2. ENTRANCE TO THE PIECE

HOW DO YOU FIND YOUR ENTRANCE INTO THE PIECE? DO YOU LOOK FOR ANYTHING SPECIFIC?

- I usually ask, What compels me? What challenges me? What makes me hot under the collar? What affects my fellow collaborators? What has the potential to make the audience uncomfortable?

- You have to ask, "Why am I doing this play?" You have to find a way to articulate these reasons.

- I usually read and go over the piece many times. It's what I used to do as an actor and still do when I have to do a scene or sing a song. I do it over and over again, and in that repetition the layers start to peel away, and hopefully the heart of the piece reveals itself (or at least what you think is the heart) or the viewpoint speaks to you. Then after you get that, all design elements start to come together.

- Usually around the third read-through of a piece, I walk it out alone. If I can physicalize it, and add vocals, or movement, then I can kinesthetically connect to the piece. It usually grows from there

- Sometimes it's a line in the play or an image or a moment that sparks me, and the process.

- Look for the spine of the piece and go from there.

- All of this depends on the show. Sometimes it's the line of a song, a painting, or a conversation that drives the piece. It can be anything, really. There are no rules here.

- I always find the key line for the play to inform my way into the rehearsal process. I also like to settle on the metaphor of the piece. For example, in one play I directed a few years ago I worked with the metaphor "a hard and solid gold heart softening."

- I write down the ideas I had immediately when I read it.

- Something that surprises me.

- Write what strikes you about the play so you can preserve those qualities. This is what will strike the audience—e.g., language, character, subject matter.

HOW DO YOU TRUST THAT YOUR INSTINCT/INTUITION IS CORRECT?

- There is no alternative. Alternatively, surround yourself with quality people who will call you on your bullshit.

- You have to train the interpretive impulse. You have to be a person with a good connective mind. Use all the theatre you've seen in the past to create work.

- Ha . . . I convince myself that my instinct is *mostly* correct. I need that to be able to lead effectively. But I say "mostly" because I try to be open to a better idea and will be the first person to say I was wrong. But I think when it comes to making a decision as a director, you have to be able to take the responsibility of making a decision. There are always so many people with so many opinions and agendas that will challenge that "instinct" and so trusting yourself is very important.

- My body tells me the truth. If the instinct isn't correct, my body tightens.

- Time has given me trust in my instinct. Whenever I have doubted it and not followed it, I've regretted it. I take comfort in the fact that there is no right or wrong anyway.

- Trust your gut! Unless your gut is stupid, then get a second opinion.

- I think this happens with some trial and error. Experience is your best friend.

- Practice.

HOW DO YOU CHOOSE A CONCEPT? DO YOU HAVE TO CHOOSE A CONCEPT?

- The concept will emerge from the language.

- Again, this depends entirely on the project. But no, I don't think that it's always necessary to have a concept or for the director's point of view to be at the forefront for a project. Sometimes it's enough to simply serve the play/lead artist.

- I choose a concept I can relate to as an artist and as a human being.

- I don't believe that a concept is necessary. I let the writing style and story inspire me to proceed.

- Whatever the concept is, it has to serve the piece. You can't just put a party theme on a project and call it a concept. Even if the piece is about a party.

- The question I need to answer is, why this play, why now (2018), and why here (in a New York City space, in Alabama, etc.). Answering this question might lead to a concept as a way of making the play immediate for the audience. But by the concept, I don't mean "Hamlet in Space" or something.

3. HIRING YOUR TEAM

HOW DO YOU CHOOSE AN ASSISTANT DIRECTOR? WHAT DO YOU ASK THEM OR WHAT HAVE YOU BEEN ASKED?

- I've been asked several times, "What makes you different from any other director?"
- Why now? Why you?
- What is the story of the play?
- I've been asked if I am patient enough to assistant direct many times. I thought I was . . . until I did it.
- Are you willing to say nothing the entire rehearsal process but also ready to jump up at a moment's notice and tackle something?
- What do you want to learn from me?
- What can I learn from you?
- Which director do you most admire and why?
- How do you speak to actors?

- How do you run the rehearsal room? What is your style?
- What is the last non-theatre book you read?
- What is a play that has majorly influenced your directing and why?
- What are your strengths as a director?
- What are your weaknesses? (Always a trick question!)
- Describe a challenge you have faced in a production and how you handled it. Or some other version of "what is the best/worst experience you have had directing?"
- Tell me about your process, and how you like to work.

WHAT ARE THE PROS AND CONS OF ASSISTANT DIRECTING?

- It's a wonderful way of getting inside the artistic process.
- Watching other directors work is invaluable.
- You get to watch different approaches to the work and, in turn, can find your own.
- It teaches you about individual style and how it works for some directors and not for others.
- It's a wonderful way to observe what works and what doesn't without the pressure of performance.

- You can watch different personalities and the relationships that people forge in the room.

- You can really get stuck in the assistant role. You have to be careful.

- If you do too much of it, you can get resentful of the position.

- It's the best way to learn what *not* to do.

- You must have tremendous patience and confidence, because sitting in a room, basically without a voice until you are asked, is a very daunting task.

- You have to be willing to be completely silent, but always available.

- It can be a torturous experience depending on the director you are working with. Make certain to set expectations prior to beginning rehearsals or be prepared for utter frustration and resentment.

- It's definitely a job for someone who hasn't directed much.

- Be kind to your assistants. They have opinions. Lots of them. As the director, you are worrying about all the elements at once. Give certain tasks to the assistant so they don't feel neglected or invisible. It's the one job in theatre that can feel like an extra appendage if the director allows it to happen. I had one experience where I felt like nothing but an intrusion and it was painful minute to minute.

HOW DO YOU CHOOSE A CHOREOGRAPHER OR MOVEMENT COACH TO WORK WITH?

- Make sure you go and see that choreographer's work prior to working with them. Otherwise they might not be the right one for the job and it all goes to hell. Or you end up, or they end up, trying to please. And as soon as you try to please in any of your work, it's just not going to work.

- Get to know the choreographers in your community and figure out which ones you'd like to work with.

- I like to ask them how they see movement contributing to the story.

- I ask them, "If this piece were only movement, how would you tell the story?"

WHAT DO YOU LOOK FOR IN YOUR DESIGNERS?

- I always encourage directors to pursue designers that are dramaturgical. This way they contribute their own dramaturgical insights with the costumes, lights, props, set, and so on to bring to the production as a whole.

- Choosing your designers is just as crucial and important as choosing your actors. Casting the people around you is everything.

- I can't have good ideas on my own. I need to speak with a designer about it and receive their feedback and ideas. So I look for very proactive designers with lots of ideas.

- Someone excited at the prospect of solving problems and challenges. Solution-oriented designers.

- Someone who understands metaphors and how to make them theatrical.

- You have to manage all the great minds/designers/actors to go with your vision. Use the forces of design in the service of the story you are telling.

- A true collaborator. Someone who will do their best to give you what you want, but strong enough to tell you when it's not possible. But then I want an alternative.

- Someone to push me and my ideas even further.

WHEN MEETING WITH THE DESIGNERS, WHAT LANGUAGE DO YOU USE? HOW DO YOU COMMUNICATE/SHARE YOUR VISION WITH THEM?

- I ask the designer what they think the show is about.

- I break the script up into events—this is a stageable event. Then I ask, "How do we stage this event?" That begins the discussion.

- Limitless brainstorming.

- I ask a lot of questions and find that the really difficult questions sometimes yield the best results.

- I bring photos and artwork that best illuminate my feelings for the piece or the atmosphere I hope to invoke or create.

- I bring them music that I connect with the piece.

- I have a big blank piece of paper and markers and we take turns drawing images that we find from the piece and then spend time connecting them.

- I bring in movies that have a semblance of what I'm looking for.

- Bring in any visual information that you think will help them on the right path.

HOW OFTEN DO YOU MEET WITH DESIGNERS?

- Meet early and often, whenever possible in your process. The earlier everyone's communicating and working together, the better. Small discrepancies between what the team members expect and what a designer actually ends up doing can become major issues if they aren't discovered until tech.

- I meet as often as I can. The design directly influences my directing ideas and my directing ideas directly influence the design. They go hand in hand. They become intertwined and work dramaturgically with each other.

- Depending on the project, I like to give them space to create without too much pressure. But I like to be kept in the loop by seeing/hearing ideas as they come to them.

- During rehearsals, things change. Sometimes drastically. It's important to keep your designer informed and engaged during this process to make necessary changes as you go.

ANYTHING YOU SHOULDN'T SAY TO A DESIGNER?

- We have no money and we can't do anything.

- I drew the set myself on this napkin.

- If I were designing this, this is what I would do.

HOW DO YOU LEAVE ROOM FOR THE DESIGNER'S CREATIVITY WHILE STILL MAINTAINING YOUR VISION?

- I think the idea of a director's "vision" is wildly overrated. Not to completely disparage the idea of an auteur director with a grand idea, working with a crack team all working in sync to bring that vision to vivid theatrical life . . . but I think it's a rare project when that works. If I walk in to the first production meeting knowing exactly how everything should work . . . well, I'm presuming that my ideas are the best ideas. In that case, I don't need designers; I just need technicians, because I've done the design work already. My preference is to take in all the ideas in the room—from the actors, the playwright, the designers, the technicians, stage management, everyone—and find a way to make them work together as a whole.

- Because I worked primarily with a music director during my time in New York, the relationship was quite different than a traditional director/designer relationship, not the least because he was an incredibly talented composer with the musical versatility to flow between classical, jazz, and electronic music production. My input into his work was mainly conducting research into different types of instrumentation that would fit into the context of the play or, in the case of sampling production, work on material use with him to mirror visual influences in the work on a sonic level. Through this though, music and sound has a huge impact on my work and how I understand the theatrical process. For a certain kind of methodology and headspace, it can be important to allow the sounds being generated not only from performers but from the composer's work to impact your vision of the piece.

- Of course, if you're working with a designer or composer in a healthy, symbiotic relationship, you'll influence each other and develop a shared understanding of the work that surpasses artistic ego and brings the work to a new height.

FROM THE DESIGNER'S PERSPECTIVE WITH ADAM SPENCER

FROM A DESIGNER'S PERSPECTIVE, WHAT DO YOU WANT FROM AN INITIAL MEETING WITH THE DIRECTOR?

- On the first meeting with a director, I want them to express to me why we are doing this play. What is it about this play that is important at this date and time, and what is it about this story that is worthy of telling? Beyond that, I want to hear them talk about some of the strong images that pop up in the show, things that got their attention as far as the imagery of the show. If there is something that is really strong conceptually and they want our opinion of how that concept may shape out, I don't mind that either, if that concept is something they want to get to together.

DO YOU LIKE WHEN DIRECTORS BRING IMAGES, MUSIC, AND SO ON? SOME KIND OF EXAMPLE OF WHAT THEY ARE LOOKING FOR?

- If there is something the director has latched on to and feels very strongly about, absolutely. I want to hear that music or see that image. The only struggle comes when they say, "This exact thing has to be represented." Basically, I love to see imagery that they present, but I don't want them to say this imagery exactly needs to be used on the stage. If it's a piece of artwork I want them to say, "This is why this piece of artwork speaks to me about this show." Or if it's music, "This is why this piece of music works for this show." That way I can jazz on what they throw out there and put out my feelers about what strikes me about what they presented and what strikes me about what's going on in the show.

DO YOU BRING MATERIALS WITH YOU FOR THE FIRST MEETING TO SHOW THE DIRECTOR?

- I usually will have something in my pocket if the time's right. I will read the play and have a great understanding of the structure of it and what's going on with the work and I might have started looking for some imagery that speaks to me about it but I am not going to pull that out until it seems like the director wants me to pull that out, because the imagery that I've pulled up and researched might not fit the director's imagery of it at all. I do my homework, but I don't pull it out unless it's needed.

IS THERE A CERTAIN KIND OF LANGUAGE YOU FEEL IS HELPFUL OR HURTFUL IN A FIRST MEETING?

- I will start with the things I don't like that a director says. I'm almost always fine with any and all language a director uses to communicate. Like, "The play feels very pink." Or, "It sounds like white noise." That will make sense to me. I don't want a director throwing out vocabulary. If I'm doing lighting design, I don't want the director to say, "I want this gobo." I'd rather have them say, "I want to see a lot of texture." A gobo is texture. I want them to understand where that design language is derived from so that the gobo is texture. I'd much rather talk about the design and feel of the work than the technical execution of it. I want a director to say, "The world feels askew," rather than, "I feel the stage should be on a rake." If you say, "I want the stage to be on a rake," then my mind instantly goes to that rake, but if you say, "I want the world to be askew," then maybe I decide that instead of a rake there's a giant ramp that comes out of the set. The technical words actually limit the creativity because it throws the technical solution into the mix rather than the design solution.

- I think asking, "Does that make sense?" and, "Is what I said clear?" is also helpful for communication.

HOW DO YOU WANT THE DIRECTOR TO SHARE THEIR IDEAS WITH YOU?

- Any way the director feels they can share their vision works. I had a director once bring in a bowl of dirt and say, "The show smells like this bowl of dirt." And that worked for me. It's earthy, it's rustic, I can get a sense of what that means for the look of the show. I know some designers don't like things like that but I do.

HOW CAN THE DIRECTOR LEAVE ROOM FOR THE DESIGNER'S CREATIVITY WHILE STILL MAINTAINING THEIR VISION?

- The director is in charge of getting us all on the same boat.

- At the end of the day, my name is not first billing. At the end of the day, it needs to be the director's vision. It might sound horrible for the designer, but it's the director's show, so sometimes you have to say, "Okay, this is what you want." If I'm not giving them what they need, I'd rather they say, "I need something like this," to get me on the right path, instead of waiting until the end and not getting that stage picture they'd hoped for.

WHAT DO YOU LOOK FOR IN A DRAMATURGE? CONVERSELY, WHAT SHOULD YOU AVOID?

- Someone who embraces and supports the story.
- Do they have a narrative brain?
- Do they have a strong aesthetic?
- Dramaturges must love the material.
- Find out what the writer is trying to accomplish and have them write that.
- I ask them to tell me about rhythm in the text.
- Are they trying to navigate and be faithful to the playwright's vision?
- Some are trying to turn it into a different play—avoid them.
- If they have an agenda, run!
- You have to be careful. It can be a dangerous thing and can kill a great deal of talent.
- A great dramaturge will show you things about your work that you didn't know.

HOW DO YOU CHOOSE YOUR STAGE MANAGER? ANY SPECIFIC QUESTIONS YOU ASK?

- Your stage manager is your best friend for the duration of that particular production. Sometimes they need to give you tough love. Look for someone clear, concise, and intuitive.

- Highly organized and a great communicator.

- Someone who can manage people effectively.

- Empathetic but not a pushover.

- I usually ask them how they might deal with conflict in the room.

4. PREP WORK

HOW DO YOU BEGIN YOUR RESEARCH?

- I research the artist, first. To really know the piece, you should know its parent.

- Researching for a show is one of my favourite parts of the process. I enjoy delving into the story and the characters, and the words the playwright has chosen. I begin my research there, getting specific with even the most basic things I'm sure I already understand so I can be sure I'm seeing them through the lens of the play. Then I dive into the ancillary research—topics, history, allegory, corresponding texts—this is the part that I love most because I get to learn new things I might never otherwise have known. I also enjoying using this research to build the world of the play, sometimes hiding Easter eggs that only others that have a similar experience or expertise may find, but I find deeply satisfying to know are there to be found.

- Just begin.

- With questions. Always questions. And the Internet. That's usually the first place. The Internet is rich with truth and lies and it often leads to surprising things. Which hopefully lead you to primary sources. Or at least the library.

- I jot down my own questions that I don't know the answers to off the top of my head and start there. Then I jump down the rabbit hole of the Internet. We have the history of the world at our fingertips, so there is no excuse for not doing your research.

- Historical relevance is extremely important to me. Once we do this thing, it will become history as well. Document everything. Honour the past while innovating for the future.

- I start with the way that time works in the play.

- If I have the time, I will read all that playwright's plays in the sequence that they wrote them. This will give you a great idea of what their grand ideas and questions are.

WHERE DO YOU GET YOUR INSPIRATIONS FOR THE PARTICULAR PIECE?

- That could come from anywhere. Usually, it jumps out of nowhere and doesn't let me ignore it.

- The bathroom is my inspiration palace. Especially with some difficult projects. If my mind is stuck, taking a bath always gives some new ideas back to me.

- Usually a word or phrase inside the piece will incite something in me. Then I fall into the Google rabbit hole of images and research.

BEAT WORK—HOW DO YOU DIVIDE BEATS? BESIDES ENTRANCES AND EXITS, HOW DO YOU CHOOSE THE NEXT BEAT?

- Ugh. Beats. I feel like that word gets overworked in the worst way. I prefer to use the word "moment." I just finished a production where there was only one entrance and one exit, so we really had to divide the play into moments. "What is happening in this moment? Where does the moment end? What does your character want in this moment? Why are they acting this way in this moment?" It just works for me. At Bread and Puppet Theater, we "chaptered" things, which also works.

- When does something change?

- I think watching people in real life and being very aware of what real people do in real life is a great tool in how beats work. So when I go through a piece I try to find the natural beats as I hear the text being read.

- Whenever there is a shift in objective.

OTHER PREP TECHNIQUES?

- I type out the entire script myself so I become intimately familiar with each word. It becomes part of my DNA. I discover so much nuance when I retype it.

- Allow yourself to read it several times, focusing on a different aspect each time.

- I "verb" each line so I know what the action is before I go in. Whether or not I use that particular verb always changes but I've done my homework.

- I make a collage for each page of script and it goes on the opposite side of the dialogue page.

- Read the playwright's earlier plays to see where they are coming from.

- I always ask myself, what is the basic question of the play? What does and doesn't fit into the world of the play?

- Find the *spine* of the play.

- I look for patterns and decode what they mean.

- You need to understand the characters and who they are at the time of the play.

- You have to ask, what is the atmosphere of the play, the scene, of the time?

- Seek to understand each moment in the play—even a character that initially seems weak and lazily written. Maybe the playwright intended it.

- When directing opera, I put one page of translation in English and on the other side, one page Italian.

- I do my best to figure out time in the play and how it works. When is it set? What time of day is each scene? How much time has passed between scenes?

- I figure out what pushes the action into the next scene.
- I find the theme of the play in one line that encapsulates the entire piece.

HOW DO YOU APPROACH NEW PLAYS?

Also see Master Class with Andrea Romaldi, p. 99.

- The director's job is to make what the creator creates. It's not your job to tell the writer what the characters say or do.
- Work with what's in front of you. Sometimes the best idea is at the end of the process.
- What is the story and what is the story we are telling?
- Find your own aesthetic and do your own work.
- Everything is its own autonomous work of art.
- As the writer you want carte blanche to try anything so allow the writer to do what his impulses want.
- A workshop is a laboratory for the writer.
- Let the director retain the authority; don't let the actor question the director or the writer.
- I always ask the writer (if it's a new play) to read the play to me. All the parts. Stage directions. Everything. You'd be surprised what you learn.

- It's different every time! What does the play want? What are the questions? I ask the writer and the dramaturge: What are our goals? How can we support one another?

HOW DO YOU PLAN/ORGANIZE THE REHEARSAL DAYS EFFICIENTLY?

- From the macro, I look at my entire rehearsal period. How much time do I have, total? What are the limitations to that time (schedules, money, space, stuff)? What do my collaborators and I need in order to accomplish our goals of bringing this play to fruition? Does that fit into the time that we have? Answer those questions, and you've got your schedule. Always budget too much time whenever possible. Continue to adjust constantly as needs change and new information becomes available.

- *Calendar and daily goals!* This is mostly for me. If I don't have it together, rehearsal is bound to be a mess. Stick to what you've planned as much as you can.

- I usually have a master plan but I'm always willing to change that according to what's happening in the room on the day. But I try not to deviate too far and lose track of my goals, otherwise you can end up with a mess.

- Rely on your stage manager to help stick to your plan.

5. AFTER YOU'VE HIRED/ ASSEMBLED THE TEAM

HOW DO YOU BOUNCE/EXCHANGE IDEAS WITH YOUR DESIGNERS? HOW DO YOU SPEAK TO THEM?

- Make sure you understand the logistics of the space so you can realistically design the piece.
- I do my best to speak to them dramaturgically.
- I bring in books, music, pictures, paintings, anything that resonates with me for the piece.
- Find a use for the stage and space. Don't fight the space—use it.
- Be sure to create a set that can be malleable as the process evolves so you are not stuck with something that has to change. A design that can listen to the play as it evolves. Especially for new work.
- Is the space a metaphor? Realistic? It must be fluid in a singular space.
- How does the set interact/contribute to the storytelling?
- How can we make the applause happen?

- "She settles into the couch and sits down"—how can we help the audience along?
- Is it a good idea to have a metaphor on the set?
- How does the lighting establish tone?

6. CASTING

WHAT DO YOU LOOK FOR IN AN ACTOR?

- Auditions are like speed dating. You know immediately if you want to see them again.
- Auditions are a form of curation.
- I love when actors come in completely prepared.
- Bold choices. Something that excites me that I wouldn't have thought of myself.
- I look for a connection and the way they interact with me.
- Someone who can be responsive to direction.
- I want someone to surprise me and be the kind of character I could never have imagined myself.
- Sense of humour and a sense of play.
- I want someone who I want to spend a month with every day, eight hours a day.

WHAT ARE SOME OF THE AUDITION TRICKS?

- Do some group work and see how they communicate and play with the other actors.
- I've pretended to leave the room and watched them from somewhere they couldn't see me. You see how they behave when you aren't there. Their nature will emerge.
- No tricks. You need to have a conversation with them.

WHAT DO YOU ASK FROM YOUR ACTORS AT THE AUDITION?

- I like to do both prepared pieces but also love to have an improvisational element to it in order to see their impulses and how willing they are to play.
- I make sure to work with them, even if they give a wonderful audition, to ensure they are playful and ready to collaborate.
- I think group work is very important. I want collaborators and team players. You can find out immediately who fits into the team you are trying to build.
- I always make sure to do group exercises so that I can see instantly who will be on board during rehearsals. If there is any resistance during the audition it will only amplify tenfold during the rehearsals.
- You must do group work. How can you not do group work? Rehearsals are all group work.

- I almost never ask for a monologue. I've been fooled by them many times. I usually do sides so that I can see them in action as they might be in rehearsals. If they do a monologue, I usually radically change it to see how they adapt to changes and suggestions.

WHAT HAVE YOU DISCOVERED IS THE MOST HELPFUL THING YOU'VE LEARNED TO LOOK FOR AT AN AUDITION FROM THE ACTORS?

- The slightest sign of negativity or resistance will only amplify once they are hired.
- If someone doesn't take direction well after you've given them a few suggestions, I worry.
- I make sure to have them do an exercise or technique I know I use in rehearsals and see how receptive they are to it.

7. FIRST DAY OF REHEARSAL

HOW DO YOU ENTER THE ROOM ON THE FIRST DAY AND PUMP YOURSELF UP FOR THE EXPERIENCE?

- The director is the ambassador of the culture in the room. I shake the hand of every actor every day to say, "I'm glad you're here and sharing this with me."

- I go individually to every person in the room to welcome them.

- I think of it as taking people camping. It's going to be a great trip, bags are packed, or "fuck it, we aren't going to use a map."

- I used to feel like I needed to be the voice of authority in the room. But this quickly made itself visible in the work. It became impersonal. Now I walk into the room like I'm a bit of an idiot. A step ahead of the cast. But let them know that we are all going to get out of the mud together.

- Being a woman, I felt like I had to prove and almost desex myself. I was full of tension and fear. That has, fortunately, dissipated over the years. Now I want a laughter-filled environment. Now I like to make space for conversation and exchange.

- I try my best to be relaxed and excited and present for the experience.

- Once I realized that everyone is filled with anxiety and doubt on the first day, it released me.

- I generally get to the studio or rehearsal space early. I sweep the room; I set up the tables, chairs. Whatever it is we're using I take care of it. I like doing this—it gives a sense organizational calm, sure, but more than that preparing the space enables me to begin humbly and with a sense of open anticipation for the process.

- I just sit down with my coffee, maybe put on music that makes me think of the piece, or some other sample of recording that works in the context of what we're about to do. Then I just hang out until people arrive. I greet them, catch up, chat. The air of the room should be light and convivial when approaching a new piece, and it's good to let some little pieces of magic flow in—the aforementioned music/sounds, opening the windows or curtains, or maybe placing an object of import to the work on the table or in the room.

- Day one is really all about saying hello, to one another and to the work. Hellos are about finding the positive and embracing the opportunity to greet someone or something with the right foot forward. Given most of the shows I work on, I like to leave all the sombre, difficult shit out of the hello. We'll all get there, probably over the course of the first read-through. But for that reason, those first moments of meeting for the day need to be clean and fresh in order to delve into the kind of work I like.

WHAT KIND OF ATMOSPHERE DO YOU TRY AND CREATE AND HOW DO YOU ACCOMPLISH IT?

- I make eye contact with every person before I start. How can you collaborate unless everyone's been acknowledged?

- Create a sense of comfort in the room and be open so that the actors can be open.

- A sense of value. A director I assisted once said, "In this room there are no second choices. This is my dream team." It was very self-affirming and made you feel like you belonged.

- Be as collaborative as possible. There are sometimes twenty people or more involved in the production, which means you have twenty or more people's imaginations to use. You'd be insane not to use that. They see the piece with just as much intelligence and creativity as you do, so your job as the director becomes somewhat editorial, vetting all those ideas and choosing the best ones to tell the story you want to tell.

- You want positive energy, but happiness is not the goal in rehearsals.

- I'm hosting on the first day. I've brought muffins. They get excited about this and I win them over. It's my way of welcoming them to enjoy the experience.

- I try my best not to be afraid to say, "I don't know, but we will figure it out."

- I want to create an atmosphere of intimacy and trust. How can I make people feel safe? How can I make people "arrive" in the room? These are the questions I try to answer.

WHAT IS THE FIRST THING YOU DO AFTER MEET AND GREET?

- I try to lift the room and excite them to work with me. Then I set a few parameters and discuss how the collaboration is going to work.

- Allow the designers to chat about the world we are creating together. I also post photos of inspiration around the room that the team and actors can reference when needed.

- I launch into the table read and get it out of our systems.

- I play a game to get rid of any butterflies and anxiety, get people in the room together.

- I like to tell everyone what excites me in the piece, things I want to investigate. I ask designers to present their ideas, then we read the piece out loud, talk about themes, and ask questions.

- I table read, then ask everyone to write down questions that arise during the read. After we're done, we go around one by one and put each person's two pressing questions on a little piece of paper and put them up on the wall so that we can answer them bit by bit, every day, until they are all gone.

- I talk about what the goal of the piece is. Then I tell them that I hope and expect that everyone will make offers and work collaboratively.

- I don't like to start staging on the first day. So, I generally have a short first day, using the time for the usual read-through, design presentation, and so on, then having a discussion about first impressions of characters and relationships. I find this gets the actors' minds thinking and puts them in the right headspace to start on their feet on day two.

- I play some exercises to get the nerves out, something physical to get them out of their heads.

- I ask everyone to introduce themselves and tell a fun fact about themselves. Or a secret, if they dare.

WHAT ELSE DO YOU USUALLY DO ON YOUR FIRST DAY OF REHEARSAL?

- I try to get us to relate to one another about things that aren't just based on the text we are working with; getting everyone in the room and letting them each have their voice that day; letting the actor speak as themselves first instead of as the character, because we'll get to that.

- I tend to go in and be pretty cynical about first day of rehearsals. What I want is for everyone to be present by the end of the day. The real work starts the next day.

- I want to have a conversation about the play, hear what the actors think it's about, and what struck and intrigued and confused them. I want them to change my mind, in a sense, about all my preconceived notions and make things more complex so we can figure it all out together.

- I always try to make them come to me and want to rehearse. I'm very prepared, but I won't tell them anything. I don't want to close them. I want their thoughts. It gives me the opportunity to rethink what I thought instead of exposing my thoughts immediately. And them slowly adapting. I always try to make them discover and not tell them what to do. The reading of the words isn't the most important thing. I watch the actors and see what they want to talk about and what they are wearing and how they are moving, and I use that to explore.

- I do a lot of devised work so I like to set up some expectations of what the process is going to be like. I learned early on to tell the actors that, of course, I want to learn about how they work and collaborate, but I also give some specific things about me that won't change. This is how my brain works. These are the five things about my brain that I need to share.

- I like to create a common vocabulary with the actors so we are on the same page.

- I do a lot of site-specific work, so my first day of rehearsal I want them to touch the space, get the character of the space. I get them to know the space. Touch the space. Love the space. Then they have the space in their minds.

- I introduce a morning warm-up. I always do that regardless of what we are doing each day.

DO YOU DO A TABLE READ? ANY TRICKS OR ADVICE ON HOW BEST TO APPROACH IT?

- Yes. On the first day, I need to hear it from beginning to end. Get it out of our system.
- Table reads can be very intimidating for an actor. I prefer to do something physical to get them comfortable with one another.
- In the first read, ask them to switch characters so the show isn't done after that first reading.
- If I do a table read, I sometimes get them to switch roles, eliminating the need to perform or make instant choices.
- I ask them to read through it, but each actor takes one line and we go around in circle until it's done. The goal is to *hear* the piece, not perform it.
- I ask everyone, while reading the script the first time together, to make a list of all the words that encapsulate the piece. It can be thematic or anything that feels relevant.

WHAT ARE ALTERNATIVES TO THE TRADITIONAL TABLE READS?

- I prefer to play games, get to know who is in the room. Get moving, get physical, and explore.
- Find four moments from the play and create a still picture in groups based on those moments that inspired you or that you felt compelled by. Show the pictures, then do that scene.

- I ask the cast to take fifteen minutes to work together and create/perform the show in two minutes. Then they perform it all as quickly as possible and we've now already "performed" it. The rest is all finessing. It's a great way to distill the show down to its basic plot points.

DO YOU SHARE ALL YOUR RESEARCH WITH THE CAST? IF NOT, WHAT DO YOU SHARE AND WHY?

- I do share what I think is relevant to them at that time. I try to space out my research so as to not overwhelm them.

- I like to post pictures and articles on the wall so they can look at them when they want.

- I try my best to find the appropriate moments to share research when it's pertinent to the moment at hand. I don't vomit it all out at once to them.

- I like to fuel the actors with some research before we begin so we all have some reference points.

WHAT TOOLS HAVE BEEN MOST SUCCESSFUL TO ERADICATE STATUS?

- You want to be careful not to dominate or micromanage everyone's contributions.

- Well, the easiest and most obvious thing for an independent production is not to have any material published for the show proclaiming that it is "starring" anyone. I like "performed by," "directed by," "written by," all in the same font and size. I know starring roles can be important when introducing higher end professional work, but at least for independent artists that is something to avoid at all costs as it places import on one person rather than on group cohesion. One of those is clearly more valuable. In the room, however, my own directing style works to my advantage, because I generally resist the Strasbergian idea that inner emotional truth leads to outward expression. I like my late Stanislavsky, Grotowski, and Meyerhold, the whole idea that it is the doing of things, alone or in relation to another person, that creates emotional truth (true also for vocal exploration—sound is generated by muscles, after all). Taking that approach can really get rid of the idea of status quickly. Just because an actor has more lines than another doesn't mean they can be unresponsive and out of sync with their partner, or the scene as I'm directing it will collapse. By moving away from the Strasberg style, I don't indulge a single person as much naturally and focus rather on the collective dynamic. Furthermore, the focus on collective dynamic can lead to interesting moments where I find people who have a wide array of skills that get used in rehearsal and the creation of images. For example, if we have two dancers and a singer, there is no reason not to use them to create images and sound while another actor holds forth in a soliloquy. Whether these experiments stay or change, or become bigger or smaller, considering everyone's skills and allowing them to experiment with them in context gives an immense sense of satisfaction and ownership to cast members.

- I ask everyone, designers, stage managers, anyone on the team, to do exercises with us to become as comfortable as we can with one another. We are all building the same show. We are all on the same team.

HOW DO YOU GET EVERYONE ON THE SAME PAGE AND INTO THE "WORLD OF THE PLAY" YOU ARE TRYING TO ACHIEVE? ARE THERE RULES OR PARAMETERS, OR IS IT A FREE FOR ALL?

- Start with what you want to explore with the show, what interests you.

- I like disguising the parameters and letting people go a bit wild at first. After all, it's harder to add something later than it is to subtract. But there are little things there—objects I may have brought in, lines of music that float through the space for certain exercises or moments. A bit of chaos is good, but always subtly suggest a direction by influences strategically placed in the room.

- I start with some of the questions and themes I have of the piece. Then I propose that we all do our best to answer these questions.

- I tell them what interests and intrigues me about the piece.

- Depending on the piece, I ask the cast to share any personal stories that relate to the themes of the piece. This instantly engages them with a true investment.

- I try to give the actors a very strong sense of time and space. You have to make sure that everyone is working with the same time and space.

HOW DO YOU DEAL WITH NUDITY IN A SCRIPT?

- I ask, "What do you feel comfortable with?"

- This is something you need to deal with at auditions first and foremost.

- You have to have a fight director for violence, so the same goes for intimacy.

- Encourage incredible communication.

- You need to give them ultimate power to tell when something is hurting them or making them uncomfortable.

- This is when an intimacy director comes in very handy.

8. BUILDING AN ENSEMBLE

HOW DO YOU CREATE A UNIFIED ENSEMBLE? DO YOU BUILD IT SPECIFICALLY OR ALLOW IT TO EMERGE ORGANICALLY?

- Give each actor agency over storytelling.

- Never let any ensemble member feel *less than*.

- I ask the cast in pairs to share stories at first: their happiest moment; saddest moment. Then they share them with the group as the other person told them. That way they are truly listening.

- I ask them to bring in an object or poem or song or dance, picture—anything that reveals who they are as a person and an artist—and share it with the group. They get one minute each to tell us about it, otherwise you'll spend the entire day with that one exercise.

- Partner up and tell the other person where your name came from and why your parents named you that. Then share your partner's name and etymology with the group. Wonderful way to build intimacy.

- Games, games, and more games!

- I bring in a jump rope and one by one we jump into it like a child would. Then we add two, then three and so on, until we get as many as we can in there. It's a fantastic way to build fun into the ensemble. We often forget to have fun, forget the importance of nurturing play into rehearsals.

DO YOU WANT DESIGNERS IN THE ROOM WITH YOU FOR ALL REHEARSALS?

- Not all, or even many rehearsals; it can freak out some actors, I've found. But I do like when everyone on the team gets together early, so actors aren't meeting designers only at tech, and the earlier designers can see a run, the better. I've often been on the other side of this equation, as a sound designer, and just getting the tone of a rehearsal and where the process is headed can really help to give me an idea of where my design should be going, to complement the sound of the actors and the movement of their bodies in the space.

- I make sure all the designers are there on that first day so we can all hear the play together and unify the entire team. We assume that designers read or hear the same way that we do, but that might not be true. They approach the story through their own lens and it can bring a valuable perspective to your own interpretation.

- I wish! Good designers are always welcome in my room and if it were financially possible I would ask them to be there all the time. They can provide valuable insight, plus help solve problems. They also become as fully immersed as you are, so I think the shorthand between director and designer would be so essential in creating the world together.

FROM THE DESIGNER'S PERSPECTIVE

DO YOU WANT TO GO TO ALL THE REHEARSALS? HOW OFTEN DO YOU WANT TO BE THERE?

- It depends on what role I'm filling. If I'm a scenic designer I want to see rehearsal so I know that what I'm building jives with what's being done. Or if something on stage is not being used the way I intended it to be used, we need to rethink the construction in the shop.

- As a lighting designer, I like to see two to three rehearsals before going into tech. I don't feel like I need to be part of the process all of the time. I want the director to have a chance to get through their process before I step in and start having opinions about their process.

- I just want to come in and watch when I can. I learn so much from watching the actors and their interpretations.

- Sometimes I want to "audition" design elements into the rehearsals, but the director needs to be clear with me about how much of that they can handle so it's not distracting. Sometimes the nature of the rehearsal doesn't allow for that. So it's very helpful for the director to say, "Yeah, come in. Watch. Respond. But maybe on a Wednesday for this period of time." There's a lot of information to be gained from seeing the rehearsal. But be clear to a designer about what you need.

HOW MUCH DO YOU LIKE TO MEET WITH THE DIRECTOR DURING REHEARSALS?

- I like having weekly meetings. I like to bring images I find and say, "Okay, you like images five, twelve, and nineteen. Great, let me narrow down my research there and do some quick sketches. Okay, you like sketches two, five, and six. Let me compile those and put those sketches into something and next week I can come with a more fully realized image of what the set might be." The key to me is that I like to have meetings with all the other designers present as well, because the costume designer might have an idea about how to approach the show that is absolutely brilliant and effects how I'm going to pursue my work. We influence one another with our work. I work much better when I can talk to and collaborate with the designers together; all the designers working in the room together with the director.

9. GETTING THE CAST ON ITS FEET

WHEN DO YOU KNOW YOU'VE HAD ENOUGH TABLE WORK? WHAT IS THE MOMENT YOU PULL THE TABLE ASIDE AND START THE TERRIFYING LEAP TO MOVING BODIES IN TIME AND SPACE?

- I often work on devised, physical work that begins with bodies moving through space, but when I direct from a script I often find it helpful to move from working with scripts at a table to working with scripts in hand as quickly as possible. This way bodies can start relating to one another in space, but without any staging. This is basically book work, but without a table so that actors can have better access to their bodies, but focus on relationships rather than worrying about the stage. I avoid furniture and try to play with varying distances that have nothing to do with the logic of any real space, but force the actors to respond to one another. Once I have a clearer idea of the moments that really spark for the actors, I can start thinking about blocking the scene in support of that. It exposes my bias towards Relationship over Narrative, but in the end they usually balance out anyway.

- When I see the actors tuning out. You can actually watch actors tuning out the table work because they are ready to go. Also, just stating very clearly at the beginning, "We are going to start blocking on this day," makes me more accountable as a leader. I can't ignore the deadline I set for myself and the production.

- I actually *love* staging. So I leave the table as soon as possible.

- As soon as possible. Day one, two, or three.

- I keep the table available at all times so if you get stuck in a moment, you can pull it out and have a seat and dissect it.

- I'm always shocked when I hear that teams take weeks to table work. I try to get us on our feet in the first rehearsal, after a read-through; second rehearsal at the absolute latest. Unless it's a radio play. Of course, there will be times when we have to go back to the books, and sit down and talk through the ideas of the play, but in my experience many actors don't immediately translate the ideas they get from table work into their work on their feet. They need to be moving to understand how to embody and voice the ideas—they're actors. It's what they do. I'll sit around over a beer all night, shooting the breeze about what's going on in a script, with anyone, but in order to make those ideas come alive on stage, we have to be on our feet. That includes me, as well. Best piece of advice I've ever grabbed out of a book, I think: Anne Bogart's suggestion to always stand in rehearsal.

- It can get boring at the table, so when energy is low at table we get up. Sometimes we read while moving in space.

- Second rehearsal. I say, "Let's continue the discussion but on our feet."

- When you sense that the actors are becoming too analytical you should jump up and get them on their feet. You want to keep the ship moving and not have things fizzle out.

WHAT ARE THE FIRST EXERCISES YOU DO WITH THE ACTORS?

- Breathing. Being inside the body. Placing the body in space. Seeing one another. Speaking.

- It depends on the project. For the last play I directed, we did a lot of getting-to-know-you exercises and trust work because the show was emotionally straining and difficult. For the next show, we will be doing lots of physical work and pantomime. Most beginning rehearsals will start with a getting-to-know-you exercise. You can't go wrong with that.

- I warm them up at the beginning of rehearsals using music—different pieces and styles and let them move and discover the space and see what style suits the piece.

- I like to get them in their bodies and give them specific images to play with. Like an image of worms inside your body—any image that keeps your body alive and active is useful.

- I try my best to create an ensemble immediately so we play fun get-to-know-you games where we are as silly as possible and gain trust.

DO YOU LET ACTORS MOVE ORGANICALLY OR DO YOU DICTATE WHERE THEY GO/BLOCK THEM PRIOR TO REHEARSALS AND ALLOW THEM TO DISCOVER WHAT THAT DOES TO THEM?

- I let them explore first. I watch and I ask questions: "Why did you move there?" "What is your personal space and boundary with each character?"
- I tell them where to go and make them figure it out. Action and text are linked.
- All spatial relationship is a response and tells a story so I encourage them to explore the space that way. How do you manifest your relationship spatially on stage?
- I have other actors read their lines so they are free to move and explore physically and not be bound by the book.

HOW DO YOU CREATE YOUR WORLD AND THE VISUAL LANDSCAPE OF THE SHOW FOR THE ACTORS?

- I let the actors create their space. It helps them connect with it. So if the set consists of a room in a house, I ask them to set up the space the way they think the characters would. Then we work with the designer from there to finesse it.
- I use different exercises to create gestures and images for specific themes or moments in the show that create a common

vocabulary or glossary for that specific piece. We name them and then we can pull them out when we need them.

- I show them pictures or images that inspire me and ask them to embody that image on stage.

- I like to begin with really elemental materials—sand, dirt, fruit, linens, childhood toys, and simple light sources. Then I just watch how the performers relate to those things, and we slowly strip out excess until we get to the bare bones. A lot of movement may go into reaching for a doll, and that's free at the start—do whatever. But slowly we isolate certain impulses, certain shapes. So it's gradual, never a hard didactic response.

- Over the course of rehearsal, the visual spectrum continues to grow, and sometimes if the work is going well, and I have some ideas I know I want to explore with lighting for example, I'll rig something for the next rehearsal and see how it works—like if I want to see her shadow fall to her right side and that's what makes the image with the man and little girl on her left, then I want all of us to see and understand that in rehearsal and collectively experience how it changes the scene.

DO YOU GIVE HOMEWORK TO THE ACTORS?

- I always ask each actor to create a mixtape for their character. Sometimes it ends up in the show, but sometimes it just gives some insight into their views on the character.

- I ask actors to bring in a bit of different research to share about the time period of the show.

- I ask them to choose books that the character would read. Make a list.

- I encourage them to create diaries and backstories to discuss with one another as reference points.

- It really depends on the age and experience of the actor, but even then it would always be optional. I might suggest an exercise to an actor if I think it would help them with their character work.

10. SCENE WORK

ANY SPECIFIC TECHNIQUES OR CONVERSATIONS YOU HAVE WITH THE ACTORS TO GET THE RESULTS YOU WANT IN THE SCENE?

- You have to know the pace of the entire piece—how fast and slow does each scene go? Find the proper tempo for each scene.

- Ask the actors what their *desired outcome* is in the scene, then how will they get it.

- We read the scene and then I ask, "What did you hear in the text? What did you see? What images come to mind?"

- We read and any time there is an intention change, we stop and talk about it.

- When staging, I often use a dance analogy —this is a "tango," this is a "rumba" and so on—as metaphor for combining dialogue with staging.

- I remind them there is always agenda behind what we say, do, wear. Choose wisely for the characters.

- The characters/people want to alter, to affect, to change, to provoke something.

- Always ask what keeps characters talking? What keeps them from leaving a situation? The room? Always ask why the character is behaving this way.

- All language/dialogue is disagreement. We only speak to change someone's mind.

- We are always trying to prove someone wrong.

- What's at play in the scene? What balls are you juggling? What's happened?

- Characters have an urgency/immediacy to their needs to help pace and flow.

- Don't try to give the actors the most comfortable experience. They should be at a loss so they continue to work. Comfortable equals complacency.

- Work in layers as opposed to segments—adding more and more difficult tasks.

- Create the world of the play—space and time. Be clear about what they need to discover with each exercise, then let them play.

- Give them open-ended questions that take time to answer.

- Remind the actors that what they say is coloured by what they just heard.

- Use as many verbs as possible to speak to the actors. Make them active. Theatre is action.

- Verbs serve the character's objective.

- I use a lot of Theatre of the Oppressed techniques inside scene work. I create sculptures with them. I use "Cops in the Head" exercises to examine certain moments.

- Everything they do on stage is done to meet their objectives.

- Encourage curiosity, problem solving. A lot of times, actors get their backs up out of fear when something is not working in a scene. So I encourage them to tackle obstacles with positive curiosity to solve the problem, like detectives.

VARIOUS OTHER SCENE WORK TECHNIQUES WE'VE ENCOUNTERED.

- If it's an intimate scene between two people, have them swap characters. It's a wonderful way to have them connect and understand what the other is saying to them.

- I ask them to do the scene using only breath. Trying their best to encapsulate the feeling or intention of the line through an audible breath. Then redo it with the lines and incorporating the breath.

- Tape the actors saying their lines, then play it for them as they move around the space responding to one another listening to the dialogue.

- Giving the beats/unit/section an active title for that beat helps the actors get invested and promotes active investigation. Like a bunch of really great cops in the room trying to solve the mystery.

HOW DO YOU DEAL WITH SILENCES AND BEATS THAT ARE WRITTEN INTO THE SCRIPT?

- Silence comes when we are shamed and there is no need for words.

- I put measures on them. A count for each. Three seconds for a beat and seven seconds for a silence. We play around with these counts, of course, but it's a wonderful way to explore what happens in those beats when they are required to fill that time.

- I will observe them as much as possible if they are guideposts and insights into what the playwright is trying to tell.

- What are they not saying or stopping themselves from saying in the silences?

WHEN IS IT TIME TO GET RID OF THE BOOKS?

- When rehearsing Shakespeare, I always get them to paraphrase in as simple language as possible.

- I ask them to read the scene and then we do a quick improv of it to filter down to the points that instinctively stuck out.

- For most plays I've directed I like to start with everyone mostly off book, but it depends what we're working on. Right now I'm on the other side of the director/actor parallel preparing for a Shakespearean role and never in my life have I wanted—as a director or an actor—to do as much table work as I am now.

- Ultimately the safety of the table has to be swept away and that's where, for me, physical improv comes into play. To me, it's one of the most important processes of theatre—discovering character or group movement within and without the confines of the text.

- Ideally we move into this gradually—I like Grotowski-influenced exercises like stream-of-consciousness warm-ups and slow-motion exercises. Later, we incorporate physical exercises that work across a spectrum of ideas: like using animal exercises, or trust-building physical exercises become important to the choreographic life of the play, which is just as important as any text being spoken.

DO YOU WORK SEQUENTIALLY?

- I do. I find it's not only helpful for me but also tremendously helpful for the actors, to give them a sense of time. How can you work on the end without knowing how and why you got there?

- I think there's a lot of value in working sequentially. Sometimes, in musicals especially, you learn a dance or music before you've stitched the piece together and you have to work backwards, but that is the nature of rehearsing musicals.

- I try my best to keep it all sequential and go moment to moment and beat by beat to layer and scaffold their emotional world and make sense of their actions.

- If you mean sequentially as in the order the play is written, generally yes, at least to start. I want the actors to understand the flow and rhythm of the play. If the timeline is told out of sequence, and if I think it will help the actors with their journey, I will rehearse scenes chronologically at least once.

- Sometimes . . . depends on the show. I usually start with the most complex or intricate group scene first and then go around it.

- For me, scheduling is a creative act. I have a very hard time letting a stage manager create the rehearsal schedule because the process depends on the project and must be strategically planned. But, I would say that I tend to work sequentially within certain sets or subsets of material, and non-sequentially in others. If the piece requires a lot of movement/ensemble work or live foley/vocalized sound,whether song or soundscape, then this work tends to form a foundational element of the whole project and is not typically sequential. It will be placed in regular intervals from the very beginning and throughout the process. We may start with a melodic theme, or developing together the physical and gestural "language" of the piece. Work of this nature requires time and repetition for it to sink into the bones, so it's important to thread it throughout the process. Because I am often asking the ensemble to collaborate in the creation of this material, we must build a secure base of trust and playfulness and rigour. Sometimes the depth of this work only becomes clear later in the process as it becomes deeply rooted. I then balance that work with intensive, focused scene work. With spoken text, I like to work sequentially, but always looking forward and backward as we consider what is impacting this particular moment.

HOW DO YOU HELP THE ACTORS BUILD CHARACTERS AND RELATIONSHIPS?

- Endless questions for the actors.

- Make the decision of who's driving the scene.

- Do the scene dozens of different ways and it will all stick with the actors.

- I create relationships through pictures. I think visually about relationships and so on. Do they start together and then go apart or do they begin apart and come together?

- All language fails so what is your body saying?

- Why does the character choose that particular word or language over another?

- What is their necessity to speak in public? The urgency to be heard?

- We are always trying to prove someone wrong, to have our say or state our perspective. Otherwise we won't speak.

- I like to exploit and figure out who the actor really is and try to bring the actor's nature out . . . so I can see how this ingredient will mix with the others.

- Ask questions until they have to make choices beyond first instincts and really confront one another.

- Talk to the actors a lot. Figure out where they are in their journey. Sometimes they'll say that they don't know, then you can guide them in a direction of self-discovery. Sometimes they are extremely eager to share where their character is going. I think it's helpful to ask questions when your actors are in a group and also when you can pull them aside during down time. Everyone develops a relationship with their characters in their own way, so try to find that way and help it grow.

DO YOU HAVE A TIMELINE FOR EACH SCENE? EACH DAY? DO YOU DEVIATE FROM THIS BECAUSE OF INSPIRATION OR ARE YOU BOUND BY TIME CONSTRAINTS?

- Time is your enemy when things are going great because you never have enough time, and when things are going wrong, you also don't have enough time. Planning and having a great stage manager to help you is very helpful.

- I need a fence, so time constraints are good for me. I can chapter out moments pretty easily. Whatever happens, we have to respect the time allotted, otherwise everything can fall apart.

- I am usually very specific about scheduling and I do this as part of my show prep. I break down my allotted rehearsal time into an ambitious but doable daily schedule that is my "best case scenario" strategic plan. It definitely starts my rehearsals off on the right track and, while I have rarely had to deviate from it, I do plan for some flextime so that I can adjust the schedule based on the needs of the show without derailing my big-picture plans.

DO YOU INTRODUCE PROPS AND COSTUMES EARLY? AND WHY DO OR DON'T YOU?

- As soon as possible. I hate the stuff but the stuff also changes everything. Actors love stuff. Let's try not to let them get too attached.

- It depends on how they are being used in the play. If we need costume pieces to block certain parts of the show, I'll ask for a rehearsal costume early. Same with props. The earlier, the better.

- I would love to introduce props and costumes as early as possible. It just gives the actor more time to familiarize themselves with the objects and also for the director to see if objects and costumes are telling the right story. It would save time during tech. Generally budget and resources are the hindrances here.

- When I enter a new project, whether it is an existing play or a devised piece, I am always interested in fluid storytelling. I am always looking for the most elemental, pared down way to communicate. What are the objects that are essential to this story? Can these few objects move and shape-shift to become different things at different moments? So I often find myself working on object-heavy shows, where objects (i.e., props, costume items, simple furniture pieces, etc.) are signifiers, and part of the exploration is figuring out how they can be used and what they mean in each context. They tell us something about location or time or character or subtext. A length of wood becomes a walking stick or a line in the sand, a bucket can hold water or be a mask/hiding place, a suitcase can be filled with clothes or papers or with dirt in which to plant a garden. In these cases, I definitely introduce these objects as early as possible, even from the very first day, as they become our tools. Once we've chosen the tools and they are there, available to us, they take on a life of their own. We find ways to use them that we may have never envisioned before they were in the room.

11. MONOLOGUES

HOW DO YOU APPROACH MONOLOGUES IN YOUR PIECES?

- I treat a monologue like a piece of music. We add rests and rhythm and breaths in the right places. It's also not a fixed product and can be altered at any time to suit the needs of the moment. It's always evolving.

- How do you approach humans in real life? I approach a monologue in the same way. For me, it's an ongoing investigation with the actor. Hopefully, by the end of a process, we've dug so far into the storytelling minutia of it that the words spin off the tongue naturally and with as much grace as the moment calls for. Achieving authentic truth is always the goal.

- I begin with basic questions: What/who are they responding to? What are they working through? What is the question of the monologue? Why do they need so many words to solve it? Then, of course, something drastic has to change by the end of the monologue.

- Monologues can have 100 moments. And you need to know what each is.

- What/where is the revelation or breakthrough?

- By having the actor identify each thought in the monologue and then having them discuss what comes in between the thoughts expressed in the monologue. I also have them play with experimenting which word to stress and to keep changing it up to see how it feels to say.

- I think of monologues as I would a book. Just as there are many chapters to the story in a book, there are many chapters to the story inside a monologue. For me, specifically identifying those chapters and understanding how they serve the story as a whole creates the detail and specificity needed for an actor to really bring a monologue to life in a magnetic way.

- I go for the words that give me the image first, and start from that. Movement exercise, or a melody could help to stretch it.

HOW ABOUT WHEN YOU ARE WORKING ON A MUSICAL? HOW DO YOU APPROACH SOLOS?

- Very similar approach as in monologue work. I always ask them to first say the lyrics as a monologue, which is usually quite difficult. Encourage them not to speak it in the rhythm of the song. Once they've explored it as a monologue, then they sing it with all the complexities and discoveries you would in a monologue.

- I ask them why they need to sing it instead of say it at this particular moment. What does the music do for them? Why do they need it? What would happen if they didn't sing it?

- Pull it back so you have somewhere to go. Don't give it all at the top or there will be no journey.

- Tell the story.

- Don't just play the tone of the song.

- Make sure there is a sense of purpose to what you are saying and singing.

- Because it's internal, it gets to be uglier. It's inside so it's the truth.

- Work against the beauty of the music to reveal the complicated guck inside you.

- Don't forecast the moment.

- Cook up a plan in the song if you need to.

- You can be feeling more complicated about it.

- Make the most muscular entrance into the song.

- Why do you *need* this song?

- Why does the character need to keep singing?

12. REHEARSALS

FAVOURITE REHEARSAL TECHNIQUES

- Put "No" in front of every word so you can find what is needed.
- Take a line out until you see why it happened. Why it's needed.
- Throw objects and sound cues that are foreign to the actors so they can react and play with them. It's directing without words.
- I use gestures to get people out of their heads. Then you can use those gestures when needed.
- In rehearsals, get actors to do things physically—six people to hold them up or give them resistance physically, and so on. Get the actors to get into their body after the text is done.

"FEEDING IN" TECHNIQUE

- Two actors are on stage then two people feed the lines to them from "offstage." This frees the actors from the book and allows them to move freely.
- Use large gestures to just get them moving, especially if they are blocked and you want to unlock the actor.

ATMOSPHERE EXERCISES

- First, walk on the grid.

  - After they've done this for a bit start adding:
  - Now the air is charged with mourning.
  - Become mourning (can be physical, might release a sound).
  - Imagine you are in Penn Station.
  - First you are commuting, in a rush—activate your destination—going to work or coming from work?
  - Add circumstances—this affects tempo—throw out examples like, "It's right after 9/11 and you are walking to the subway," or, "It's a Friday night or Monday morning." How does this affect the way you walk and interact?
  - Change that tempo.
  - Check the clock (which you place in the room).
  - List given circumstances—add a new element/circumstance
  - First day trains are running since 9/11—how does this change the atmosphere?
  - How do we create that atmosphere? Fill the air with a feeling. Of loneliness. How? Then when someone enters change it to something else. Danger? Continue to explore.

- Keep butcher paper all along the walls in rehearsals so actors, designers, and so on can draw or write whatever they want during rehearsals.

- I like to try scenes using proximity between the actors/characters. I try them very close to one another on the floor, then far away standing up, and little by little we find the distance that plays best for the characters and scene.

- I like to use Le Coq techniques. Put the actor into a body that they would *never* be in: bubble wrap meets a fire in a bus stop, for example.

- What is the secret behaviour of each character?

- Choose the opposite physicality reading to what you think the character would do.

- Get actors to do other characters so they understand what the other is saying.

- Go in a circle. One by one someone goes in the middle of the circle and closes their eyes and responds physically to whatever sounds the person in the outside circle makes. It's a great way of connecting everyone and getting them in tune with their surroundings.

- Choose four images that relate to the piece. Put an image on each wall. Then the actors move to each wall and see the image and react/respond physically to it. Then once they've explored all four, ask them to go to the image they most gravitate towards, the one they are plugging into.

- Now imagine that image surrounding you. It's everywhere you look. Respond to that as you walk around the room. How do you connect the image to your body? How does it respond? How does it respond when you approach or are confronted with other bodies that either share the same image or have another.

FAVOURITE TIDBITS OR ADVICE YOU REMIND YOURSELF OF OR GIVE TO THE ACTORS

- Don't moralize—the characters can't tell us what to think.
- Keep flipping the coin of the character.
- Resist the urge to "fix" things quickly. Trust that sometimes the actors know better than you. If you try to fix it fast, you'll lose many special moments.
- Identify the small action that leads to the big action.
- Start with a big open space then slowly close the doors till there's no other option to focus on.
- Just stay animated and alive.
- After a while actors get to realize what is right in their mouths.
- Never let the actors carry the words—let the words carry the actors.
- The audience can smell recycled truth.

- Live in a perpetual state of ambiguity and "I don't know" in rehearsals. Deprogram the actors.
- When something fails, don't go away from it, walk through it.
- You get your muscles from failure.
- Don't act the language: act the stakes.
- What are the good questions that open up the scene instead of close doors?
- The stage is a metaphoric space; theatre cannot reproduce reality.
- The urgency pushes the words out of the character.
- Stay in the gray zone. Make it muddy, then find your way out.
- Look for the narrative potential of objects, the poetry in objects.
- As adults we so rarely get to "play." Remember, the audience wants to play.
- Theatre allows the opportunity and privilege for an audience to witness/watch/observe people's behaviour when they are alone, truly alone. Like watching someone from a window. So explore real solitary behaviour. Behaviour is always interesting to watch on stage. Allow the audience to be the voyeur.
- Try not to repeat yourself. Allow the piece to inform the way you direct it instead of having a concept you impose on it.
- Surround yourself with the right people so you don't have to shout at them!

- Nothing is more exciting than combining elements simultaneously. Someone gets touched and the stage explodes with music and light and set change at that exact moment.

- Remember you are directing for the audience. But in the rehearsal room you must forget about them and try to direct for yourself. It's a fine balance.

- You do the work and the audience finds it.

- Try to find the truth in the storytelling. The human truth.

- What is the atmosphere of the language?

- There is fidelity of the words.

- Why is a word repeated?

- Can we land in the sound of the story?

- Find the "why" in the word. In that scene. In that moment. In that play.

- Work from the micro to the macro.

- How does the sound hit your body?

- If the writing is imagistic, then contrast what we are actually seeing.

- Don't replicate the image on the page.

- The second you give someone an objective like "find someone you are looking for," the focus becomes clear to audience too.

- Biology of emotions—physical behaviour might indicate an emotional state.

- It's dangerous to be one-sided or have an affinity for one part of the play and not interested in other parts. Don't just focus on one element that interests you.

- The first image that hit you when you read the script—always go back to it.

- A play is a series of moments that can last a second to a minute. Find the moment-to-moment work.

- Rehearsing is learning what you're *not* going to do.

- Respect what is going on in the room. Don't deny it.

- Write what keeps you up at night!

- The actor's job is to replicate spontaneous original thought.

- The minute you start thinking about a directing "style," you're in big trouble.

- Lighting in diagonals always works. It's emotional.

- You have to be transformed by the time you leave the show.

- Memorization comes from making choices. So don't make definitive choices too early.

- As a director you should relish acquiring information and continuing to learn.

- Start with questions. Explore the movement of the questions; pay attention to details. Ask a question. The answer is in your body.

- When you are done, ask yourself: What did I do? What did I see? How did I feel?

- The audience is paying eighty-five dollars to hear your verb!

- The cast needs repetition, not change.

- Anger leads to energy, and energy leads to action.

- Directors need one foot in the past (research) and one foot in the future.

- You have to learn the interpretation of the text.

- Attention to detail in the text is most important.

- Get the audience into the active nature of the story.

- Change the architecture. Punch the audience with image or something to get them into the story.

- Know what the intention is.

- Difference between subtext and surtext—everything is in the subtext. It's where all the information lives.

- Planning is for amateurs.

- You, the director, don't need to know everything.

- How can theatre create transcendence?
- Use circles and lines and repetition, composition, to create an emotional response/visceral reaction. Use geometry, symmetry.
- Two-thirds of the way through in theatre, mass, and so on, something happens
- Combine all your influences.
- Work in depth, images, layering—as in, using a volleyball net to double as barbed wire.
- What is the psychological nature of gesture?
- Show me brief, short seconds of real life, so believable that we believe this is the character.
- Brain and heart combined with the body is always the goal.
- Feeling is the most important. Theatre without feeling is dead.
- Shocking the audience is important.
- Make everything feel alive on stage.
- You have to stay a student all your life.
- Continue to train and warm-up with cast—intellectual, physical, vocal warm-ups
- Always set tasks that are impossible so you can travel longer to achieve them.

- Art does not exist without exercise, but exercise could not exist without art.

- Psychological and physical need to meet.

- Explode the scene from the inside.

- Make it as expressive as possible.

- Rhythm is vital.

- How does the rhythm of the play influence the performance?

- How true is the actor's breathing and speaking?

- Words are only an embellishment on the tapestry of movement. Movement is an embellishment on the tapestry of life. When the former two combine, theatre happens.

- The only way to answer the director's question is to improvise the scene—oral answers are worthless.

- Theatre is about being shocked and to make it happen you have to make your actors shock themselves.

- Contradictions are so important—love, hate, sex, and violence all mixed up.

- Filter as many situations and feelings through rehearsal using different techniques.

HOW DO YOU DEAL WITH A MOMENT THAT'S NOT WORKING?

- If a moment is not working I take it as a sign that there is a manner in which I am not serving the artists or the process. Finding the solution for that moment can only happen once I've identified how I need to adjust my part in the process.

- Ugh . . . . Lately I just walk away and come back to it later. Most of the time that works. If not, I try to find another opinion I can trust.

- Put it away for a minute if possible. If that's not possible, is there another approach? Can we let go and address it from a new angle? Are there other ideas in the room? Let's brainstorm. There are no bad ideas.

- If nothing tried is working and the actors don't have any thoughts, I leave the moment and sleep on it. I find that eventually the answer comes. Usually it boils down to simplifying.

- I close my eyes and listen to it. Usually, I'll find it there. If not, I can't work it to death. If we've reached an impasse, we will return to it on our designated "Punch Day" where we knock everything out before tech. Oftentimes, the solution appears between those times, which is always good.

- Sometimes a scene gets stuck when it becomes too cerebral or academic. This is when you can unlock a scene through physical work. You can release the scene physically and the actors can relate to one another in a new way.

- I follow Stephen King's advice and kill my darlings. This is difficult in theatre, for anyone in theatre—whether you're a director, a writer, or an actor. The moment that isn't working could be something you look at and go, "Yeah, that sucks, whatever, throw it in the rubbish pile," but it requires far more bravery to let something go if it's a cherished image, line, or movement that you really believed in.

- Ultimately you can't spend all day trying to shove a square peg into a round hole, and somehow, by holding on so tightly to the idea as you had imagined it at the start, it becomes suffocated and works even less than it did before. So it's better to let some air in and try something totally different in order to regain the joy and intrigue of navigating the moment.

- Oftentimes I find this newfound exploration helps me to circle back to the original idea I had, but without the rigidity that was keeping it from connecting to begin with.

HOW DO YOU DEAL WITH CONFLICT OR A "DIFFICULT" ACTOR?

- This, I find, is the hardest part of the job. There's no one single answer for this question, either, in my experience. The worst thing is for that actor to become isolated from the rest of the cast, however, so that's important to avoid. My goal is to make that actor feel like they're part of the ensemble, and getting them there can be via a number of paths.

- The best answer, though, is not to work with difficult actors in the first place. If they show themselves to be a problem early enough in the process that you can replace them, then replace them.

- Never bring it up with the rest of the cast present. That, I know for sure.

- Conflict is trust and stems from power struggle.

- I deal with conflict as compassionately as possible.

- Don't be reactionary. No matter what, as the director, you can't lose your cool. It's your job to keep the room safe and free from drama, instead of contributing to it.

HOW ABOUT CONFLICT BETWEEN ACTORS?

- Observe, then ask questions. Separately. Figure out the root of the problem. They may just be exhausted, or struggling with a particular scene. Don't let it fester.

- Again, make sure this is not made public. Find a time and space outside the rehearsal room to address the issue with only those involved.

- Honesty. This is always tricky and one should definitely have the stage manager involved. The stage manager is the first line in resolving conflict. If they are unable to resolve the situation, I will have a private chat with actors separately to see if I can find out the source of the issue. Being honest and kind are very important, as most problems arise from actors' own insecurities. Also making it about the well-being of the whole company, and not just individuals, usually helps. You don't want to single people out, and getting people to work towards a common goal outside of themselves is useful.

HOW DO YOU CREATE A SAFE SPACE TO PLAY AND EXPLORE WITH RISK OF FAILURE?

- One of the first things I tell my actors is that in the rehearsal process we are here to fail . . . and fail and fail again . . . Now, let's start.

- Say yes. One of the greatest lessons I learned from a director I worked with early in my career was how important it is for the director to be able to hold space for everyone in the room to move through their own artistic process in a manner that doesn't hold your own process hostage. We all have different needs as artists—we learn, create, and explore in different ways. Saying yes to the other artists in the room to give them the space they need to be the artist you've brought into the process is imperative to allow people to give you their best work.

- This is *always* the goal, isn't it! That needs to be clear from the very beginning. My hope is that I approach every project, every person, with love and compassion. So that we can do the hard work together. I'll never ask an actor to do anything on stage that I'm not willing to do myself.

- Don't be a dragon.

- Don't let sarcasm guide you when someone attempts something new. Your reaction will colour their next steps.

HOW DO YOU GET YOUR ACTORS TO GIVE YOU WHAT YOU WANT?

- Oh, man, this is hard . . . If I truly believe they are trying their best . . . that is all I can ask for, and I applaud them for that. If I sense that they aren't trying, I call them on it. Usually, after that they are more open to my direction.

- How can we all come from a place of giving and relinquish wanting?

- I find being blunt and honest and just asking for what I want generally works—a sense of humour also helps.

- Figure out who they are as people. Become very good at identifying interpersonal communication styles. Some actors might want you to be gentle and encouraging, while some actors might need a strong push.

WHAT LANGUAGE DO YOU FIND HELPFUL? IS THERE ANY SPECIFIC LANGUAGE YOU USE WITH THE ACTORS THAT YOU FIND WORKS BEST TO ACHIEVE RESULTS?

- Clear, concise language. If you aren't sure, don't bullshit. Just say, you aren't sure, but you'll figure it out.

- Three questions I always ask the actor in every moment: "What do I want? What's my obstacle? How am I going to get it?"

- Questions. Positivity.

- Use the words "clear" or "not clear" with the actors instead of "good."
- I tell the actors, "You're the experts of the inside world."
- What is the music of this character's/person's voice?
- What energy do they have when they enter the scene?
- Pressurize the moment or the talk.
- "What's important to me is ______________"
- "What interests me in this scene . . . or in this character . . . or in the show is _______"
- You can be feeling more complicated about it.
- I want to make sure the moment is happening for you.
- Heat up the moment.
- Use the real estate here.
- Be clear in your storytelling of the moment to moment.
- Don't forecast the moment.
- Always search for opportunity of feelings—to feel.
- More muscular attack on the language.

- I use phrases like: "Is there value in . . . "; "This might be a terrible idea but . . . "; "What would happen if . . . "; "We need to trial-and-error this . . . "

HOW DO YOU INCORPORATE MOVEMENT INTO THE PIECE?

- I incorporate live music, soundscape, and movement into most pieces I direct or create. They are evocative storytelling tools, but I always want to make sure that they serve a strong and clear dramaturgical function. They must move the story forward in some way, even if that dramaturgical function doesn't become clear until late in the play. It's important to acknowledge the unconscious, or subconscious, effect that music or sound and movement can have on a viewer. Repetitions and variations of particular gestures, physical sequences, or melodic lines trigger the autonomic nervous system and can complement text by communicating ideas on a sensory and intuitive level. In order to incorporate these effectively, you need time. Explorations of movement—physical embodiment—and music or sound are usually where I begin a rehearsal process. Sometimes these elements are preplanned, or possibilities are, but usually they are developed in collaboration with the performers, based on specific prompts and the performers' instinctual reactions to the material. I take note of those images, phrases, and moments that are evoking a key idea or emerging as a redolent motif. We latch on to those that communicate most strongly, they begin to recur and evolve and are gradually and carefully shaped and built into the piece—structured over the course of rehearsals through trial and error.

WHEN DO YOU DO A RUN-THROUGH?

- Typically I will do a run-through (or rather a "stumble-through") once we've completed the initial table work and after we've had a bit of time to touch on each scene or section individually. Something I do with some regularity now, instead of a read-through on the first night of rehearsal, is a "play-through." A play-through is exactly what it sounds like. Rather than sitting around a table, we are on our feet, usually in a large circle or on the taped-out stage space, with scripts in hand. The stage manager (or other volunteer) reads all the stage directions, and if you're in the scene you just enter the space and try to be fully present with the other people there. It's very improvisatory and low-stakes. It can feel like a bit of a disaster at the beginning, as people get their footing, but it doesn't take long for everyone to click in and begin to listen closely to what's happening, to be fully present and play. Relationships emerge and it encourages physicality and playfulness from the start. I find that I always make discoveries about the play when I do this, and it's a more lively and engaged way to begin a process.

INTO THE DARKNESS/TECHNICAL REHEARSALS—FROM THE DESIGNER'S PERSPECTIVE

HOW DO YOU PROCEED INTO TECH EFFICIENTLY? WHAT IS THE BEST WAY TO ENTER TECH REHEARSALS?

- Efficiency during tech rehearsals is key because you have to worry about the actors' time, the technicians' time, and so on.

- It's important to recognize which notes need to be solved now and which can be solved tomorrow.

- The director has to remember that, during tech, all the designers will be taking notes as well. But if the director does have a note, I don't mind them coming up to me and saying, "Hey, that didn't seem to work," so we can stop and fix it if needed, if it's a big enough thing to warrant that. If it's about the lights being too bright in one scene, then that can wait. If it's a note that you know is going to take a long time to address, then you should mention it so plans can be made to fix it after rehearsal or the next day. But ultimately, it's recognizing what note needs to stop the show and what note can wait.

DO YOU DRY TECH? DO YOU FIND IT HELPFUL?

- I definitely do a cue-to-cue with the director, with both lighting and scenic. I think dry tech is helpful, if for no other reason than to get some of the clunky bits out of the way before the actors are in the space. It helps with the efficiency of the tech, as well. If the tech screeches to a halt with the actors on stage, everyone feels a little uptight because we're wasting people's time. The more you can iron out those details before the actors step onto the stage the better.

WHO IS THE CAPTAIN DURING TECH: STAGE MANAGER OR DIRECTOR?

- There's the first day of tech where we're all in the room and getting a feel of what's going on up there. Then after that, once we've gone through the entire thing and spaced it and all the looks are right and we know how things are working, I want the director to step back and let the stage manager take charge.

- After that, I'd much rather the director give notes about what didn't work—give those directions to me, the stage manager, since we've already established some form of communication up to this point.

13. TECHNICAL REHEARSALS

CAN YOU TELL US SOME THOUGHTS ON YOUR TECH EXPERIENCES?

- Technical rehearsals can be daunting and laborious and frustrating; but it's also an exciting time when you can finally see all the elements together (costumes, lights, set, and staging). It's a wonderful time to see how and if all these separate departments meld into one and how they contribute and tell the story. Sometimes you find that the costumes distract from the story. Sometimes a piece of the set is too much. Sometimes it's a wig that needs tweaking. Look for what enhances the storytelling best.

- The rehearsal room becomes this safe cocoon while you're in there. Suddenly you're plunged into an entirely new environment where tape that indicated stairs becomes actual stairs. It's a drastic change. You must have tremendous patience during this period so people can adjust to that.

- So many moving parts and people meeting and working with one another for the first time—it sometimes takes a bit to figure out that collaboration.

- Make sure to at least introduce the entire crew by name to everyone so there is a moment of recognition and connection before the insanity of tech begins.

- In musicals especially, the synthesis of music and orchestra with lights and dancing and singing and technical aspects to create fluid and elegant transitions takes tremendous effort and patience.

WHO IS THE CAPTAIN DURING TECH: STAGE MANAGER OR DIRECTOR?

- The stage manager should be at the centre of the communication between designers, creative team, and actors.

- In larger regional theatres, there are sometimes dozens of crew and union members running around trying to build the show. It can be pandemonium if you don't find a way to streamline communication. In these instances, the production stage manager needs to be in control. Of course, you are still in charge of the artistic decisions, but the communication should be driven through the PSM. This was the hugest change for me from independent theatre to regional. It's a big jump, especially when dealing with union members.

WHEN DO YOU GIVE NOTES AND WHAT KINDS OF NOTES DO YOU GIVE TO KEEP THE DISCOVERIES FLOWING FOR THE ACTORS UP TO OPENING?

- It depends on the project and the moment. I tend not to hold back on notes at this stage of the game, but I do usually become more insistent about leaning into choices and being consistent when necessary. I'm also more likely to give explicit direction at this stage rather than ask questions and make new discoveries. Time is usually of the essence and actors usually crave this directness.

- At that point, we are refocusing our efforts. If an actor feels safe in their costume, I can ask questions that make them excited for the future, not spring something on them about their technique.

- Try not to give opposing notes from rehearsals during this time or it can embed doubts in the actors.

- Encourage the actors to keep searching and digging. Sometimes the new space itself can inspire new ideas and curiosities.

HOW DO YOU WORK WITH THE DESIGNERS DURING TECH?

- Collaboratively. Designers are amazing, and so much smarter than I am. They are also usually coming in with fresh eyes and I so appreciate their candour in the room.

- Remind everyone that change is good. Don't impose anything but continue the spirit of exploration, and remember that everyone is there to serve the story.

- I try to stay away from correcting actors during tech and just allowing the designers to do what they need to do. This is not my moment.

- I stay as calm as possible and let them feel like their work is not being judged or criticized.

HOW DO YOU KEEP THE ATMOSPHERE HAPPY AND PRODUCTIVE?

- I always start the day with some lighthearted banter, then buckle down and work in a very focused manner. I always keep my energy levels high and keep a sense of humour. I keep a fairly open rehearsal and any members of the team can feel free to pop in whenever they like. I will also entertain any and all offers from any member of the team. I acknowledge when I use someone else's ideas.

- By any means necessary.

- Take care of yourself. If you come in all freaked out, or angry, or whatever, it will seep out into the rehearsal process. Also, make an effort to keep "please" and "thank you" as a habit in the rehearsal room. We forget about that too often.

14. PREVIEWS

WHAT KIND OF CHANGES/NOTES DO YOU GIVE THE CAST? HOW DO YOU DECIDE WHICH ASPECTS TO FOCUS ON CHANGING DURING THIS PERIOD? OR DO YOU THINK ABOUT THAT AT ALL AND JUST CHANGE WHATEVER IS NECESSARY?

- Notes come when it's fully realized, because there is more to see and observe. But actors want repetition. Layer things in. Don't change things drastically.

- I listen for moments when the audience gets distracted and try to figure out why they happened. Then I will tackle those moments in rehearsal. How can the cast deny what is a clear response from an audience?

- I do what I can to clarify the storytelling. Whether that's acting moments, set, costumes, lights, or transitions.

15. OPENING NIGHT

DO YOU GIVE NOTES BEFORE THE SHOW? IF SO, WHAT KIND OF NOTES?

- I think theatre is always alive and in order to stay alive it needs to be adaptable and changeable. So until the second the lights go up on opening, I do what I need to do to achieve that. I use the previews to determine and gauge what I hear and see from my own perspective but also from the response to the audience. Setting moments in stone, unless it's from a technical and safety standpoint, is utter death in theatre.

- Usually I don't. It depends on the person and the note. Sometimes I will give some positive feedback on a moment and perhaps a push to keep moving in that direction, or a purely technical note—for example, you missed your light, or don't forget to move an object at a particular moment. I find that giving any significant note right before a show doesn't give time for the actor to process it. It's better to get those notes out the night before or at the latest in the morning before the show.

DO YOU GIVE THE CAST A RITUAL OR TASKS TO DO BEFOREHAND?

- I never mandate anything but I do encourage some sort of group warm-up to get them all connected.

- This is something you have to foster in rehearsals. If you don't have a daily ritual in rehearsals, you can't expect them to start in the theatre.

- I usually do some kind of fun physical group warm-up just to help relieve a little stress. And then I always thank the cast and team for their hard work and officially pass the show on to my stage manager. It's my way of letting go and also giving the power, and immense gratitude, to the SM.

16. AFTER THE STORM

AFTER OPENING NIGHT, THERE IS THE MOMENT OF RELEASE FROM A PROJECT. HOW DIFFICULT IS IT TO LET GO? OR NOT? ANY TIPS ON HOW TO LET GO?

- Before the show opens, especially in the last couple of weeks leading up to it, you often feel like God. Everyone needs you. You are fixing things. But once opening night is over you have to let go.

- The moment the show opens, you are dead weight.

- It's a terrible, tortuous moment once the show opens. You're job is done and there is a grieving process of letting go.

- I dive full force into my next project, hoping that will distract me from my grief.

- I love letting go. It is freeing for me, and freeing for the actors. Yes, it's hard, especially if the play is not where you want it to be, but if you have done the job right, the actors should be prepared enough to get where they need to go. Immediate self-care after opening is a great way to let go. Book a massage or hole up in your house and turn off social media for a day.

- I start applying for grants and getting ready for whatever is coming next. It's a sad day when the show is over, especially if it was a great experience.

- I have definitely learned over the years to let go more, to hold less tightly. Because I do tend to take on large, unwieldy shows, I have gotten better at planning and foreseeing where I might encounter difficulties and pushing early to find resolutions. If things are going relatively smoothly by the time we reach tech, I find it is easier to give it over on opening night. The more stress I feel during tech, the more prone I am to run over and over in my head what I could or should have done differently. It's always challenging if the final "product" doesn't quite live up to your hopes and expectations or what you have envisioned as the full potential of the piece, but I've learned to embrace the process and appreciate the journey. I try to think of performances as one of many points, or stopovers, in the process of making a piece, and actively take stock of both successes and lessons to apply the next time around.

DO YOU READ REVIEWS? HAVE ANY HELPED OR HINDERED YOUR PROGRESS OR NEXT PIECE?

- I do everything I can to *not* read them. It never works. As the old saying goes, "If you believe the good ones, you have to believe the bad ones."

- I've found that sometimes the worst reviews have some shred of constructive input that has helped me. You will know instinctively what resonates with you and will help you in the future.

- I would be lying if I said no. How can you not read them? Unfortunately they are the lifeblood for most productions. I try to be open and sometimes, in retrospect, once the dust has cleared, I will find a morsel of truth in some of the harshest of critiques. Still, I hate them.

17. KEEPING YOURSELF INSPIRED

HOW DO YOU KEEP INSPIRED AND EDUCATED BETWEEN GIGS? ANY TECHNIQUES TO SHARE?

- I watch movies. I go to theatre, art galleries, museums, concerts, sporting events.
- I live my life and keep my tank full of experiences outside theatre. It's important to have a balance.
- I travel as much as I can afford. I'm always inspired by what I don't know or haven't experienced before.
- The technique of living.

FROM THE MOVEMENT-BASED DIRECTOR'S PERSPECTIVE

I asked Allyson McMackon some of these same questions since I wanted to compare her answers as a director whose lens is much more movement based than others to see if they would be any different. Here are her answers.

WHAT ARE THE FIRST EXERCISES YOU DO WITH THE ACTORS?

- My work is physical, so all of the exercises are physical. I do a warm-up that I have done for twenty-five years to get the body present, strong, and available and then I begin with impulse work and the work that I do with Theatre Rusticle that is called source work or "river work." All are improvisations connecting the imagination to the body and expression. For actors I have worked with before, it's all shorthand and the work can be connected directly and quickly to the text or character we're working with. If they are new to me, there is a little teaching component of introducing the work and then building on it. We don't do table work with my company, so the physical work in relation to image, character, situation, and so on, is all critical and very much the first thing we do.

HOW DO YOU HELP THE ACTORS BUILD RELATIONSHIPS AND CHARACTERS?

- Again, all physical work and all based on play. I like to start in a solo fashion, however, with the actors working very much on their own stream in order to get it strong and rooted. Then we begin games with sticks, opening up eye contact, and improvising together. The river is a way to build character directly by sourcing physical language, vocabulary, gestures, bodies, voices, and so on and then finding the expression. The process nurtures relationship and character implicitly because we begin with the bones and muscles. The head and ideas about character and relationship are not really on the table. It's all built on its feet, so character and relationships have an authenticity and engagement that is energized.

WHAT LANGUAGE DO YOU FIND HELPFUL?

- Not sure how to answer this question. We have to develop the working language in the room and, for me, that means the ability to speak plainly, respectfully, and with transparency. My language is very much gestural and built on metaphor. In physical work if we can't speak plainly and also discover the language and ways to speak as we go, we're doomed.

WHEN IT'S NEARING END-OF-DAY AND EVERYONE'S LOSING STEAM, DO YOU: JUST PUSH THROUGH THOSE MOMENTS; USE THEM TO RUN THROUGH THINGS YET AGAIN AT THE RISK OF EXHAUSTING PEOPLE; LET PEOPLE OUT EARLY? OR ARE THERE BETTER WAYS TO USE THAT TIME?

- I never push through unless we're really far behind. I am not a fan of exhaustion. I can't work that way and I know the company can't. The best ways to use the time are to create gestation periods, frameworks where the actor can gather and reconnect or suss out what we did physically. An exhausted company is of no use.

WHEN DO YOU DO A RUN-THROUGH?

- When we're ready. I like to review, daily, what we've built, so the actors are always running some little sequence. The big run happens when the show is built. We need accurate timing and the actors need to be able to fall into the world of the show full on.

HOW DO YOU PROCEED INTO TECH EFFICIENTLY?

- I'm lucky that my designers are in the room a lot with me. We are real collaborators so I never feel like there are surprises. Our communication and decision-making makes the tech efficient and clear.

WHO IS THE CAPTAIN? DO YOU ALLOW THE STAGE MANAGER TO TAKE OVER?

- After opening, yes. There is a period of weaning that is important. I rely heavily on my SM and trust her implicitly.

WHAT KIND OF CHANGES OR NOTES DO YOU GIVE THE CAST? CREW?

- Whatever we need.

HOW DO YOU DECIDE WHICH ASPECTS TO FOCUS ON CHANGING DURING THIS PERIOD? OR DO YOU THINK ABOUT THAT AT ALL AND JUST CHANGE WHATEVER IS NECESSARY?

- It's really whatever is necessary. Ideally by a preview situation, I am looking for a show that could open and run at any time during our run. My notes during previews are historically small, unless something really terrible happens. Audiences help me see new things, so notes can come up with regard to things the audiences may make us accountable for that we did not anticipate or could use more attention.

DO YOU GIVE NOTES BEFORE OPENING? IF SO, WHAT KIND OF NOTES?

- No. I hug everyone or leave cards in secret and let the show go. I don't like rehearsing on opening and usually we're in a place where we don't need to. We have to be so mindful of people's physical energy in our shows. Pulling back is sometimes better.

DO YOU GIVE THE CAST A RITUAL OR TASKS TO DO BEFOREHAND?

- I say, "lotsa breath," "see you on the other side," "find what you need to say."

AFTER OPENING NIGHT, THERE IS THE MOMENT OF RELEASE FROM A PROJECT. HOW DIFFICULT IS IT TO LET GO? OR NOT?

- Depends on the show. We did a production of *Our Town* in 2017 that I loved and that felt seminal and it was not too difficult to let go of. It felt complete, so it was a little easier. I just finished a production of *Threepenny Opera* with some musical theatre students at Sheridan College, and I am missing them and having a very hard time letting go of the show. It, too, felt complete, but I still want to get back in.

DO YOU READ REVIEWS? HAVE ANY HELPED OR HINDERED YOUR PROGRESS OR NEXT PIECE?

- I always read them. As a producer, I need to. I don't give them that much value, I have to say. They have helped progress, but on a creative level, they don't do much. As a younger person, I felt just debilitated by bad or no reviews. Now, I stand tall in my work regardless of the review.

ANY TECHNIQUES TO CONSTANTLY KEEP YOU INSPIRED AND EDUCATED BETWEEN GIGS?

- So hard right now . . . but I have to move. I have been studying gyrotonic for four to five years now and it keeps me myself and in my body versus in the body that everyone else received during a rehearsal period. It keeps me plugged in. Because my "off" life is full of care-giving my husband, the doing nothing, thinking nothing is actually a gift and it keeps me inspired. I see theatre. I see dance, music. I walk. I try to connect with and make a little sense of the world.

CLOSING REMARKS

So there it all is. I hope you were inspired. Or ignited. Or agitated. Or all of it. Because it's up to us to keep this ancient tradition alive in this age of Netflix. To continue to tell stories to people who will listen and to those who need to listen, like we did around the fire for millions of years. It's our job to stoke the perpetual theatrical flames and keep them burning. Theatre, in this technological age, feels in constant peril of extinction. It's up to us to continue the work.

Some people create theatre for fun; some for survival. Some change lives. Or legislation. Or minds. Or hearts. Or souls. But it is always about change. It's about connection—our hearts beating together in a room. Feeding off one another. Reflecting one another. It's about us sitting in front of that fire and sharing stories with others. If we don't do it, who will?

Every year we end the Lab in one of our traditional circles where we pass a squishy toy shaped like a tomato (it's actually a stress ball that we found the first year and used as a "conch" and it just stuck) and throw it to each Labbie to give a final thought of the week and experience. Some people give thanks, some take their moment to look at each and every one of us, and others share a thought or idea that sparked for them that week.

Here is mine.

Thank you to all the phenomenal artists who contributed to this book and have passed through the Lab over the last decade. Each connection and word has imprinted itself into my psyche and been tattooed onto my theatrical soul. The passion and dedication and rigour that I've seen has been awe-inspiring. It's a privilege to share your words and minds and souls with the people who read this. Readers, I hope the ideas and words you've read become embedded in you as they have in me. These artists have seeped their way into my theatrical DNA, and I am humbled and grateful to you all.

Now go. Make theatre. Tell the stories. It's up to us. I throw the squishy tomato toy to you now . . . Catch it.

THANK-YOUS

Always, and most importantly, thank you to my mother, Dimitra Argiros, who has always been my constant source of strength and inspiration and the reason I have had the ability to pursue my dreams. To my other sources of inspiration: my sisters, Alexandra Tsitsias-Rotskas and Georgia Tsitsias-Fineman; my nephews, Aaron and Josh; my other rock, Kevin Grillo; and all my friends who've listened to me chat away incessantly about this process with open ears, especially Sue Dunstan, Mark Allan, Shelly Meichenbaum, Donna Marie Baratta, and Lisa Baylin. To Richard Rose, who has generously donated the Tarragon Theatre Studios to us since the inaugural Lab. To the Luminato Festival, who have partnered with us the last several years and donated countless tickets to their shows for all our Labbies and given us tremendous access to their artists. To all the members of my steering committee and artistic associates over the years. To our outstanding stage managers, Gloria Mok, Victoria Wang, and especially Daniel Bennett for his constant smiles in the middle of the madness. To every guest artist who has shared their experience, wisdom, and anecdotes with us, and, of course, to the Labbies, the heart and soul of it all, who pour their passion and guts each and every year into this Lab and provide one another and the world with theatrical magic. Thanks to Elif Işıközlü for founding the Lab with Esther and me. And most of all, thank you to my partner-in-crime and brilliant collaborator, Esther Jun, who has stood side by side with me as co-artistic director all these years. We took the seed of an idea and created a ten-year journey together with this passion project. I could not have done this without you. Eternally grateful to share this wild ride with you. To

Playwrights Canada Press—Blake Sproule and Annie Gibson—for the tremendous support, faith, and effort they put into publishing this book. Lastly, my undying gratitude to the visionary and theatrical titan, Anne Cattaneo, the mother of the Labs, who had the inspiration to start it all in the first place. You've created an unprecedented space for exchange and created a global network of artists, shaping the landscape of the theatrical world in ways we can't begin to imagine. Thank you from all of us. It's because of you that any of it exists.

SPECIAL THANKS TO

Richard Beaune
Robert A.K. Gonyo
Elizabeth Kirkland
Fiely Matas
Nancy McAlear
Allyson McMackon
Adam Spencer
Laura Tesman Gillette
Leta Tremblay
Sam Wilson

OUR INCREDIBLE STEERING COMMITTEE OVER THE YEARS

Donna Marie Baratta
Heather Cant
Andrea Donaldson
Allegra Fulton
Stephanie Graham
Andrew Lamb
Shelly Meichenbaum
Jen Quinn
Rupal Shah
Matthew Tiffin

ALL OUR LABBIES OVER THE YEARS

Manolis Antonio
Lara Arabian
Aviva Armour-Ostroff
Sahar Assaf
Donna Marie Baratta
Mimi Barcomi
Herbie Barnes
Megan Barrios
Jerry Beal
Georgina Beaty
Richard Beaune
Conrad Belau
Justen Bennet
Rebecca Benson
Tamara Bernier Evans
Alice Bever
Catherine Blake Smith
Heather Braaten
Erin Brandenburgh
Wesley Broulik
Briana Brown
Christine Brubaker
Colin Bruce Anthes
Kent Burnham
Katia Café-Fébrissy
Heather Cant
Joao Carrolo
Jill Carter
Rod Ceballos
Kristy Chambrelli

Brenley Charkow
Harmony Cohen
Amanda Connors
Trevor Copp
Nick Crisafulli
Brandon Crone
Jeff Culbert
Evan Cummings
Rebecca Cunningham
Rozie Curtis
Chelsea Dab Hilke
Katrina Darychuk
Heather Davies
Joanna Doak
Andrea Donaldson
Charlotte Drover
Marissa Emma Smith
Sten Erik
Zoe Erwin-Longstaff
Sabrina Everett
Floranina Ezzell
Alex Fallis
Kayla Feldman
Joel Fishbane
Monique Fisher
Genevieve Fleming
Gianna Formicone
Jessie Fraser
Teri-Lynn Friesen
Allegra Fulton
Annie G. Levy
Brian Gillespie
Jessica Glanfield
Ara Glen Johansen
Sam Godfrey
Valmai Goggin
Amanda Goldberg
Robert A.K. Gonyo
Charlotte Gowdy
Taylor Graham
Jack Grinhaus
Graydon Gund
John Gundy
Cory Haas
Chelsea Haberlin
Ingrid Hansen
Alix Harris
Michele Hawkins-Jones
Julia Heinrichs
Ryan G. Hinds
Janet Howe
Patrick Hughes
Jennifer Hunter
Lois Hunter
Kate Hurman
Melee Hutton
Shanti Ikwe Gonzales
Cole J. Alvis
Christopher Jackman
Pomme Johansson-Corvellec
Charlie Johnson
Kelly Johnston
Kendra Jones
Nancy Jones
Pam Joyce
Mimi Kammer
Liam Karry
Anthony Kennedy

Michelle Kennedy
Ilana Khanin
Jamie King
Lillian King
Alan Kinsella
Elizabeth Kirkland
Janet Kish
Sarah Kitz
Kevin Klassen
Conrad Kluck
Ann Kreitman
Anita La Selva
Ulla Laidlaw
Courtney Laine Self
Jeannette Lambermont-Morey
Mika Laulainen
SG Lee
Susan A. Lock
Daniel Macdonald
Ken MacKenzie
Natasha MacLellan
Deborah Magid
Buffie Main
Gabe Manthrop
Marta Mari
Heather Marie Annis
Dian Marie Bridge
Natasha Martina
Alexsandra Marzocca
Fiely Matias
Alisa Matlovsky
Heather May
Nancy McAlear
Clara McBride
Christine McBurney
Tamara McCarthy
Charlie McGrath
Aileen McGroddy
Griffin McInnes
Julie McIsaac
Brenda McLean
Laura McLean
Kenn McLeod
Brendan McMurty-Howlett
Jordan Merkur
Gabrielle Metcalf
Anna Michael
Jon Michaelson
Nicole Miller Marks
Antonio Miniño
Jenny Montgomery
Leora Morris
Elenna Moseff
Macey Mott
Robert Motum
Nicola Murphy
Ciarán Myers
Chang Nai Wen
Dawn Naser
Elise Newman
Elizabeth Newman
Kristina Nicoll
Sonia Norris
Jay Northcott
Morgan Norwich
Dayane Ntibarikure
Marilo Nuñez
Zita Nyarady

Ingrid Oslund
Catherine Paskell
Peter Pasyk
John Jack Paterson
Rachel Peake
Eric Perron
Christina Pichler
Leonie Pichler
Megan Piercey Monafu
Sean Pollock
Bo Powell
Jefferey Pufahl
Jennifer Quinn
Maya Rabinovitch
Karin Randoja
Alex Randrup
Nicole Ratjen
Benjamin Rexroad
Ali Richardson
Jennifer Roberts
Sheena Robertson
Emily Rollie
Jesse Roth
Mandy Roveda
Jason Schlafstein
Nathan Schwartz
Tyler Seguin
Julia Siedlanowska
Daniel Sileshi
Rouvan Silogix
Anthony Simpson Pike
Michela Sisti
Ralph Small
Laureen Smith
Shana Solomon
Jodi Sprung-Boyd
Isabella Stefanescu
Rebecca Steiner
Jay Stern
Jonathan Strayer
Taylor Sutherland
Tony Tambasco
Chadwick Taylor
Eric Taylor
Samantha Tella
Harrison Thomas
Sarah Thorpe
Matthew Tiffin
Alec Toller
Julie Tomaino
Barbara Tomasic
David Tompa
Leta Tremblay
Chiamaka Ugwu
Raluca Urea
Thomas Usher
Paul Van Dyck
Rona Waddington
Dawn Walton
Caroline Williams
Joanne Williams
Kaitlin Williams
Danielle Wilson
Lee Wilson
Samuel Wilson
Cole Wimpee
Chris Woodworth
Vici Wreford-Sinnott

ALL OUR GUEST ARTISTS OVER THE YEARS

Chris Abraham
Philip Akin
Cole J. Alvis
Stafford Arima
Daniel Brooks
Nicole Brooks
Erin Brubacher
Ronnie Burkett
Naomi Campbell
Jill Carter
Anne Cattaneo
Ben Chaisson
Leah Cherniak
Micheline Chevrier
Derrick Chua
Kim Collier
Mitchell Cushman
Vincent de Tourdonnet
Joanna Falk
Brad Fraser
Dean Gabourie
Dennis Garnhum
Sky Gilbert
Linda Griffiths
Brendan Healy
Peter Hinton
Eda Holmes
Matthew Jocelyn
Jane Johansen
Anika Johnson
Britta Johnson
Natalia Kaliada
Beth Kates
Jillian Keiley
Akram Khan
Jung Kim-Hye
Camelia Koo
Jeannette Lambermont-Morey
Nina Lee Aquino
Richard Lee
Daniel MacIvor
Ross Manson
Jackie Maxwell
Allyson McMackon
Jim Millan
Hannah Moscovitch
Yvette Nolan
Lisa O'Connell
Morris Panych
Soheil Parsa
Steven Prengels
Brian Quirt
Michelle Ramsey
Tina Rasmussen
Joseph Recinos
Siobhan Richardson
Josephine Ridge
Andrea Romaldi
Richard Rose
Thomas Ryder Payne
Kat Sandler
Albert Schultz
Erin Shields
Bill Shmuck

Lyon Smith
Julie Tepperman
Judith Thompson
Kelly Thornton
Emma Tibaldo
Lezlie Wade
Michael Wheeler
Aaron Willis
David Yee

ALL THE ACTORS WHO HAVE WORKED WITH US

Wade Bogert-O'Brien
Jasmine Chen
Dillan Chiblow
Sochi Fried
Allegra Fulton
Cynthia Jimenez-Hicks
Chanakya Mukherjee
Miquelon Rodriguez
Rachel VanDuzer
Jeff Yung

ALL THE GUEST ARTISTS FROM LINCOLN CENTER THEATER DIRECTORS LAB

Andre Bishop
Lev Dodin
Sheldon Epps
Andy Paris
Sarah Ruhl
Ntozake Shange
Bartlett Sher
Kate Whoriskey
George C. Wolfe

ABOUT THE CONTRIBUTORS

Born in Toronto, **Naomi Campbell** grew up in Sackville, New Brunswick, and Ottawa, and has called Toronto home for the last thirty-five years. She has a degree in political science from the University of Toronto and over thirty years of programming, touring, and producing experience, both nationally and internationally. She has worked with a range of performing arts companies including Nightswimming, Mammalian Diving Reflex, DVxT Theatre, the late Paul Bettis's Civilized Theatre, and VideoCabaret, and with numerous independent artists. She's also worked at festivals throughout her career including Bread and Butter (Guelph, 1989), World Stage (1994–2000), and as curator for Buddies in Bad Times's Rhubarb! (2003) and Magnetic North Theatre Festival's Industry Series (2008–10). Naomi joined Luminato as company manager in 2011 and subsequently produced large-scale productions for the festival including *The Life and Death of Marina Abramović* and *Apocalypsis*. In 2013 she was appointed Luminato's first ever director of artistic development, commissioning, developing, and producing works for the festival. She was appointed deputy artistic director in 2017 and artistic director in 2018.

Jill Carter (Anishinaabe/Ashkenazi) is a theatre practitioner and researcher, currently cross appointed to the Centre for Drama, Theatre & Performance Studies; the Transitional Year Programme; and Indigenous Studies at the University of Toronto. She works with many members of Tkaron:to's

Indigenous theatre community to support the development of new works and to disseminate artistic objectives, processes, and outcomes through community-driven research projects. Her scholarly research, creative projects, and activism are built upon ongoing relationships with Indigenous elders, artists, and activists, positioning her as witness to, participant in, and disseminator of oral histories that speak to the application of Indigenous aesthetic principles and traditional knowledge systems to contemporary performance. The research questions she pursues revolve around the mechanics of story creation, the processes of delivery, and manufacturing affect. More recently, she has concentrated upon Indigenous pedagogical models for the rehearsal studio and the lecture hall, the application of Indigenous [insurgent] research methods within performance studies, the politics of land acknowledgements, and land-based dramaturgies/activations/interventions. Jill also works as a researcher and tour guide with First Story Toronto; facilitates land acknowledgement, devising, and land-based dramaturgy workshops for theatre makers; and performs with the Talking Treaties Collective (Jumblies Theatre, Toronto).

Anne Cattaneo is the dramaturge of Lincoln Center Theater and the creator and head of the Tony Honors for Excellence in Theatre nominated Lincoln Center Theater Directors' Lab. A three-term past president of the Literary Managers and Dramaturgs of the Americas, she is the recipient of LMDA's first Lessing Award for lifetime achievement in dramaturgy. She has worked widely as a dramaturge on classical plays with directors such as Bartlett Sher, Robert Wilson, Adrian Hall, Jack O'Brien, Robert Falls, Mark Lamos, and JoAnne Akalaitis. As the director of the Playworks Program at the Phoenix Theater during the late 1970s, she commissioned and developed plays by Wendy Wasserstein (*Isn't It Romantic*), Mustapha Matura (*Meetings*), and Christopher Durang (*Beyond Therapy*). For the Acting Company, she created two projects: *Orchards* (published by Knopf and Broadway Play Publishing), which presented seven Chekhov stories adapted for the stage by Maria Irene Fornes, Spalding Gray, John Guare, David Mamet, Wendy Wasserstein, Michael Weller, and Samm-Art Williams, and *Love's Fire* (published by William Morrow) a series of responses to Shakespeare sonnets by Eric Bogosian, William Finn, John Guare, Tony Kushner, Marsha Norman, Ntozake Shange, and Wendy Wasserstein. Her own translations of twentieth century German playwrights include Brecht's *Galileo* (Goodman Theater, 1986, starring Brian Dennehy) and Botho Strauss's *Big And Little* (Phoenix production starring Barbara Barrie, published by Farrar, Straus and Giroux). She is currently on the faculty at Juilliard. In July 2011, she was awarded the Margo Jones Medal given annually to a "citizen of the theater who has demonstrated a significant impact, understanding and affirmation of the craft of playwriting, with a lifetime commitment to the encouragement of the living theatre everywhere."

Chang Nai Wen, trained in Taiwan, Edinburgh, and Germany, works internationally as a freelance director and producer. In 2008, she founded the independent company Sisyphos, der Flugelefant (SdF) in Berlin, which constantly investigates the most diverse facets of "home" through various performative and participatory formats. As a founding member of the international directors' collective the World Wide Lab (WWL), she has developed different methods of co-directing with ten other directors from New York City, Rome, Syros, New Taipei City, Toronto, Thunder Bay, and Berlin. Since 2016, as a part of the model project ZUsammenKUNFT—a coalition of asylum seekers, social workers, and creative artists in a German Red Cross–run building in Berlin—she has created the cooperative networking format MindLab# in collaboration with Artist Training for Professionals of UdK Career College. The aim is to bring together Berlin-based artists and new arrivals from different artistic disciplines in a practical collaborative context, using methods from the performing and visual arts. She later applied such playful and creative environments to an ongoing theatre workshop called Young Mind Lab for ages four to eighteen, run by SdF artists, some of whom found their way to SdF through MindLab#. In the summer of 2019, SdF and WWL came together to create a participatory performance with the participants of Young Mind Lab, exploring Berlin from the perspectives of young people of various cultural backgrounds at FELD—Theater for Young Audiences. Chang is a member of the International Forum of Theatertreffen in Berlin, the Lincoln Center Theater Directors Lab in New York, and a board member of Berlin Independent Performing Arts Association (LAFT Berlin).

Brad Fraser is a maverick, openly gay playwright born in Edmonton, Alberta. His early work about teenagers living on the margins, entitled *Mutants*, was produced at Edmonton's Walterdale Playhouse in 1980. He then wrote *Wolfboy* for Paul Thompson's Theatre Passe Muraille. Brad Fraser hit the big time with *Unidentified Human Remains and the True Nature of Love* in 1989 (Alberta Theatre Projects, directed by Bob White). The work became a sensation playing across the country and in London and Chicago. The French translation of *Unidentified . . .* was a hit at Théâtre de Quat'Sous. It was made into a movie by Denys Arcand in 1994, with a screenplay by Fraser. Recently, the play was produced in Brazil in Portuguese. In a provocative and often humorously angry way, Brad Fraser has spent much of his career to date throwing stones at the status quo. Other plays include *The Ugly Man* (Alberta Theatre Projects, subsequently in Brighton, London, Edinburgh, Brussels, and New York) and *Poor Super Man* (Ensemble Theatre, Cincinnati). *Martin Yesterday* has been performed in Toronto, Edmonton,

Manchester, and San Francisco. His adaptation of the movie *Outrageous* opened at Canadian Stage in autumn 2000, and his commissioned work *Snake in Fridge* opened at the Royal Exchange Theatre in Manchester, England, also in autumn 2000. *Cold Meat Party* and *True Love Lies* also premiered at the Royal Exchange. The latter was nominated for best new play at the *Manchester Evening News* Theatre Awards. It premiered in Canada at Factory Theatre and was nominated for best new production. *5 @ 50* premiered at the Royal Exchange in 2011. Its Canadian premiere was by Ruby Slippers Theatre and Zee Zee Theatre, Vancouver, in 2016. *Kill Me Now* premiered at Workshop West Theatre. Fraser has also been a scriptwriter for the TV gay sitcom, *Queer as Folk*. Brad Fraser has twice received the Chalmers Award (*Unidentified* . . . and *Poor Super Man*) and was nominated for the Governor General's Literary Award (*Poor Super Man*, 1995). He is a five-time winner of the Alberta Culture Playwriting Competition and five-time winner of the Alberta Writers' Guild Drama Award. He also received the London *Evening Standard* Award for best new play and the Los Angeles Critics' Award (both for *Unindentified . . .*) His plays are published by NeWest Press and Playwrights Canada Press.

Director, dramaturge, and playwright **Peter Hinton** has worked across Canada with many theatre companies. He has been the associate artistic director at Theatre Passe Muraille and the Canadian Stage Company in Toronto, artistic director of Playwrights Theatre Centre in Vancouver, the dramaturge in residence at Playwrights' Workshop Montréal, and artistic associate of the Stratford Festival. From 2005 to 2012 he was artistic director of the National Arts Centre English Theatre, where he created a resident English theatre company with actors from across the country and programmed the NAC's first season of Canadian plays. His own plays for the stage include *Façade*, *Urban Voodoo* (written with Jim Millan), and a trilogy of three full-length plays entitled *The Swanne—George III: The Death of Cupid* (2002), *Princess Charlotte: The Acts of Venus* (2003), and *Queen Victoria: The Seduction of Nemesis* (2004). Eleven years in the making, all three plays premiered under his direction at the Stratford Festival. In 2006, he co-created with Domini Blythe, and directed the solo work *Fanny Kemble*, about the life of the famous British actress and abolitionist. Peter has also written the librettos for two operas with composer Peter Hannan: *The Diana Cantata*, and *120 Songs for the Marquis de Sade* (awarded the Alcan Performing Arts Award in 2002). Since 1985 he has directed over eighty productions of new plays, classical texts and operas, including premieres of works by Allen Cole (*Hush*, *The Crimson Veil*), Blake Brooker (*Serpent Kills*), John Mighton (*Possible Worlds*), Michael McKenzie (*Geometry in Venice*), and Marie Clements (*Burning Vision*). His production of Gloria Montero's *Frida K.* premiered at Toronto's Tarragon Theatre in 1995 and subsequently played to sold-out houses in Canada, Mexico City, and Madrid. His productions have twice been invited to the prestigious Festival TransAmériques in Montreal: Greg MacArthur's *girls! girls! girls!* in 2001, and Marie Clements's *Burning Vision* in 2003. In 2007, he partnered with Britain's Royal Shakespeare Company in the world premiere of Margaret Atwood's *The Penelopiad*. In 2009, he directed Sam Shepherd's *Buried Child* in a National Arts Centre and Segal Centre for Performing Arts co-production. He made his directing debut at the Shaw Festival in 2011 with *When the Rain Stops Falling*. He returned in 2013 to direct Oscar Wilde's *Lady Windermere's Fan*. Other Shaw directing credits include *Cabaret*, *Pygmalion*, and *An Octoroon*—a startling interrogation and reversal of racial stereotypes by Branden Jacobs-Jenkins. In 2018, he directed a Canadian adaptation of *Oh, What a Lovely War!* by Joan Littlewood, with clowns playing soldiers fighting in significant Canadian battles, and exposing racist policies on the exclusion of Black and Indigenous volunteers. In March 2017, he directed the premiere of *The Millennial Malcontent* by Erin Shields at the Tarragon Theatre. For the Canadian Opera Company, he directed a revisionist production of *Louis Riel* by Harry Somers (music) and Mavor Moore (libretto). It questions why we need to keep retelling our history, and focuses on the colonial expropriation of Indigenous land, more than the conflict between French-speaking Metis and English-speaking federal politicians. Hinton was the recipient of the Jessie Richardson Award for directing in 1995 for his production of Gordon Armstrong's *Scary Stories*. In 2009, he was made an Officer of the Order of Canada.

Akram Khan is one of the most celebrated and respected dance artists today. In just over eighteen years he has created a body of work that has contributed significantly to the arts in the UK and abroad. His reputation has been built on the success of imaginative, highly accessible, and relevant productions such as *Until the Lions*, *Kaash*, *iTMOi* (in the mind of igor), *DESH*, *Vertical Road*, *Gnosis*, and *zero degrees*. An instinctive and natural collaborator, Khan has been a magnet to world-class artists from other cultures and disciplines. His previous collaborators include the National Ballet of China, actress Juliette Binoche, ballerina Sylvie Guillem, choreographers/dancers Sidi Larbi Cherkaoui and Israel Galván, singer Kylie Minogue, visual artists Anish Kapoor, Antony Gormley, and Tim Yip, writer Hanif Kureishi, and composers Steve Reich, Nitin Sawhney, Jocelyn Pook, and Ben Frost. Khan's work is recognized as being profoundly moving, in which his intelligently crafted storytelling is effortlessly intimate and epic. Described by the *Financial Times* as an artist "who speaks tremendously of tremendous things," a highlight of his career was the creation of a section of the London 2012 Olympic Games Opening Ceremony that was received with unanimous acclaim. As a choreographer, Khan has developed a close collaboration with the English National

Ballet and its artistic director, Tamara Rojo. He created the short piece *Dust*, part of the *Lest We Forget* programme, which led to an invitation to create his own critically acclaimed version of the iconic romantic ballet *Giselle*. Khan has been the recipient of numerous awards throughout his career including the Laurence Olivier Award, the Bessie Award (New York Dance and Performance Award), the prestigious ISPA (International Society for the Performing Arts) Distinguished Artist Award, the Fred and Adele Astaire Award, the Herald Archangel Award at the Edinburgh International Festival, the South Bank Sky Arts Award, and six Critics' Circle National Dance Awards. Khan was awarded an MBE for services to dance in 2005. He is also an honorary graduate of the University of London as well as Roehampton and De Montfort Universities, and an honorary fellow of Trinity Laban. Khan is an associate artist of Sadler's Wells, London, and Curve, Leicester.

Jeannette Lambermont-Morey has directed productions in theatres across Canada and the United States, from the Stratford Festival to the Virginia Stage Company; including such theatres as the Citadel, Great Canadian Theatre Company, Atlantic Theatre Festival, Manitoba Theatre Centre, Theatre Aquarius, Thousand Islands Playhouse, Talk is Free Theatre, Theatre By the Bay, the New World Theatre Project, and Huron Country Playhouse; and Toronto theatres Factory Theatre, Canadian Stage, Harbourfront Centre, and the Toronto International Fringe Festival. Significant Stratford Festival productions include *As You Like It*, *Pride and Prejudice*, *The Miracle Worker*, *Henry V*, *Titus Andronicus*, *The Grand Inquisitor*, and *Swan Song*, as well as serving as collaborating director on *The Comedy of Errors* and *The Relapse* (1989) and assisting Richard Monette on *The Taming of the Shrew* (1988) and John Neville on *Othello* (1987). Her hit production of *The Syringa Tree* (Citadel) won a Sterling Award for Liisa Repo-Martell; and her productions of

Twelfth Night in High Park (Canadian Stage) and *Digging For Fire* (Paramour Productions) were both nominated for Dora Mavor Moore awards for Outstanding Production. Favourite projects have included *The Tempest* and *The Merchant of Venice* for the New World Theatre Project in St. John's, Newfoundland; *As You Like It* for Blue Bridge Repertory Theatre in Victoria; *Private Lives* at the Atlantic Theatre Festival; *The Beauty Queen of Leenane* at the Virginia Stage Company with Eileen Brennan, and also at the Manitoba Theatre Centre with Rosemary Dunsmore; *Doc* (Great Canadian Theatre Co., Ottawa); *Moving Day* by Cathy Elliott (TIFT); and *A Midsummer Night's Dream* (Juilliard School, New York), to name only a few. She also produced and directed the CBC's live show *Get Set for Life* for a cross-Canada tour and the Milk International Children's Festival of the Arts at Harbourfront. Jeannette works extensively in college and university theatre programs as a director and instructor. Among them are George Brown College; Memorial University, Grenfell Campus; York University; the Juilliard School (NY); the University of Alberta; Ryerson University; Dartmouth College (NH); and the University of Victoria. At George Brown College Jeannette has directed several shows and has helmed the Annual Period Study exercise for over fifteen years. Jeannette is passionately devoted to the development and dramaturgy of new work, and is currently working with several George Brown graduates on various projects. Jeannette was artistic director of the New World Theatre Project in Newfoundland in 2012/13. She was also executive director of the Shakespeare Globe Centre of Canada from 2000 to 2015.

Annie G. Levy is a theatre maker and director whose work often revolves around modern mythology, historical turning points, and scientific breakthroughs. Her pieces include *Six Seeds: The Persephone Project*, (Space on White, NYC; Theatre @ The Tank, New York City; Catnip Divadlo, Prague) *Tree Army: The CCC*

Project (FIGMENT, New York City; Alabama State Park Tour), and, most recently, *Meteorite | Doorstop* (Lady Fest @ The Tank, New York City). Levy is a founding member of the World Wide Lab and has co-directed as part of the collective since 2011. With WWL, she has created work for the Irondale Center in Brooklyn; Teatro Due in Rome; the Syros Institute on the Greek island of Syros; 453 Art Zone in New Taipei City, Taiwan; and for the Superior Theatre Festival in Thunder Bay, Ontario. She has also created and directed new, award-winning work with theatre incubator warner | shaw, the Northwood Theatre Company, and various other New York City theatres and institutions, including City Center, Dixon Place, HERE, New Ohio Theatre, Terra Nova, and Access Theatre. Levy's writing has appeared in *The Cambridge Handbook of Creativity Across Domains*, AATE's *Incite/Insight* journal, and the *SDC Journal*. Past developmental residencies include the Paul Artist Residency at Indiana University, Bloomington, and a Lower Manhattan Cultural Council's Uptown/Downtown Artist, among others. She is a member of the Lincoln Center Theater Directors Lab and an associate member of the Stage Directors and Choreographers Society. Levy is Artistic Director of Boston's Emerson Stage.

Daniel MacIvor is a prolific and highly versatile actor/playwright/director who was educated at Dalhousie University and George Brown College. He has been writer-in-residence at Buddies in Bad Times, the National Theatre School of Canada, and more recently at the Tarragon Theatre. His plays, many of them solo works in which he acts variations on himself, play in theatres across the country and abroad, including Australia, Israel, Europe, Britain, and the United States. His work has been translated into French, Portuguese, Spanish, Czech, German, and Japanese. He was the founder and artistic director of da da kamera and is also a film and video artist. His best-known play, *Marion Bridge*, has been performed across Canada, including at

Mulgrave Road Theatre (1998) and Theatre Network in 2004. His monologues are extraordinary performances in which he assumes diverse roles that project aspects of his psyche in terms of multiple personae: *Monster* (1998) is a study of evil, combining humour, frightening (albeit very simple) stage effects, and a story line that seduces and delights. Other plays include: *See Bob Run, Yes I Am and Who Are You?* (Buddies in Bad Times); *Wild Abandon* (Theatre Passe Muraille); *Somewhere I Have Never Travelled* (Tarragon Theatre); *Never Swim Alone* (da da kamera), *2-2 Tango* (Buddies in Bad Times); *House, Jump* (Theatre Passe Muraille); *This is a Play*, *The Lorca Play, In On It* (Edinburgh Festival), for which he was awarded a Village Voice OBIE Award; *Cul-de-Sac* (da da kamera); *A Beautiful View* (da da kamera, 2006); *His Greatness* (Arts Club Theatre, Vancouver, 2007, Jessie Richardson Award); *How It Works* (Tarragon, 2007); and *This is What Happens Next*. Other work includes: *Confession*, *Redemption*, *Communion*, *Was Spring* (Tarragon); *Bingo!,The Best Brothers* (Stratford Festival); *I, Animal*, *Arigato Tokyo* (Buddies in Bad Times), *Something Small*, and *Who Killed Spalding Gray?* MacIvor has adapted several of his plays for film, including *House* (1996). His feature film, *Past Perfect* (produced by Camelia Frieberg) premiered at the 2002 Toronto International Film Festival and played in theatres across Canada in 2003. He also shot his second feature, *Wilby Wonderful* in 2003. His screenplay adaptation of *Marion Bridge*, directed by Wiebke von Carolsfeld, also premiered in Toronto in 2002. More recently, he wrote and starred in the film *Whole New Thing* (2005) and appeared in the Halifax film *Growing Op*. MacIvor has twice won the Dora Mavor Moore Award, is a Chalmers Award laureate, and in 2006 won the Governor General's Literary Award for his collection of five plays, *I Still Love You*. In October 2008, he was named the recipient of the Elinore & Lou Siminovitch Prize in Theatre, Canada's largest annual theatre award.

Director, theatre maker, and educator, **Allyson McMackon** is based in Toronto and is the artistic director of the multi-Dora nominated Theatre Rusticle. Specializing in physical theatre and the collision points between text and the body, Allyson's work has taken her across the country. She has received a Dora Mavor Moore Award nomination for Outstanding Direction, been nominated three times for the K.M. Hunter Artist Award, and received a Harold Award from Vikki Anderson in 2008. Recent Rusticle projects have included *The Stronger Variations*, *Dinner at Seven-Thirty* (in association with Buddies in Bad Times), *Peter and the Wolf* (Theatre Centre), *Birnam Wood* (in association with Theatre Passe Muraille), and *April 14, 1912* (with Harbourfront Centre, Magnetic North Theatre Festival, Supernova Theatre Festival, Rotary Arts Centre, Artspring, and Intrepid Theatre). She is a frequent outside eye for various dance companies, coached on the multi-Dora Award winning *If We Were Birds* (directed by Alan Dilworth), and has worked with DVxT Theatre, Soulpepper, and Theatre Passe Muraille. She was the original director on Brooke Johnson's acclaimed *Trudeau Stories*, which has toured to the National Arts Centre, Centaur, and across the country. Allyson has been on faculty at York University since 2008 teaching movement and physical theatre in both the Theatre Studies and Acting Conservatories. She has also taught at the University of Toronto, the Centre for Indigenous Theatre, and the Koffler Centre for the Arts, and she is a frequent workshop leader at the Directors Lab North. She has directed *The Stronger Variations* (York University) and *Anna Karenina* (George Brown Theatre School) and she leads workshops regularly with the Rusticle Gym training programs. She has taught at the Globe Theatre Conservatory in Regina since 2012. Allyson has a BA in drama and English from the University of Toronto and an MFA in theatre performance from York University.

Yvette Nolan launched her career as a playwright at the Winnipeg Fringe Festival in 1990 where her play *Blade* premiered. She has worked at various theatre companies throughout Canada including Agassiz Theatre, Manitoba Theatre Centre, Nakai Theatre in Whitehorse, and Native Earth Performing Arts. As a director, Nolan has contributed significantly to the development of Indigenous theatre. She has directed plays by George Ryga (*The Ecstasy of Rita Joe*), Turtle Gals Performance Ensemble (*The Only Good Indian*), and Marie Clements (*Tombs of the Vanishing Indian* and *The Unnatural and Accidental Women*), Kenneth T. Williams (*Café Daughter* and *In Care*), and Melanie J. Murray (*A Very Polite Genocide*). From 1998 until 2001, Nolan was president of the Playwrights Union of Canada (now called the Playwrights Guild of Canada). She was artistic director of Native Earth from 2003 to 2010. She was president of Indigenous Performing Arts Alliance and has served on the boards of the Saskatchewan Arts Alliance and the Saskatchewan Association of Theatre Professionals. Nolan is an artistic associate at Signal Theatre and co-director with Michael Greyeyes of a dance opera (*Bearing*) at the 2017 Luminato Festival. She also directed (*Nôhkom*) with Signal Theatre. Nolan has been a writer-in-residence at several institutions including Brandon University (1996). During this term as writer-in-residence, Nolan wrote *Annie Mae's Movement*. She was also playwright-in-residence at the National Arts Centre and resident at Mount Royal College in 2009. In 2011 she began a nine-month term as writer-in-residence at the Saskatoon Library and playwright-in-residence at the University of Regina. Nolan's commitment to Indigenous and feminist live art is attributed to the first time she saw an Indigenous character on stage during the Royal Winnipeg Ballet's adaptation of *The Ecstasy of Rita Joe*. In 2017 she was awarded an Honorary Lifetime Membership to the Canadian Association of Theatre Research.

Morris Panych graduated from Creative Writing at UBC in 1977 and had his first professional production in 1982 with *Last Call* for Tamahnous Theatre in Vancouver. Since that time, he has written twenty plays and adapted half a dozen others. He has twice won the Governor General's Literary Award for Drama, the highest honour for playwriting in Canada. Playwright, actor, and director, Panych is a man for all seasons in Canadian theatre. He has directed over ninety productions across Canada and written thirty plays that have been produced throughout Canada, Britain, the United States, Europe, Asia, Australia, and New Zealand in a dozen languages. Other plays include: *7 Stories*, *The Necessary Steps*, *Lawrence & Holloman*, *The Ends of the Earth*, and *Vigil* (which won the Jessie Richardson Award for best play and has been performed in over thirty theatres in Canada and the United States). In 1998 he co-created and directed *The Overcoat*, a physical theatre piece in which choreographed movement and music function in place of dialogue. This production toured across Canada. Panych also directed the television version of *The Overcoat*. *Earshot* premiered at the Tarragon Theatre and *Girl in a Goldfish Bowl* at the Arts Club Theatre (Jessie Richardson Award and a Dora Mavor Moore Award). Further plays include *The Dishwashers*, *What Lies Before Us*, *The Trespassers*, *Gordon*, *In Absentia*, *Wanderlust*, *Sextet*, *The Shoplifters*, and *The Waiting Room*. He has won the Jessie Richardson Award fourteen times for acting and directing. He has won Toronto's Dora Mavor Moore Award five times, three Sydney Risk Prizes, and a Chalmers Award. In 1995 he was awarded the Governor General's Literary Award for Drama for *The Ends of the Earth*, and in 2004 for *The Girl in the Goldfish Bowl*. Panych's plays are published by Talonbooks.

Joseph Recinos (kab' lajuj b'atz'—twelve monkeys) was born and raised on Turtle Island with Maya roots from Iximulew (Guatemala). A creator, performer, advocate, administrator, and facilitator for the performing arts of T'karon:to, whose television credits include roles on *Mayday*, *Dual Suspects*, and *The Strain*. Joseph is a Harold Award recipient whose passion for the arts extends behind the scenes, and whose commitment to equitable and diverse practices within the arts has led them to speak at YouthREX and several other panels and to publish articles with *NOW Magazine* and *Intermission*. A trained facilitator, Joe has delivered various workshops on diversity, inclusion, and self-care with Goodmans LLP and with youth and communities across Ontario. A Humber Performance graduate, their extensive experience in the performing arts led them to found Creative Mafia.

Josephine Ridge was born and educated in Melbourne, Australia. Her love for working in the arts started from a chance placement with the BBC's Radio 3 while she was travelling in Europe, and what was supposed to be a two-week long engagement turned into a three-year job and a lifelong commitment. Returning to Australia in 1986, her first role was with a Melbourne theatre company, Playbox, before moving to Sydney to work with the national opera company, Opera Australia. In the three decades since she has worked in the performing arts across a variety of sectors in theatre, dance, and music. Considered one of Australia's most experienced arts professionals, her experience has encompassed marketing, communications, sponsorship, philanthropy, general management, and artistic direction. Other companies Josephine has worked with include the Malthouse Theatre, Australian Chamber Orchestra, and the Australian Ballet. In 2003 she was appointed as general manager, later executive director, of Sydney Festival, an international multi-platform arts festival. She worked there for nearly ten years and her experience led to an invitation to move back to Melbourne to curate three editions of the Melbourne Festival as artistic director (2013–2015). In 2016, she was appointed artistic director of Luminato Festival in Toronto where she curated the 2017 and 2018 festival programs. Josephine is a fellow of the Williamson Community Leadership Program (1993). She has held board positions with the Australian Centre for Contemporary Art (1999–2004) and Critical Path (NSW), an organization supporting choreographic research (2004–2011) where she was chair from 2006, and she was a member of the board of TarraWarra Museum of Art (2009–2016).

Andrea Romaldi is a dramaturge, teacher, and artistic leader who, during her fifteen-year career in theatre, has also worked as an independent producer and director. Prior to becoming Director of the Playwriting Program (English Section) at the National Theatre School of Canada, she spent ten seasons as literary manager at Toronto's Tarragon Theatre, directing the theatre's extensive roster of play development programs, and assisting in the development of over eighty new plays, with almost thirty produced. They include Governor General's Literary Award nominated plays by Sean Dixon, Brendan Gall, Jonathan Garfinkel, Michael Healey, Joan MacLeod, and Hannah Moscovitch, and Governor General's Literary Award-winners Erin Shields and David Yee; eleven Dora Award Outstanding New Play nominees and three winners; and a Trillium Book Award winner. She has mentored both graduate students and professional theatre makers through university training programs, internships, and play development programs at a variety of theatres, and was a regular panellist for the Directors Lab North. Previously, she has worked with Brian Quirt at Nightswimming and with Maureen Labonté and Neil Munro at the Shaw Festival. She was Artistic Director of Hudson Village Theatre's 2018 season, ran the Alumnae Theatre's New Ideas Festival for two seasons, and contributed to Canadian Stage's inaugural Festival of Ideas and Creation. Andrea also participated in workshops at the National Theatre Society (Dublin) while she pursued her MPhil in film and theatre at Trinity College, Dublin.

Richard Rose is the artistic director of Tarragon Theatre. Prior to joining the Tarragon in 2002, Richard was founding artistic director at Necessary Angel (a position he held from 1978 to 2002), associate director for the Canadian Stage Company, director of the Stratford Festival Young Company, and spent ten seasons directing at the Stratford Festival. He has directed plays across Canada, the United States, and in London's West End in styles ranging from the environmental to the classical. Richard is well known for developing new work, including four plays that won the Governor General's Literary Award and nine other nominated plays. He is a four-time Dora Award winner for direction and production and has had numerous nominations.

Kat Sandler is a playwright, director, and the artistic director of Theatre Brouhaha, based in Toronto. Kat attended the University of Toronto Schools, where she wrote and directed a musical; and graduated from the Queen's University Drama Program. She then worked with Theatre Gargantua in Toronto, which develops multi-faceted works. Since 2012, she has directed twelve of her own plays, including Toronto Best of Fringe hits *Bright Lights*, *Punch Up*, *Help Yourself* (winner of the New Play Contest), *Delicacy* (Summerworks Spotlight Award), *Liver*, *Cockfight*, and *Retreat* (Storefront Theatre). She was a member of the Tarragon Playwrights Unit, where she developed *Mustard* (Dora Mavor Moore Award, Outstanding New Play) and has been the playwright-in-residence at Tarragon Theatre. *Bang, Bang* premiered at Factory Theatre in 2018. Kat Sandler was the 2015 recipient of *NOW Magazine*'s Audience Choice Award for Best Director and Best Playwright.

Judith Thompson is one of Canada's most highly regarded playwrights. Her plays are performed across the country in both official languages. Her first work, *The Crackwalker*, premiered at Theatre Passe Muraille in 1980. She has twice won the Governor

General's Literary Award for *White Biting Dog* (1984) and the anthology *The Other Side of the Dark* (1989); and the Chalmers Award for *I Am Yours* (1987) and *Lion in the Streets* (1991). *Sled* (1997), *Perfect Pie* (2000), and *Capture Me* (2004) all premiered at the Tarragon Theatre, the company with which she has had the closest links (all directed by Judith Thompson). *Habitat* played at Canadian Stage, and *Enoch Arden* at Toronto's Theatre Centre. In 2008, the Canadian Stage Company premiered *Palace of the End* on its Berkeley Street stage. *Such Creatures* premiered at Theatre Passe Muraille in 2010. In 2013, *The Thrill* opened at the Stratford Festival. *Borne*, which features all actors in wheelchairs, opened at Soulpepper in 2014, in a co-production with her own company, RARE Theatre. *Watching Glory Die* was produced by Canadian Rep Theatre and premiered at the Vancouver East Cultural Centre in April 2014. Judith Thompson has written many radio plays, including *Tornado* (1987), which won the ACTRA Award for Best Radio Drama, and *White Sand* (1991). She has also adapted and directed Ibsen's *Hedda Gabler* for the Shaw Festival (1991). In 2007 she was awarded the Walter Carsen Prize for Excellence in the Performing Arts. The $50,000 prize, administered and presented by the Canada Council for the Arts, recognizes the highest level of artistic excellence and distinguished career achievement by Canadian artists who have spent the major part of their career in Canada in theatre, dance, or music. In 2008 she was awarded the Susan Smith Blackburn Prize for *Palace of the End*. In 2012, she was awarded the Herbert Whittaker Award for Distinguished Contribution to Canadian Theatre by the Canadian Theatre Critics Association. She was awarded an honorary degree by Queen's University in November 2016.

Vincent de Tourdonnet is a Canadian musical theatre writer. He is known for large-scale historical musicals, as well as intimate, cabaret-style musicals. He frequently also serves as stage director. De Tourdonnet's current historical project is *The Musical McCoy*, adapted from Andrew Moodie's award-winning hit play *The Real McCoy*. De Tourdonnet's epic musical *Pélagie*, co-written with Allen Cole, premiered at Canadian Stage in Toronto and the National Arts Centre in Ottawa, and de Tourdonnet directed an Eastern Canada touring production produced by Two Planks and a Passion with a bilingual cast alternating performances in French and English. His first production of *Snappy Tales: Short Satirical Musicals* (book, lyrics, and direction) at Factory Theatre in Toronto was nominated for seven Dora Mavor Moore Awards. De Tourdonnet's largest musical to date was the Joan of Arc musical, *Jeanne*, which went on to large-scale production at the Place des Arts , Montreal, and La Capitole in Quebec City in 1997 and was seen by over 100,000 people. While living in New York City, de Tourdonnet taught musical theatre writing at Long Island University. He is now based in Prince Edward County, Ontario, with his wife, Beth Easton.

ABOUT THE EDITOR

Evan has been Co-Artistic Director of Directors Lab North in Toronto for the last ten years. His plays include *Aftershock*, *The Murmuration of Starlings*, *Unstuck*, *Strange Mary Strange*, the musical *Inge(new)*, and the short film *Bagged*, which aired on CBC. As a founding member of the World Wide Lab, he has spent the last decade travelling across the globe co-directing, co-writing, and co-creating site-specific, immersive pieces in Greece, New York, Taipei, Thunder Bay, Rome, and Germany. In Germany he's also co-created, directed, and written *I am Invisible*, *Berlin Bound*, *My Berlin*, and *We Are The Play*. Evan has worked across Canada and the US with companies such as the Houston Grand Opera, the Musical Stage Company, the New York City Centre Encores Series, and more. He trained at York University, Sheridan College, and has his Professional Training Certificate in Theatre of the Oppressed from London, England, where he trained with Augusto Boal. He is a member of the Lincoln Theater Center Directors Lab, Chicago Directors Lab, the Playwrights Guild of Canada, the Tarragon Playwright's Unit, and an associate member of the Stage Directors and Choreographers Society, as well a resident artist at Robert Wilson's Watermill Center. He's been nominated for a Dora Mavor Moore Award, the John Hirsch Directing Prize, the Tom Hendry Award (Stage West Comedy Award), the Herman Voaden National Playwriting Prize, the Broadwayworld Awards, and was a finalist for the Charles Abbott Directing Fellowship. He's spent the last several years at Theatre Under the Stars in Houston, where he's directed, worked as an associate in the Education Department, has been Artistic Assistant for the company, and Head of Acting on the faculty of the Humphreys School of Musical Theatre. He is currently Artistic Director of Eclipse Theatre Company in Toronto. His work has been published in Germany, Canada, and the USA. www.evantsitsias.com.